TAX STRATEGIES FOR THE SMALL BUSINESS OWNER

REDUCE YOUR TAXES AND FATTEN YOUR PROFITS

Russell Fox

Apress®

President and Publisher: Paul Manning
Acquisitions Editor: Jeff Olson
Developmental Editor: Robert Hutchinson
Editorial Board: Steve Anglin, Mark Beckner, Ewan Buckingham, Gary Cornell, Louise Corrigan, Morgan Ertel, Jonathan Gennick, Jonathan Hassell, Robert Hutchinson, Michelle Lowman, James Markham, Matthew Moodie, Jeff Olson, Jeffrey Pepper, Douglas Pundick, Ben Renow-Clarke, Dominic Shakeshaft, Gwenan Spearing, Matt Wade, Tom Welsh
Coordinating Editor: Rita Fernando
Copy Editor: Laura Poole
Compositor: Bytheway Publishing Services
Indexer: SPi Global
Cover Designer: Anna Ishchenko

Distributed to the book trade worldwide by Springer Science+Business Media New York, 233 Spring Street, 6th Floor, New York, NY 10013. Phone 1-800-SPRINGER, fax (201) 348-4505, e-mail orders-ny@springer-sbm.com, or visit www.springeronline.com. Apress Media, LLC is a California LLC and the sole member (owner) is Springer Science + Business Media Finance Inc (SSBM Finance Inc). SSBM Finance Inc is a Delaware corporation.

For information on translations, please e-mail rights@apress.com, or visit www.apress.com.

Apress and friends of ED books may be purchased in bulk for academic, corporate, or promotional use. eBook versions and licenses are also available for most titles. For more information, reference our Special Bulk Sales–eBook Licensing web page at www.apress.com/bulk-sales.

Any source code or other supplementary materials referenced by the author in this text is available to readers at www.apress.com. For detailed information about how to locate your book's source code, go to www.apress.com/source-code/.

To Brett Fox
for his support throughout the years.

Introduction

When I was just out of college, my father gave me Charles Adams's classic book on the history of taxes, *For Good and Evil: The Impact of Taxes on the Course of Civilization*.[1] Since then, I've been fascinated with taxes and am something of a tax nerd. As one of my clients said to me, "We're glad *someone* enjoys taxes."

That's not really accurate. I like working in tax, but I don't know anyone who truly enjoys paying taxes. I suspect we would all like to pay less. Meanwhile, many Americans are facing the specter of tax increases on the federal, state, and local levels.

That's where this book comes in. This is a commonsense, practical guide to taxes for the small business owner. The goal of the book to give small business owners an understanding of what he or she needs to think about regarding taxes—from when the business is formed to when it is sold.

The book is divided into four parts. "Before the Business Opens" focuses on the types of business entities (and how they are taxed), the taxes a small business owner faces, and the start-up phase and record-keeping requirements. "Day-to-Day Expenses" looks at deductions you can take and what's required to take them. The third part, "Payroll, Payroll Taxes, and Benefit Plans," looks at paying yourself and employees, payroll taxes you must pay, retirement plans, and medical expenses (with a focus on the new Affordable Care Act). The final part, "Other Items," reviews the documentation you generally need for taxes besides the federal income tax, what to do when a tax agency contacts you, and other topics (including electronic filing, foreign issues, using a tax professional, and selling your business).

I tell my clients that tax is a combination of common sense and arcane rules. I've tried to keep the minutiae of the rules, regulations, and laws to a minimum in this text. I hope this book will set you on the course of paying the least amount of tax you legally can.

---

[1] Charles Adams, *For Good and Evil: The Impact of Taxes on the Course of Civilization (2nd Edition)*, (Toronto: Madison Books, 2001).

Before the Business Opens

There are several different types of business entities for a small business owner to choose among, including sole proprietorships, partnerships, corporations (both C and S), and limited liability companies. This is perhaps the most critical decision a business makes, and Part I begins by exploring this important area.

Chapter 2 looks at the types of taxes a small business owner must pay, the definitions of income and expenses, and cash versus accrual accounting. The last chapter in Part I covers the rules of the start-up phase: that part of the business before you receive any revenue. The final part of Chapter 3 examines the recordkeeping requirements of a small business in dealing with tax agencies.

The Business Entity

The business of America is business.

—President Calvin Coolidge

You've been in business or you're just starting out. You've picked up this book because you're wondering how to deal with taxes. You might expect the book to start by looking at taxes; however, we won't look directly at them at all in this first chapter. That's because the most important decision a business owner can make is about the structure of the business.

You may have been told, "The best structure for a business is an LLC." Perhaps your buddy told you he has an S corporation, and it works great. If you choose your business entity based on someone else's business, you may be making a major mistake. *There is no one right business structure.* Like many things in tax (and business), the correct answer to "What is the best structure for a business?" is: "It depends."

Generally, all businesses calculate their income in the same manner: Figure out the gross income, subtract all ordinary and necessary business expenses, and whatever is left is profit. Of course, this is a simplification, but the general principle holds. Why, then, is the choice of business entity so important?

- *Different tax treatments.* Though *income* is generally calculated identically across business structures, the *tax* may not be.

- *Legal consequences.* Not only will different entities be treated differently under the law, but the treatment can vary state by state.

- *Your goals*. Depending on your goals, you may be able to only use one specific type of business entity.

In this chapter we take a look the different types of business entities, the requirements for each, their pros and cons, and how they are taxed. We discuss how you can change your type of entity and conclude with how you should choose your form of business entity.

The Sole Proprietor

If you alone conduct your business without forming a separate legal entity, you are a *sole proprietor*. This is the simplest form of business entity. Any business conducted by an individual that is not another form of business entity will be a sole proprietorship.

There is no such thing as wages or salary with a sole proprietorship. You are the business, so wages would just be moving money from your left hand to your right hand.

This is by far the simplest form of business entity. It's just you conducting a business. Of course, you must truly be conducting a business and not just trying to make a hobby into a business.

Hobby Loss Test

Most of us have hobbies—activities we pursue for enjoyment, not to make money. Many individuals attempt to turn their hobbies into businesses; after all, activities we pursue for enjoyment can make the best businesses. That said, to have a business for tax purposes, you *must* be trying to make money at it. The Internal Revenue Service (IRS) is naturally skeptical of a "business" that loses money year after year. A nine-factor test is used by the IRS and the courts to determine whether an activity is being conducted as a business or a hobby:[1]

1. The manner in which the taxpayer carried on the activity;

2. The expertise of the taxpayer or his or her advisers;

3. The time and effort expended by the taxpayer in carrying on the activity;

4. The expectation that the assets used in the activity may appreciate in value;

---

[1] Treasury Regulation §1.183-2(b).

5. The success of the taxpayer in carrying on other similar or dissimilar activities;

6. The taxpayer's history of income or loss with respect to the activity;

7. The amount of occasional profits, if any, which are earned;

8. The financial status of the taxpayer; and

9. Elements of personal pleasure or recreation.

The effect of these rules for a business that's considered a hobby is that gross income is taxable but the expenses might not be deductible. Most of the time you do *not* want your business to be considered a hobby.

One of the most important ways of avoiding this is to *document all of your expenses.* My mother, a realtor, says that the cliché that real estate is location, location, and location is true. Similarly, the most important thing for a business owner is to document, document, and document.

▓ **Tip   Keep good records!** I cannot overemphasize this. You will see this point recurring throughout this book because it really is that important.

Let's look at a business that is a hobby. Say you've decided to buy a lot of cosmetics, and you decide to become a distributor for a multilevel marketing (MLM) company. By becoming a distributor for an MLM that markets cosmetics, you can make a little bit of money on the side. MLMs typically pay a residual to you for every product you order (and for product ordered by others you recruit to the company). However, in this example you do not have a profit motive: Your goal is solely to purchase cosmetics for your own use. This "business" would clearly be a hobby.

I deliberately chose an MLM for this example because they have a reputation for abuse with tax agencies. That does *not* mean that you should avoid MLMs as your choice when starting a business. On the contrary, many people have done quite well with businesses that are structured as MLMs. If you honestly conduct your business with the goal of making money, you will likely be considered to be running your business for the purpose of making a profit, not as a hobby.

Sole Proprietorship: The Advantages

The main reason for choosing a sole proprietorship is its ease. The moment you "hang up your shingle," you've formed a sole proprietorship. Other than a local business license[2] and/or a fictitious business statement,[3] there are usually no other requirements to form a sole proprietorship.[4] This makes it one of the easiest businesses to create.

From a tax perspective, a sole proprietorship reports its income and expenses on a Schedule C. This is part of your personal tax return, so no separate business entity tax return is required.

A sole proprietorship is usually one of the least expensive businesses to run from an organizational standpoint. Because there are few (if any) legal filings required, legal costs are usually limited. Because there's no separate tax return required, there can be a savings on tax preparation costs.

It's also easy to close a sole proprietorship: You simply stop working in that business and don't include the Schedule C on your tax return (though you may need to cancel your business license or fictitious business statement).

Sole Proprietorship: The Disadvantages

The ease of forming a sole proprietorship is also one of its negatives. A sole proprietorship is you conducting a business. You can be held personally liable for anything that is conducted by your business.

Indeed, protection from legal liability is one of the main reasons that people form business entities. I am not an attorney, and nothing written in this book is meant as legal advice. That said, it's safe to say that most individuals do not want to be exposed to potential liability issues.

Second, a sole proprietorship is, by definition, you conducting a business by yourself. With one exception,[5] there cannot be any other owners if you file as a sole proprietorship.

Finally, according to IRS statistics, a business that files a sole proprietorship has on average five to ten times the audit risk of a corporation or a partnership.[6]

---

[2] Business licenses are generally issued by cities and counties, though some states (such as Nevada) also require them.

[3] A *fictitious business statement* is required when you conduct a business in anything other than your own name. In most jurisdictions, these statements are issued by counties.

[4] A business conducted out of a home may be subject to zoning and/or homeowners association restrictions. Consult an attorney familiar with your jurisdiction and legal issues to determine whether this is a concern.

[5] A married couple living in a community property state jointly conducting a business can file their business as a sole proprietorship. The income and expenses of the business would be split onto two Schedule C's. I discuss this in the note in the next section.

[6] 2011 Internal Revenue Service Data Book: October 1, 2010, to September 30, 2011, accessed at http://www.irs.gov/pub/irs=soi/11databk.pdf, page 22.

Why is this the case? The IRS has found that tax returns for sole proprietorships tend to have more errors than do corporate or partnership returns. The IRS is a collection agency; they go where the money is. They get more bang for their buck by examining sole proprietorships than investigating other business entities (except for the largest C corporations). Audits are covered in detail in Chapter 17.

Partnerships

A *partnership* is when two or more persons conduct a trade or business. Note that I did *not* say "two or more individuals"; a partner in a partnership can be a business entity, such as a corporation or an LLC (though this is rare). A business does not have to have a written agreement to be considered a partnership. Most states do not require partnerships to register with the state; however, partnerships have the same requirements as sole proprietorships in obtaining business licenses and fictitious business statements.

Partnerships file an *information return* (Form 1065) noting their income and expenses, but they generally do not pay income tax.[7] The income and expenses from a partnership flow through to the partners' own tax returns. Thus, a partnership is a *flow-through entity*. A partnership issues Schedule K-1's noting each partner's share of the income and expenses so that these items can be reported on each partner's personal tax returns.

As in sole proprietorships, individual owners in a partnership cannot be paid wages. Instead, owners take *draws* of money from the business. Note that a draw is *not* an expense; rather, it is the movement of earnings from the partnership to the partners.

▥ **Note   The married couple exception in community property states.** There is one business with two owners that can, if it wishes, file a Schedule C (sole proprietorship) rather than a partnership return: a business operated by a married couple in a community property state (Arizona, California, Idaho, Louisiana, Nevada, New Mexico, Texas, Washington, and Wisconsin; Alaska and Puerto Rico allow for community property but it is not the default status). Such a business can file a partnership return (Form 1065) or two Schedule C's on their individual return (Form 1040). If the owners choose to file Schedule C's, the income and expenses would be split equally on the two Schedule C's. The pros and cons of this should be carefully considered before choosing a filing method. Be aware that community property law is *not* identical in each community property state.

---

[7] A few jurisdictions, such as Illinois, do charge tax on partnerships. Illinois calls its tax the "Partnership Replacement Tax."

Partnerships: The Advantages

The positives of a partnership are similar to those of a sole proprietorship. If two individuals go into business together, they have formed a partnership. I recommend that a business partnership create a written partnership agreement; it will make things far easier if the partnership should dissolve.

First, a partnership is easy to form. Although you *should* have a written partnership agreement (ideally, reviewed by an attorney), you don't have to. Two individuals who go into business together absent some other form of business entity will have a partnership.

A partnership is usually easy to dissolve. The partners simply dissolve (close) the entity.

Partnerships have a low audit risk. In fiscal year 2011, only 0.4% of partnership returns were examined by the IRS.[8] Compare that to 3.6% of sole proprietorship returns with income of $200,000 to under $1 million and you can see why you might prefer a partnership return to a Schedule C.

Finally, a partnership is a flow-through entity. The partnership itself generally does not pay tax; rather, each partner pays tax based on his or her share of the income. Thus, a partner pays tax on the partnership income based on his or her marginal tax rate.

Partnerships: The Disadvantages

The ease of forming a partnership can also be a negative. When a partnership splits, it can be messy—especially if there was not a written partnership agreement.

There are other potential legal issues. A partnership does not give a business liability protection. Additionally, each partner can be held personally liable for another partner's actions.

A business entity that is similar to a partnership—a limited liability company (LLC)—gives liability protection while usually allowing for a partnership tax return. However, an LLC does require an operating agreement; the operating agreement should be prepared by an attorney. I discuss LLCs in more depth in the "LLCs" section of this chapter.

---

[8] 2011 Internal Revenue Service Data Book, page 22.

Corporations

Corporations are separate legal entities that have their own rights, privileges, and liabilities distinct from those of their owners. Most corporations are creatures of state laws. A corporation has its own life; it has rights and responsibilities just like you and me. Most corporations issue stock, have a board of directors, and have limited liability. In general, a stockholder will not be liable for the actions of a corporation *assuming the corporation is properly run.* If you own the stock of a publicly traded entity, it's probably a corporation.[9]

For tax purposes, all corporations start as *C corporations.* The other type of corporation is an *S corporation.* A C corporation files a *tax election* to become an S corporation. From a legal perspective, generally all corporations have the same legal rights as any other corporation in that state (irrespective of their C or S status).

One of the major advantages of a corporation is the separation of legal liability. A properly structured corporation has its own legal liability. This doesn't mean that owners and officers of a corporation cannot be sued, nor does it mean there aren't circumstances in which they can be held liable for a corporation's actions—these circumstances definitely exist. That said, *generally* a corporation is treated separately from the owners of the corporation.

There are disadvantages to corporations, too. Because a corporation is a separate legal entity, it files its own tax return. The corporation will need to have annual stockholders and board of directors meetings. You have to document and keep the minutes of these meetings. There will be filings with the agency in your state that handles corporations. This involves additional work (though your attorney may be willing, for a fee, to handle the additional work).

Though C and S corporations start the same, there are significant differences in these entities. C corporations are thought to be the province of large entities, but they can be right for some small businesses. On the other hand, many small businesses choose to become S corporations.

C Corporations

As noted earlier, all corporations start as C corporations. If you own the stock of a public corporation, you own the stock of a C corporation. Though most small business owners rarely think of using a C corporation form for their business, it could be the right choice for you. Although there are some disadvantages of a C corporation, there are several advantages. These include

---

[9] There are a few publicly traded partnerships.

a low tax rate on the first $75,000 of income, advantages for health insurance and other fringe benefits, ability to use a *fiscal year* (a business year that ends other than on December 31), and some other tax benefits. There are some significant disadvantages, too: double taxation, high tax rates on income above $75,000, and certain other negative quirks.

C Corporations: The Advantages

Low Tax Rate on First $75,000 of Income. A C corporation, unlike a partnership or an S corporation, pays its own taxes; it files a Form 1120 each year. C corporations have a deserved reputation for high tax rates; income above $75,000 a year is taxed at a *minimum* rate of 34% for federal income tax. However, the marginal tax rate for a C corporation on its first $50,000 of income is just 15%; the next $25,000 is taxed at just 25%.[10] If a business is expected to remain small (or marginally profitable) a C corporation could be a wise choice.

Health Insurance and Fringe Benefits. C corporations are among the most flexible structures for a business entity. Besides the ability to have multiple classes of stock, there are some tax rules that benefit C corporation owners. Under §105(b) of the Tax Code, a self-insured medical reimbursement plan is allowed. This can cover owners' medical expenses that are not reimbursed by medical insurance, and it may allow for coverage of some over-the-counter medications.[11] If most of the employees of the corporation are owners, this can be a significant advantage.

Use of a Fiscal Year. Most business entities are required to use a calendar year; that is, the business year ends on December 31.[12] A C corporation can use a fiscal year—a business year that ends at the end of a month other than December (for instance, a fiscal year might run June 1 to May 31).

This gives the owner some ability to control when he or she receives salary and when expenses are taken. Also, tax professionals love businesses that have a fiscal year: Their tax returns will be due outside of the busy season.

---

[10] These figures based on 2012 tax rates.

[11] Everything related to medical care, medical insurance, and reimbursements therein is subject to change based on the Affordable Care Act. While the Act was recently held to be constitutionally valid by the Supreme Court, challenges to specific provisions are certain. Additionally, many Republicans vow to repeal the measure at their first opportunity. Thus, anything written concerning health insurance and medical expenses *while accurate as of the date of writing* could be inaccurate as you read this book.

[12] Other business entities can make a §444 election to use a fiscal year; however, this is rarely of value to the business.

Other Tax Advantages. There are some other tax advantages of a C corporation. Under Tax Code §1202, if the stock of the business qualifies as "small business stock,"[13] then 50% of the gain from sale of shares can be excluded from income and the other 50% is taxed at 28% (an effective 14% tax rate). Some states recognize this exclusion, and this can cut state capital gains taxes in half. Under §1244, a deduction of $50,000 ($100,000 if married filing jointly) is available as an ordinary loss if the corporation fails. This potentially allows the owners to plan for the failure in a year when this can offset other income the owners have. Finally, if you plan on taking your business "public" (selling stock to the general public), you must be a C corporation.

C Corporations: The Disadvantages

There is no perfect business entity type, and C corporations definitely have their tax disadvantages. These include the ability to move money to the owners, double taxation, and generally high tax rates.

Moving Money to the Owners. There are generally only two methods available to move money to owners of C corporations: salaries and dividends. Using wages means that you pay payroll taxes; dividends will cause double taxation (see the next paragraph). Although other methods can be devised, the movement of money from the business to the owners is always an issue with a C corporations.

Double Taxation. Taxes are bad enough the first time around. They're even worse when you have to take after-tax money (with regard to the business) to send to yourself (the owner) and then pay taxes on that! But that's what a dividend is: An after-tax distribution of funds from the business that's then taxed again on your personal return. Additionally, assets of the business can end up being double-taxed when the business is sold or dissolves.

High Tax Rates. Although C corporations have relatively low income tax rates on income of $75,000 or less, that's not the case when income rises above that. The *minimum* tax rate on income above $75,000 is 34%.

Is a C Corporation Right for You?

A C corporation can be the right business structure for a small business. That said, if you choose this structure, make sure you are fully aware of all of the advantages and disadvantages.

---

[13] Among the requirements: The stock must be held for at least five years, at least 80% of the assets of the entity must be used in a trade or business, and the business cannot be a personal service provider.

S Corporations

Most corporations elect to become S corporations. The "S" refers to the Subchapter S of Chapter 1 of the Internal Revenue Code (the Tax Code). There are some technical rules for S corporations that you *must* follow. First, all shareholders must be either US citizens or resident aliens. There can be a maximum of only 100 shareholders (spouses are automatically treated as a single shareholder; other family members can be treated as a single shareholder if any family member elects such treatment). Shareholders generally must be people, though some trusts, estates, and tax-exempt corporations qualify as shareholders.

A corporation elects S corporation status by filing Form 2553 with the IRS. This form must be filed by the fifteenth day of the third month of the tax year for which the election is to be effective. Although there is a procedure available to make a late S election, it is far easier to do it correctly the first time. Note that some states (such as New Jersey and New York) require a *separate* election to be made for state tax purposes.

▨ **Caution   What happens if your S corporation suddenly doesn't qualify?** Suppose a shareholder of your S corporation gives a share of the corporation to a nonresident alien. You will suddenly have made a "deemed election" to lose your S corporation status and will become a C corporation. If you choose to be an S corporation, make sure your stock cannot go where it would disqualify you from being an S corporation.

S Corporations: The Advantages

A C corporation pays its own taxes. Although an S corporation does have to file a tax return (Form 1120S is used for federal taxes), it *generally does not pay any tax.*[14] Instead, S corporations are flow-through entities: The profits and losses flow through to the owners' tax returns.

While S corporation officers must take a "reasonable salary," distributions can be made that are not subject to payroll taxes. This eliminates the double taxation issue of dividends that impacts C corporations.

---

[14] The most common exception is if the business converted from a C corporation and is subject to the Built-In Gains Tax. See the discussion on converting business types later in this chapter. Additionally, California taxes S corporations at 1.5%, and New York City does *not* recognize S corporations for their business tax (S corporations are treated the same as C corporations).

S Corporations: The Disadvantages

S corporations are corporations, a formal business entity. That means that you must have your annual shareholders and board of directors meetings (and keep minutes of those meetings). There are some other tax issues that negatively impact S corporations.

Required Salary. As mentioned, any corporate officer of an S corporation must be paid a reasonable salary. This has become a point of emphasis with the IRS in examinations (audits) of S corporations and their owners. What is reasonable can be debated, but clearly a salary of $0 for a profitable entity is *not* reasonable. A rule of thumb is that you should take as salary that is at least half the net income of the business, or the current FICA wage base,[15] whichever is less. This is discussed in depth in Chapter 12.

Health Insurance. Although health insurance premiums are deductible for the self-employed, S corporation owners[16] *cannot* take full advantage of this deduction. The rules are not straightforward and are the result of how Congress has made the Tax Code overly complex.

The deduction is taken *not* on the S corporation tax return; rather, it's taken on the owner's tax return (Form 1040). To take the deduction, you must include the premiums as part of your taxable income (wages) in Box 1 of your W-2. However, these "wages" are *not* included for FICA or Medicare tax. You then can take the deduction on your Form 1040. The premiums must be paid for by the employee, but can be reimbursed by the corporation.

Documentation of Loan Basis. Loans add basis to an S corporation. (I look at the reasons you want basis in Chapter 18.) Let's say you personally lend money to your S corporation. Make sure you document the loan (have a written loan agreement), the loan repays with interest,[17] and that the terms of the loan are followed. The Tax Court has disallowed loans that are not documented with signed agreements.

LLCs

One of the newest forms of business entity is the *limited liability company* (LLC). An LLC is a more informal entity than a corporation. For example, no

---

[15] The FICA (Federal Insurance Contributions Act, or Social Security payroll tax) wage base for 2012 is $110,100.

[16] Defined as someone who owns at least 2% of the stock of an S corporation.

[17] Each month, the IRS publishes the minimum required loan rates, or Applicable Federal Rates (AFRs). These are published as Revenue Rulings and can be downloaded from the IRS website at http://www.irs.gov/app/piclist/list/federalRates.html.

annual meeting of owners or officers is required. A properly formed LLC offers liability protection (similar to corporations).

The key for an LLC is its operating agreement. Though it's relatively easy to change a corporation's bylaws, it is more difficult to change an LLC's operating agreement. This means that if you form an LLC, you should carefully consider having your operating agreement professionally prepared (by an attorney).

The tax treatment for an LLC depends on its number of owners. The owners of an LLC are considered to be its *members*. A single-member LLC is generally a *disregarded entity* for tax purposes. Because the entity is ignored on the tax return, a single-member LLC files a Schedule C (just like a sole proprietorship).

LLCs with more than one member are generally considered partnerships for tax filing and will file a Partnership Return of Income (Form 1065). That makes multiple-member LLCs flow-through entities (like partnerships and S corporations).

However, LLCs can elect a different tax status. An LLC can elect to be taxed as a C corporation or an S corporation. This gives this business structure tremendous flexibility.

LLCs, like corporations, are creatures of state law. Corporate law is similar in most states, but the laws dealing with LLCs vary considerably. For example, many professionals cannot form LLCs in California. You should consult with a local attorney familiar with business formations to make sure that your LLC is legal in your local jurisdiction.

Be aware that state tax treatment of LLCs is *not* identical. Although most states will consider a single-member LLC a disregarded entity (and, thus, there is no separate tax filing), California does not. All LLCs in California must pay an $800 a year minimum franchise tax. California also has a gross receipts tax on LLCs.

The tax advantages and disadvantages of LLCs depend on how they are taxed. A disregarded LLC will have the same issues as a sole proprietorship (see "Sole Proprietorships: The Disadvantages" section); a multiple-member LLC will have the same issues as a partnership (see "Partnerships: The Disadvantages"). LLCs electing C corporation status or S corporation status will have the same issues as those entities (see the respective "Disadvantages" sections). The one special advantage that LLCs will have over sole proprietorships and partnerships is that they offer liability protection, whereas sole proprietorships and partnerships do not.

It's easy to see why LLCs have become very popular. This structure combines liability protection with the ease of a sole proprietorship and a partnership.

Other Business Entities

The types of entities noted here are the most common, but the limited liability partnership and the professional service corporation are also options.

Limited Liability Partnership

The *limited liability partnership* (LLP) is a hybrid entity between a partnership and an LLC. It offers the liability protection of an LLC with the tax filing of a partnership. Generally, only individuals in professions who cannot form LLCs will consider an LLP. These are usually professionals who are prohibited by state laws or other rules from forming LLCs.

Professional Service Corporation

A *professional service corporation* (PSC) is a special kind of C corporation. Under the Tax Code, professionals such as accountants, architects, or attorneys who form C corporations are considered to have formed a PSC. PSCs are taxed at a flat rate of 35%. Thus, a PSC loses one of the tax advantages of a C corporation (the relatively low tax rate on income of less than $75,000).

PSCs are generally used only by professionals who must have a C corporation because of benefits such as health insurance or retirement planning or are forced into this entity because of legal reasons. Most PSCs try to zero out their income each year: Usually it is less expensive to pay the owners' wages (and the associated taxes) than to pay the 35% income tax rate (plus state income tax).

Moving from One Entity Type to Another

Sometimes you form a business entity and you want or need to change it. In some cases, you can move from one kind of entity to another.

You can almost always move from a sole proprietorship to any other form of business entity. The sole proprietorship is not a separate entity, so if you move from one to, say, an S corporation, it would be like forming the S corporation from scratch. Note that for tax reporting purposes, you would use the date the new entity formed as the date you stopped reporting income on a Schedule C and began reporting it as an S corporation.

Similarly, you can almost always move from a partnership to any other form of business entity (you would become a sole proprietorship if there were only one partner remaining in the business). A partnership is a group of individuals acting as a business. Again, you would be forming a new business.

You can move from being an S corporation to a C corporation or vice versa. (Note that if you become an S corporation you must legally qualify as an S corporation; see "S Corporations" section for the requirements.) However, there can be tax consequences to doing so.

If you convert a C corporation to an S corporation, there are three major taxes that might be faced. First, there is the Built-in Gains Tax on any assets that have appreciated (above what they are shown on the books for) that are disposed of within ten years of the S corporation election. Second, any C corporation that used *LIFO inventory* must pay a tax on the benefits under LIFO.[18] (This tax can be paid over four years.) Third, S corporations that have converted from C corporations must pay a tax if their *passive investment income* (i.e., dividends, interest, rents, and capital gains) exceeds 25% of their gross receipts *and* they have accumulated earnings and profits from the time they were a C corporation. One additional factor is that any net operating losses from the time a business was a C corporation do *not* carry forward to the S corporation.

It is much easier to move from an S corporation to a C corporation. Sometimes this will be forced on you if you no longer meet the S corporation qualifications. Note that if you convert from an S corporation to a C corporation you cannot convert back to an S corporation for five years (unless the IRS approves the reconversion, something that almost never happens).

Although you can convert from being a corporation (both an S and a C) to any other form of entity (such as an LLC), there will be significant tax consequences. The corporation will dissolve for federal tax purposes; thus, the owners of the corporation may have a large capital gains tax to pay.

Finally, it's rare to convert an LLC to another form of entity because the LLC can elect to be taxed like a C corporation or an S corporation. An already existing LLC files Form 8832 to be taxed as a C corporation or Form 2553 to be taxed as an S corporation. Note that these forms have date deadlines if the entity wishes to be taxed as a corporation for the entire year.

---

[18] LIFO stands for Last In, First Out. Under this method of inventory, items purchased most recently are considered sold first rather than the oldest items. LIFO is discussed in detail in Chapter 5.

In all cases where you are considering converting your business entity, make sure you discuss your options with a tax professional and an attorney so that you understand all the rules and consequences prior to making the conversion.

Which Entity Is Right for You?

There is no one right entity for every kind of business. You have to weigh the tax issues, legal issues, and your goals to determine which form you should choose.

First, determine your goals. Let's say you've started a high-tech business that you want to take public in a few years; you would likely want to be a C corporation. Perhaps you are an architect in California, just starting out in your own business. In most states an LLC would be a good choice of entity, but you can't choose that in California. You might decide to form an S corporation. The decision will always be different depending on *your* situation.

Once you've set your goals, you should discuss them with a tax professional and an attorney familiar with business entity formation in your jurisdiction. They should be able to help you decide which kind of entity is right for your situation.

▨ **Tip**   Do not form a business entity before discussing it with a tax professional and an attorney.

Table 1-1 lists the different kinds of business entities and their strengths and weaknesses.

Table 1-1. Business Entity Types and Their Strengths and Weaknesses

	Sole Prop.	Partner-ship	S Corp.	C Corp.	LLC
Easy to form?	Yes	Yes	More difficult	More difficult	More difficult
Liability protection	No	No	Yes	Yes	Yes
Flow-through entity?	No*a	Yes	Yes	No	If taxed as partnership
Reasonable salary required?	No salary	No salary for partners	Yes	No	If taxed as S corp

	Sole Prop.	**Partner-ship**	**S Corp.**	**C Corp.**	**LLC**
Annual meeting required?	No	No	Yes	Yes	No
Tax audit risk	High	Low	Low	Medium	Low to high
Can have fiscal year?	No	No	No	Yes	If taxed as C corp
Tax rate	Owners	Owners	Owners	Low on first $75,000; high after	Owners except if taxed as C corp
Owners restricted?	No	No	Yes	No	If taxed as S corp

* A sole proprietorship is the individual alone, so this really does not apply.

An Overview of Taxation

Don't tax you, don't tax me, tax that fellow behind the tree.

—Senator Russell B. Long

When most individuals think of taxes, they naturally think of the income tax. Indeed, the federal income tax is the primary tax that most small business owners pay and is the main focus of this book. However, there are a myriad of taxes that impact businesses from all levels of government. These include state income taxes, state gross receipts taxes, payroll taxes (federal, state, and local), real property taxes, personal property taxes, business license taxes, and more. Not all of these taxes apply to every business, but most business owners will have to file and pay multiple taxes. In this chapter, we explore the taxes that small businesses face, the basis of income and expenses, and the difference between cash and accrual accounting.

There's a saying in law: *ignorantia juris non excusat*. That's Latin for "ignorance of the law is no excuse." Let's say you start a business in Lexington, Kentucky. You pay your federal and state income taxes but didn't know about a local tax you must pay (the Lexington-Fayette Urban County Government Net Profits License Fee Return). You will eventually be contacted and asked to file the past due returns (with interest and penalties, of course).

Types of Taxes

We begin by looking at the federal income tax, as most of the taxes that businesses pay are based on this tax. We then move through the remaining litany of taxes that business owners face.

The Federal Income Tax

The Sixteenth Amendment (ratified in 1913) to the US Constitution states, "The Congress shall have power to lay and collect taxes on incomes, from whatever source derived, without apportionment among the several States, and without regard to any census or enumeration."

The first income tax form was just four pages long (including one page of instructions).[1] Today, an owner of a small business almost certainly looks at a return many times this size. But the basics of the return have *not* changed. Form 1040 is still designed so that you report and pay tax based on your income over the last year.

The US tax system is a *self-reporting system*. You report your income and file your return each year. Your report is accepted at face value subject to the right of the Internal Revenue Service (IRS) to examine (audit) your return. There's a three-year *statute of limitations* on your return (three years from the due date or date of filing, whichever is longer). That's the amount of time the IRS has to audit your return.[2]

Almost everyone has heard the legal concept that you are innocent until proven guilty. Tax law works differently. Because you self-report your income, you are generally *guilty until proven innocent* when your return is examined by the IRS. This is another reason that it is so important to keep excellent records. (For more on audits, see Chapter 17.)

Self-reporting doesn't mean voluntary. Failing to file an income tax return when you are required to do so can be a crime. An individual who has a low income may not have to file a tax return, but almost all business entities that separately file *must* file a tax return every year. Suppose you are the sole stockholder of a shell corporation, Acme. (A *shell corporation* is an entity that exists but is doing no business.) You still have to complete a Form 1120 federal corporate tax return. Because your income is zero, the corporation

---

[1] Original Form 1040 available at http://taxhistory.org/thp/1040forms.nsf/WebByYear/1913/.

[2] The IRS has six years to examine a return in case of a gross understatement of income (defined as an understatement of at least 25 percent). There is no statute of limitations in cases of fraud or if you don't file a return.

will generally owe no tax. However, if you do not file the return in a timely way, you can be subject to penalties.

Note   The strange case of Wesley Snipes. In the "don't try this at home" category, consider the tax protester. They have all sorts of reasons that on their face sound great as to why we don't or shouldn't have to pay income tax. None of them work, but that doesn't stop them!

Wesley Snipes is an actor who fell under the spell of American Rights Litigators (ARL). ARL attempted to take the position that only *foreign* income is taxable. That argument is frivolous, and the courts have universally thrown it out. Snipes was found guilty of three misdemeanor counts of willful failure to file a tax return. He made millions of dollars as an actor. He was sentenced to three years in federal prison, where he'll make a few dollars an hour. It's a lot easier in the long run to file and pay your taxes than to take a frivolous position.

No matter what kind of business you have, the basic format of the federal tax is the same. You note your income and cost of goods sold to come up with your gross income (the income before your business expenses). You then note business expenses by category to determine the net income of the business. If only it were that simple.

Over time, Congress (which writes the laws) and the IRS (which writes regulations promulgated under the laws) have made taxes extremely complex. There's a scene in one of Tom Clancy's novels where the Secretary of the Treasury designate puts the entire Tax Code on a table and the table collapses.[3] Unfortunately, I don't see tax simplification happening soon, so we all must live with the current tax system.

There are layers to tax rules. The Tax Code is law (Title 26, US Code). Sections of the Code cover what income is, what expenses can be deducted, and filing requirements. The Code itself is the highest authority: It's the law.

Similarly, there are *tax treaties* between the United States and various countries. Although these are generally beyond the scope of this book (there are a few paragraphs on this subject in Chapter 18), treaties hold the force of law.

Below the Code and treaties are regulations promulgated under the Code. Congress may write a law allowing the secretary of the Treasury or his or her designee (typically the IRS) to write *administrative law*—a regulation.

Regulations are written and published in the *Federal Register*. Once written, they are open for comment by anyone for at least thirty days. Based on the

---

[3] Tom Clancy, *Executive Orders*. (New York: G.P. Putnam's Sons, 1996).

comments, the proposed regulation may be rewritten or may become the final regulation. The regulation is again published in the *Federal Register* and shortly thereafter becomes final.

Sometimes the IRS issues *temporary regulations*. These cover situations that urgently require resolution. Although titled "temporary," some temporary regulations may remain in force twenty years (or longer) after being written.

Below the Code, treaties, and regulations lie *revenue procedures*. These are official statements of a procedure that affects taxpayers under the Code, statutes, treaties, and regulations that the IRS believes should be public. Revenue procedures are published in the *Internal Revenue Bulletin.* Some revenue procedures are published annually. For example, every year there's a revenue procedure on how you obtain a private letter ruling from the IRS. Some are issued as needed. For example, Revenue Procedure 2012-11 is titled "Procedures for issuing determination letters and rulings on the exempt status of qualified nonprofit health insurance issuers (QNHIIs) described in IRC 501(c)(29) of the Internal Revenue Code."[4] Generally, taxpayers must follow revenue procedures.

Revenue rulings are the lowest form of guidance. These are official interpretations of how the IRS would apply the law to a specific set of facts. Revenue rulings are also published in the *Internal Revenue Bulletin.*

Revenue rulings usually cover a specific situation. For example, Revenue Ruling 2012-18 is titled "Tips included for both employee and employer taxes."[5] Unlike a revenue procedure, a taxpayer does *not* have to follow a revenue ruling. That said, if you don't follow a revenue ruling, you are required to note that fact on your tax return (possibly increasing your chances for an examination), and you will need basis in your position (for example, a court ruling). In reality, most taxpayers follow the guidance that the IRS gives in revenue rulings.

Finally, courts interpret the law. The ultimate arbiter is the US Supreme Court. The Supreme Court does not take many tax cases; usually, a tax case taken up by the Court is done so because two different circuit courts of appeal have issued opposing rulings. A Supreme Court ruling is precedential throughout the United States.

---

[4] See Revenue Procedure 2012-11.

[5] See www.irs.gov/irb/2012-26_IRB/ar07.html. The IRS states that the purpose of this revenue ruling is "to clarify and update guidelines first presented in Rev. Rul. 95-7, 1995-1 C.B. 185, concerning the taxes imposed on tips under the Federal Insurance Contributions Act (FICA) and the notice and demand under section 3121(q) of the Internal Revenue Code (Code)."

▓ **Note   The Supreme Court speaks: Can you be a professional gambler?** Back in 1987, the Supreme Court took up the case of Robert Groetzinger.[6] Groetzinger was a professional gambler and wanted to deduct his business expenses on his tax return. The Supreme Court took up his case, "Because of a conflict on the issue among Courts of Appeals, we granted certiorari."

The key to this case—and a major factor in hobby loss cases—are these lines from the decision: "We conclude that if one's gambling activity is pursued full time, in good faith, and with regularity, to the production of income for a livelihood, and is not a mere hobby, it is a trade or business within the meaning of the statutes with which we are here concerned. Respondent Groetzinger satisfied that test in 1978. Constant and largescale effort on his part was made. Skill was required and was applied. He did what he did for a livelihood, though with a less-than-successful result. This was not a hobby or a passing fancy or an occasional bet for amusement."

Below the Supreme Court are the regional Courts of Appeal. There are twelve regional circuits. A precedential decision of a court of appeal serves as precedent throughout that region.

The lowest rung in the regular federal court system are district courts. A decision of a district court is on a specific case and does not serve as precedent.

There are also specialized federal courts. One of these is the US Tax Court, which hears cases solely on tax issues. Full decisions of the Tax Court serve as precedent. Decisions can be appealed to the regional appeals courts, depending on where the petitioner resides.

Although thousands of Tax Court cases are filed each year, relatively few are actually heard. This is because the court urges both sides (the *petitioner* who files the claim and the *respondent,* the IRS) to settle if at all possible.

Most tax cases that make it to court are heard by the Tax Court. That's because you do not have to pay assessed tax when you file a Tax Court petition. However, if you pursue a tax case in either district court or the Court of Federal Claims (the other methods of challenging the IRS in court) you *must* pay the tax first.

Most of this book covers the specific income and expense items you report for federal income tax. This is the primary tax paid by business owners, either directly if their business entity pays tax or indirectly on their personal return if the business is a sole proprietorship or a flow-through entity.

---

[6] *Commissioner v. Groetzinger,* 480 U.S. 23 (1987).

State Income Taxes

Most states have an income tax. If you pay federal income tax for your business, you likely will have to pay state income tax, too.

A few states do not have an income tax on individuals: Alaska, Florida, Nevada, New Hampshire,[7] South Dakota, Tennessee,[8] Texas, Washington, and Wyoming. However, Alaska and Florida have a corporate income tax (C corporations must file and pay this tax). New Hampshire has a business profits tax paid by all businesses within the state. South Dakota has a tax on financial institutions. Texas has a gross margin tax that exempts sole proprietorships and partnerships; the tax also applies only to businesses with gross revenues of more than $600,000 (though all affected businesses must file a return). Washington has a Business and Occupation tax—a gross receipts tax on all businesses with a tax rate of 0.138% to 1.9% depending on the industry. Only Nevada and Wyoming truly have no state income taxes.

A few jurisdictions, such as California, have minimum franchise taxes that must be paid every year. California's minimum tax of $800 must be paid each year by every corporation and LLC in the state.[9]

For most businesses, the state income tax flows directly from the federal tax. This is because most state systems are based on the federal income tax. However, a few states, such as Arkansas, Iowa, and New Jersey, do not use federal taxable income as the beginning point in calculating tax. Many states have *conformity issues,* where state tax law differs from federal tax law. California has numerous areas in which the state does not conform to federal law. For example, Section 179 depreciation in California is limited to $25,000 a year, vs. the current federal maximum Section 179 depreciation of $500,000.

Other State-Level Taxes

Three states have taken a different approach to taxes. As mentioned in the previous section, Texas has a gross margin tax that impacts larger businesses, and Washington has a Business and Occupation tax that impacts all businesses in the state. Hawaii has a general excise and use tax that applies to all businesses. This functions not only as the state's sales tax but also as a gross receipts tax on businesses. A business in Hawaii has the joy of paying two state-level taxes: income tax and the general excise and use tax.

---

[7] New Hampshire has an interest and dividends tax of 5 percent.

[8] Tennessee has an interest and dividends tax of 6 percent.

[9] There is no minimum tax in the first year of a corporation that is registered with the California Secretary of State.

▓ **Tip   Location matters.** Suppose you are starting a business near Lake Tahoe (on the border of California and Nevada). If you are in California, you will be paying income tax and are subject to the California regulatory environment. If you are in Nevada, you will *not* be paying income tax and are subject to Nevada's regulatory environment.

Although this is a rather polarized example, where you locate your business definitely matters. I moved my business from Southern California to Nevada for several reasons (a major one was taxes). When you're choosing a business location, pay attention to *all* the requirements, regulations, and taxes that exist in your chosen location. You may decide that a different location is a better choice.

Most businesses also have to comply with sales tax laws. Five states do not have a sales tax: Alaska, Delaware, Montana, New Hampshire, and Oregon. Although sales taxes are thought of as a cost mainly for consumers, businesses must pay them on purchases for their own use. States have become increasingly proactive in collecting *use tax*. Use tax is the equivalent of sales tax when a product is purchased but no sales tax is paid. Suppose you buy a machine that you would generally resell to a customer, but you end up keeping the machine for your own use. You generally owe use tax on that purchase.

Sales tax rates vary widely throughout the country and even within a state. Most states allow local jurisdictions to charge additional sales tax. California has over 100 different districts charging sales tax!

Many businesses find they have to collect sales tax in multiple states even though they have just one physical office. In 1992, the Supreme Court decided *Quill Corp. v. North Dakota*.[10] The Court held that for there to be nexus (see definition in the note) to a state, there must be a physical presence in the state. Since that decision, states have been pushing the envelope and attempting to enforce nexus when there is no physical presence.[11] A few states now have economic nexus statutes on their books. These laws are of questionable constitutionality, but this doesn't change the fact the laws are on the books.

---

[10] *Quill Corp. v. North Dakota* (91-194), 504 U.S. 298 (1992).

[11] California and Washington are two states with economic nexus laws.

▓ **Note   What is nexus?** One of the most important concepts in tax is *nexus*. The dictionary defines *nexus* to mean "a means of connection; tie; link."[12] In tax, *nexus* means that your business has sufficient ties to the state (or local jurisdiction) and has become subject to the tax laws of that state. For income tax purposes, generally a business will have nexus with a state if it has a physical location in the state, employees in the state that are doing more than just soliciting business, or property in the state. Nexus rules vary in each state.

The rules for nexus for sales tax law are more complex. All of the factors that can cause nexus to arise for income tax can cause nexus for sales tax. Additionally, activities by affiliates and even manufacturers' representatives have been used to cause nexus for sales tax. Again, the rules vary among the states.

Complying with sales tax law requires documentation. Sales tax agencies will assume that every sale is for your own use unless you properly document resale licenses or certificates. The required procedure varies in each state. If you keep good records and follow your state's procedures, you will be far better off.

Local Income Taxes

Some local jurisdictions have their own income taxes. At the time of this writing, if you are in Kentucky, Michigan, Ohio, New York, or Pennsylvania you may have to deal with local income taxes. These are tax forms you must file and pay to a local jurisdiction. (Indiana has a county option with its income tax, but the tax is collected with the state income tax.)

New York City is the most infamous locale for local taxes in the United States. First, residents of the metropolitan area (within New York state) must pay the Metropolitan Commuter Transportation Mobility Tax (MCTMT). Though the tax rate is low, it's yet another set of paperwork and regulations for the business owner.

A resident of New York City pays a higher personal income tax rate than other residents of the state.[13] This additional tax is collected on the state income tax return (similar to Indiana).

Unfortunately, it doesn't end there. A business in New York City must file and pay business taxes to the city. An unincorporated business (a sole proprietorship, partnership, or LLC) files an unincorporated business tax

---

[12] Definition of "nexus," Dictionary.com, http://dictionary.reference.com/browse/nexus?s=t.

[13] Yonkers also has a local income tax add-on that's collected with the New York state income tax.

return. A corporation (either a C corporation or an S corporation) must file and pay New York City General Corporation Tax. New York City does *not* recognize S corporations for its tax. The tax rate isn't low; it can be up to 8.85%.

Another jurisdiction with high local taxes is Philadelphia. The City of Brotherly Love has a school district income tax, a business privilege tax, and a net profits tax.

Ohio has city and school district taxes; each local jurisdiction has a different rate. At least it's easy to determine your rate: The Ohio Department of Taxation offers *The Finder,* which allows you to look up your city, school district, and sales tax rates for wherever you reside in the Buckeye State.[14]

If you are a resident of one of the affected states, make sure you check to see if you have a local tax filing obligation along with your state and federal taxes.

Payroll Taxes

If your business has employees, you will have payroll taxes. These include FICA (social security), Medicare, federal unemployment insurance, state unemployment insurance, and possibly other state payroll taxes.

Payroll taxes are covered in depth in Chapter 13. For now, one major point to realize is that an officer or owner of a business can be held personally liable for payroll taxes. Say you use Fly by Night Payroll Service, and they properly calculate and withhold your payroll taxes but don't remit them to the government. *You* can be held liable for paying them again! I cover how to avoid this in Chapter 13.

Real Property Taxes

For most US citizens, their home is their biggest investment. Among the bills homeowners must pay are local property taxes. A business that owns real property must also pay property taxes on the land and buildings.

Personal Property Taxes

In most jurisdictions businesses must pay personal property taxes. These are assessed on machinery, equipment, supplies, and sometimes inventory; the tax is usually administered at the county level. A business files a statement of personal property annually noting the property it has (or the property it has

---

[14] Ohio's Finder, Ohio Department of Taxation, www.tax.ohio.gov/online_services/thefinder. stm.

added or retired); later, the tax agency sends the business a bill. Tax rates vary widely depending on state and local laws.

Business License Taxes

Most businesses must obtain a business license. These are usually administered at the local (city or county) level. Some jurisdictions charge a flat fee for a license; others charge based on gross receipts or payroll taxes. You should carefully check local law on obtaining a business license and the associated taxes and fees. A few states, such as Nevada, also require a business to obtain a state license (in addition to the local license).

■ **Tip   Location matters (again).** Suppose you are opening a business in Southern California. You're debating between a location in Los Angeles and one in Irvine (in Orange County). You look at the licensing requirements of both cities.

You discover there's an annual tax of just $50 in Irvine.[15] However, you find that Los Angeles has a gross receipts–based business license structure.[16]

This does not necessarily mean that Irvine is a better location than Los Angeles. The gross receipts tax (or lack thereof) is just one factor that should be evaluated in choosing the location of your business.

Excise Taxes

Businesses in a few industries must pay an *excise tax*. These were typically introduced to pay for specific items. For example, the telephone excise tax was introduced in 1898 to pay for the Spanish-American War. In 2006, this tax was eliminated for all but local telephone service. Excise taxes exist at both the federal and state levels.

A complete listing of federal excise taxes (except for taxes administered by the Bureau of Alcohol, Tobacco, Firearms and Explosives) is found in IRS Publication 510.[17] The most well-known IRS-administered excise taxes are on fuel, telephone use, and indoor tanning. There are also excise taxes on sport fishing equipment, bows and quivers, arrow shafts, and vaccines.

---

[15] Business License Application, City of Irvine, https://cityofirvine.org/ipd/divisions/business_licenses/regulartax.asp.

[16] Tax Information Booklet, City of Los Angeles, http://finance.lacity.org/content/TaxInfoBooklet.htm.

[17] See www.irs.gov/pub/irs-pdf/p510.pdf.

Other Taxes

Anything that the mind of man can make, he can also tax. Thus, taxes are always expanding. It's probably impossible to list out the unreal taxes you could face if you're in the wrong business in the wrong location. User fees (next section) are yet another form of tax.

The one other "tax" that most businesses must pay is the annual registration fee. Most corporations must register with the Secretary of State (or Corporations Commission) of the state in which they are doing business. LLCs generally fall under this requirement as well. This is usually called a fee, but for all practical purposes is an additional tax.

One piece of good news about all these taxes: Generally, any tax paid by a business is an "ordinary and necessary" business expense that can be deducted.

User Fees

In 1978 California voters passed Proposition 13. This measure limited property tax within California, which cut tax revenues. One result of this was an increase in user fees.

Most people think of user fees as the fee to go to a beach or to take the elevator to the top of the Statue of Liberty. However, there are user fees that businesses must pay. Your water bill may have various fees that you are required to pay. Your property tax bill almost certainly has several user fees (such as a lighting district) included. You may be paying a federal user fee if you are in agriculture (such as the Animal and Plant Health Inspection Service user fee). Tax professionals pay user fees to the IRS to obtain required licenses and related matters.

User fees have the same impact of a tax; the only difference is the name. I use the duck test: If it looks like a duck, swims like a duck, and quacks likes a duck, then it probably is a duck. User fees are just another name for taxes. If you don't pay a user fee when required to do so, you usually suffer the same consequences as if you didn't pay a required tax.

What Is Income?

The first step in determining tax is determining income. The Tax Code gives a starting place for this—Section 61(a) states, "Except as otherwise provided in this subtitle, gross income means all income from whatever source derived." Courts have interpreted this broadly; in *Commissioner v. Schleier* the Supreme

Court notes,[18] "We have repeatedly emphasized the 'sweeping scope' of this section and its statutory predecessors."

A simple way of looking at this is to assume that *everything is taxable unless Congress exempts it.*

I'm sometimes asked if there's a minimum threshold for taxation. There's not—if your business earns $1 of gross income, that $1 is reportable.

You do get to deduct any sales adjustments and refunds you make. For example, if a check from a client bounces, that's a deduction from gross receipts; if a customer returns a product he's purchased, that's a deduction from sales.

If you recall the definition of gross income, your cost of goods sold can be deducted against your gross receipts. This would include the material costs of items you sell, the labor costs related to that, shipping and handling to get the goods to customers, and similar costs.

But that's it. Gross income is simply your gross receipts minus your sales adjustments minus your cost of goods sold.

What Are Expenses?

The next step is to determine expenses. The Tax Code is the first resource. Section 162(a) begins, "There shall be allowed as a deduction all the ordinary and necessary expenses paid or incurred during the taxable year in carrying on any trade or business." Courts have interpreted expenses narrowly; in *Commissioner v. Schleier,* the Supreme Court states,[19] "We have also emphasized the corollary to §61(a)'s broad construction, namely the 'default rule of statutory interpretation that exclusions from income must be narrowly construed.'" In plain English this can be stated: *Nothing is deductible unless Congress allows it.* Though Section 162(a) appears broad (and it is), the rest of the Tax Code narrows what can and cannot be deducted. Indeed, most of the remainder of this book is devoted to what you can deduct for expenses and how to correctly document those expenses. Although most tax professionals would prefer a simpler Tax Code, the current Code is anything but straightforward.

---

[18] *Commissioner v. Schleier* (94-500), 515 U.S. 323 (1995).

[19] *Commissioner v. Schleier.*

Cash vs. Accrual Accounting

The final topic of this chapter is an important one: *cash* vs. *accrual*. This may seem arcane, but the difference in accounting methods can make a difference in the tax you pay.

Cash basis accounting is relatively straightforward. You recognize income when you receive it; you recognize expenses when you pay for them. This is the method that most Americans use for their day-to-day lives.

There's a second type of accounting: *accrual accounting*. Here, income is recognized when the invoice is sent out; expenses are recognized when you receive the invoice from the vendor.

Some businesses do not have a choice. You *must* use the accrual method if you have annual sales of more than $5 million or you have annual sales of $1 million and you maintain an inventory of items you sell to the public.

For the most part, the results will be the same no matter which method you use. However, there can be timing differences. Let's look at two examples with a calendar year C corporation, Acme.

*Example 1. Acme makes a $25,000 sale on December 29. The customer pays for the product on January 24. If Acme is cash basis, the sale **will not** be included in this year's income (it will go on next year's income); if Acme is accrual basis, the sale **will** be included in this year's income.*

*Example 2. Acme purchases supplies costing $20,000 on December 30. Acme pays its vendor on January 25. If Acme is cash basis, the $20,000 expense **will not** be included in the year's results (it will go on next year's expenses list). However, if Acme is accrual basis, the expense **will** be included in the year's results.*

Most small businesses use cash basis accounting. That does not necessarily make it the right choice for your business. Although cash basis is more like how you keep your books for your personal life, accrual basis accounting is better for showing your overall results without emphasizing a particularly good (or bad) month.

Before Your Business Opens

The beginning is the most important part of the work.

—Plato

You are ready to start building your business. Most people just plunge in, and taxes and record keeping fall by the wayside. "Let's get the business up and running as fast as possible," they think. The problem with this is that things we keep track of today are known tomorrow. When we reconstruct things tomorrow that occurred yesterday, we tend to make mistakes.

In this chapter we look at how to make sure your business starts off on the right foot from a tax standpoint. The focus is on the *start-up phase,* the time when you're building your business but you have not yet had any revenue. There are rules that must be followed, and we look at what you can and can't deduct.

The Start-Up Phase

The cost of getting started in a business is considered a *capital expense.* All of your costs that are both *ordinary and necessary* (see Chapter 4 for more on these standards) are deductible. This includes everything from the purchase of equipment, wages for your employees, and advertising your business. Your *organizational expenses* are separately accounted for (see "Organizational Expenses" section later).

There is an exception to start-up costs being capital expenses: *capital equipment* you purchase for your business. Let's say you are starting a pizza shop, and you buy a pizza oven. The oven would be separately capitalized as a fixed asset (see Chapter 10 for more on fixed assets and depreciation).

The start-up phase commences when you begin building your business, and it ends once you have your first dollar of revenue.

Start-Up Expenses

What are start-up expenses? The Internal Revenue Service (IRS)[1] gives the details:

> Start-up costs are amounts paid or incurred for: (a) creating an active trade or business; or (b) investigating the creation or acquisition of an active trade or business. Start-up costs include amounts paid or incurred in connection with an existing activity engaged in for profit; and for the production of income in anticipation of the activity becoming an active trade or business.

Let's put that into plain English. A start-up expense is almost anything you spend money on that is used for creating a business that will attempt to make a profit. I've already covered the major exceptions (organizational expenses and capital expenses). There are three other costs that do *not* qualify as start-up expenses: interest, taxes, and research and development. Those items are still deductible business expenses, so it's not as if you lose them.

Unfortunately, how you deduct start-up expenses is very different from how other items are deducted. The Tax Code states that start-up expenses are generally deducted over a fifteen-year period.[2] A related part of the Code[3] states that you can *elect* to take up to $5,000 of start-up expenses in your first year in business. However, if your total start-up costs are more than $55,000, you *cannot* make an election to expense up to $5,000 of start-up expenses in your first year in business. (The ability to make the election phases out as the total of start-up expenses increases from $50,000 to $55,000.)

When you make the election to amortize and expense your start-up expenditures, you will attach a statement to your tax return. A sample statement is shown in Figure 3-1.

---

[1] IRS, Publication 535: Business Expenses (for 2011 returns), www.irs.gov/pub/irs-pdf/p535.pdf.

[2] IRC §195(c)(1)(A).

[3] IRC §195(b).

▓ **Note   Start-up expense election now deemed.** Effective as of September 2008, the election to expense up to $5,000 of start-up expenses is now deemed to have been made. If you have $5,000 or less of start-up expenses, you do *not* have to attach a statement to your return (as detailed next). You can simply include those costs as "start-up expenses" on your tax return. However, if you have more than $5,000 of start-up expenses you *must* include a statement and follow the procedures as noted.

Note the detail that's required on the statement in Figure 3-1. First, it must note that the taxpayer is electing under Section 195(b)(1) of the Internal Revenue Code that the total start-up expenses were $5,830, that $5,000 of those expenses are elected to be deducted, and the remaining $830 of expenses are being amortized over 180 months (15 years). The name of the business and a description of the business must be given. The month the business began must also be provided. Finally, each expense must be separately listed.

I have deliberately made the listing of expenditures short. The sample business had just six expense items. However, it's possible to have hundreds of items. If you do, they still must be individually listed.

▓ **Tip   Accounting software to the rescue.** Typing six entries is no big deal when completing your tax return; however, I doubt you want to type 60, 600, or 6,000 entries. This is one of the benefits of using accounting software.

You can create an expense account titled "Start-Up Expenses" and simply charge all such expenses into that account. Many tax software products can import from popular accounting software such as QuickBooks. (Note that importing is generally *not* available from the QuickBooks online product). If you use accounting software, make sure you have everything set up correctly. A mistake made early in a business's life will tend to cascade and cause increasing problems over time. If you have any doubts, consider hiring a bookkeeper experienced with your software to make sure you start off on the right foot.

IRC SECTION 195(b)(1)

Name(s) shown on Return
John Smith

Identification Number
111-22-3333

Tax Year: 2012

Election to Amortize Start-up Expenditures

The taxpayer elects under Section 195(b)(1) of the Internal Revenue Code to:

1. Start-Up costs that must be amortized when paid or incurred before October 23, 2004:
   a. Amortize total start-up expenditures paid or incurred before October 23, 2004:   _____
   b. Number of months (not less than 60) to amortize expenditures incurred before
      October 23, 2004. Beginning with the month on Line 6:   _____

2. Start-Up expenditures paid or incurred after October 22, 2004:
   a. Total Start-Up Expenditures after October 22, 2004:   _____5,830
   b. Start-Up expenditures allowed or elected to be deducted in 2011 limited
      to $5,000/$50,000:   _____5,000
   c. Start-Up expenditures after October 22, 2004 to be amortized over 180 months: _____830

3. a. Total Start-Up expenditures for this business   _____5,830

4. Name of this trade or business: _____ Acme

5. Description of the trade or business: _____ Management Consulting
_____
_____
_____

6. Month in which business began: _____April

Start-Up Expenditures

7. Enter a description, an amount, and date for business start-up expenses paid or incurred for the start of a new business.

Description of Expenditures	Expenditure Amount	Date Incurred
Design of Website: Smith Web Designs	2,500	03/10/2012
Paper: Office World	30	03/20/2012
Printing: North City Printers	210	03/30/2012
Postage: US Postal Service	90	03/30/2012
Design of Website: Smith Web Designs	2,500	04/04/2012
Advertising: Daily Thing	500	04/10/2012

Figure 3-1. Sample election to amortize start-up expenses

In the first year of this business, $5,000 will be expensed as start-up expenses. Of the remaining $830, only $37 will be amortized in the first year (8/12 of 1/15 of the $830).

Notice also that the expense listing notes both a description of the expense (e.g., Design of Website) and the name of the vendor. This allows for an easy reconciliation if the return is audited.

Any tax or interest expenses incurred during the start-up phase are expensed; these items are *not* treated differently during the start-up phase. Tax and interest expense are covered in Chapter 10.

You do *not* have to elect to deduct $5,000 of start-up expenses; you can, if you wish, deduct a lesser amount. However, most business owners want to get the benefit of the expenses (the tax write-off) as quickly as possible. Thus, it is rare when a business does not deduct the maximum allowable start-up expenses.

Organizational Expenses

The second major type of expense incurred during the start-up phase is organizational expenses. Organizational expenses are incurred only if you have a separate business entity, such as a corporation, LLC, or partnership.

Organizational expenses are costs used for the creation of the business entity that would be amortized over the life of the business (if the business had a fixed life). They must also be incurred either before the end of the first tax year in which a corporation is in business or incurred prior to the due date of a partnership tax return (excluding extensions).

▨ **Tip   The left and right hands of a sole proprietorship.** You may ask, "Why can't there be organizational expenses for my sole proprietorship? I still need legal and accounting advice." The reason is that legally there is no difference between you and the sole proprietorship. If you recall from Chapter 1, a sole proprietorship is you acting as a business. The business functions as your alter ego. Although you can have costs for starting the business, these costs cannot be deducted as organizational expenses because *you haven't organized a new business!* Legal and accounting fees in the start-up phase for a sole proprietorship would be deductible as start-up expenses.

Also note that you can't pay yourself a salary when you have a sole proprietorship. You *are* the business; paying yourself a salary would just be moving money from your left hand to your right hand.

The rules for deducting and amortizing organizational expenses are identical to those for start-up expenses (though the Code section and regulation allowing for the deduction and amortization are different).[4]

The election to amortize and/or deduct organizational expenses is now deemed to have been made. If you have less than $5,000 of these expenses, you do not have to attach an election statement to your tax return. If you have more than $5,000 of expenses, you will need to attach a statement.

Figure 3-2 shows a sample statement for Acme Consulting LLC. The statement is very similar to the start-up election statement shown in Figure 3-1. There's a statement that the partnership is electing under Section 709 of the code to deduct $5,000 of organizational expenditures and amortize the remaining $550 over 180 months. The total of the organizational expenses is given along with the name of the business and a description of the business. The starting month of the business and a listing of the expenses is the last part of the statement.

The number of organizational expenditures is usually smaller than it is for start-up expenses. That's because organizational expenses are limited to only a few kinds of expenses. In practice, many businesses will not have to file the organizational expense election statement because their expenditures in this category will not exceed $5,000.

---

[4] IRC §709 allows for the amortization for partnerships; §248 is for corporations. The statement falls under IRC Regulation 1.709-1(b) and (c) for partnerships and IRC Regulation 1.248-1(c) for corporations.

Partnership Name: Acme Consulting LLC
Identification Number: 12-3456789
Tax Year Ending: 12/31/2012

Deemed Election to Amortize/Deduct Organizational Expenditures
Statement Pursuant to IRC Regulation 1.709-1(b) and (c)

The partnership hereby elects under Section 709 of the Internal Revenue Code to:
1. Amortize total organizational expenditures paid or incurred before
   October 23, 2004: _____
2. Number of months (not less than 60) to amortize expenditures incurred before
   October 22, 2004 beginning with the month on line 8: _____
3. Deduct organizational expenditures limited to $5,000 incurred after
   October 22, 2004: _____5,000
4. Amortize remaining organizational expenditures incurred after October 22, 2004
   over 180 months beginning with the month on line 8: _____550

5. Total organizational expenditures: _____5,550

6. Name of this trade or business: _____ Acme Consulting LLC

7. Description of the trade or business: _____ Management Consulting
   _____
   _____
   _____

8. Month in which business began: _____April

9. **Organizational Expenses:**

Description of Organizational Expense	Date Incurred	Date Paid	Amount
Legal Fees, Smith & Jones LLP	03/10/12	03/10/12	4,000
Registration Fees, Nevada Secretary of State	03/10/12	03/10/12	250
Business License Fees, City of Las Vegas	03/20/12	03/20/12	300
Legal Fees, Smith & Jones LLP	04/01/12	04/01/12	1,000

Figure 3-2. Sample election to amortize organizational expenses

▨ **Tip** **Consider including the elections statement when you do not have to.** Let's say you've started a new LLC, and your organizational expenses total $4,000. You can deduct those organizational expenditures without including a statement on your tax return. You should consider including the statement anyway, and the reason has to do with what would happen if you've made a mistake.

Imagine you forgot about a $1,200 invoice from your attorney, so the true total of organizational expenses was $5,200 rather than the $4,000 you included. You would be able to expense the maximum $5,000. However, you might not be allowed to amortize the $200 of expenditures that exceed the $5,000 that can be deducted in an audit.

If you include the deemed statement and you have left off the $1,200 invoice, you will be allowed to either amend your return (noting the additional expense, deducting an additional $1,000, and then amortizing the remaining $200 over fifteen years). By including the election statement, you allow yourself the ability to more easily recover from an error.

Record Keeping Requirements

Having a business means that you *must* keep records. As Ben Franklin said, "An ounce of prevention is worth a pound of cure." In this case, starting with good records will make your life as a business owner far easier. Good records allow you to see how your business is doing, prepare financial statements, know who is paying you (and who is not), keep track of business expenses, help in preparation of your tax returns, and support items claimed on the tax return.

For tax purposes, you need to be able to prove anything and everything on your return. Remember, you're guilty until proven innocent in the eyes of the IRS. Let's examine the different items on a tax return and the records you will need for each.

Income

The records you need for proving your income depend on the kind of business you have. Typical records include:

- Cash register records.
- Bank deposit records.
- Cash receipts books.
- Invoices.

- Credit card records.

- Forms 1099-MISC you receive.

Note that if your business uses the accrual method of accounting, the cash you receive might not match your income. In this case, the invoices you generate should match the income. For a cash-basis business, the money you receive should match your income, whereas the invoices you generate might not match the income.

Tip   Use a separate bank deposit for nonincome items. Although most of the deposits you make into your business bank account will be for income, you will likely have some nonincome items that you have to deposit. For example, you may have a refund of a deposit you made to a utility company. If you use a computer system for your accounting, make sure to note your bank deposit as a refund. Consider making a separate deposit at the bank so that it is readily identifiable in case of an audit.

Expenses (Including Cost of Goods Sold)

You need to be able to prove your expenses. This not only means being able to show that you spent, say, $200 for a hotel but that it was *business-related*. If there might be any doubt, write the business purpose of the expense on the receipt. If you have a business meal or entertainment expense, write on the receipt who was with you *and* the business purpose.

Documents you can use to prove business expenses include:

- Canceled checks.

- Account statements.

- Credit card sales slips.

- Invoices.

- Petty cash slips.

These are primary records and, as long as there is a business purpose, these will be accepted by the IRS. Credit card statements are *secondary records* that do *not* have to be accepted by the IRS. The problem with a credit card statement is that it only shows you spent, for example, $200 at a business. It doesn't show what was purchased or that it had a business purpose.

Electronic Records

Up until the 1990s, keeping records meant keeping the original documents. Although you can still keep original documents, the IRS allows scanned copies (and photocopies) as long as all of the information on the original document is readable.

If you use a scanning system, your system must have an index so you can easily retrieve a specific document. The IRS has the right to test your system to make sure that it accurately reproduces an original record. You should test your scanner (and electronic filing cabinet software, if applicable) to make sure that you can retrieve anything you store digitally.

█ **Tip** **Only back up the data you want to keep.** Computer hard drives can and do fail. My corollary to Murphy's Law is that your computer will crash at the least opportune moment. Make sure you are backing up all the data you wish to keep, and *test the backups!* This means you need to attempt a restoration from your backups. If you can't restore the data, your backup is worthless.

Additionally, make sure you store a backup off-site and that you regularly backup your data to the off-site location. What would happen to your backup if it's next to your computer and that room is destroyed? If you don't regularly back up your data, you may have to recreate a week or a month's worth of records when (not if) your computer crashes. You may wish to consider one of the online backup services that will automatically back up your data.

Computer Accounting Systems

The same regulations that allow you to use electronic systems for storing your data also allow computer-based accounting systems. All reputable software providers, such as QuickBooks and Peachtree, comply with IRS requirements of being able to reproduce records. Make sure that if you use a computer system that you back it up!

█ **Caution** **Two sets of books aren't better than one.** Most business owners want just one set of financial records (books). After all, that's all you need for your business. Of course, where most wouldn't consider going the Bozo contingent has no problem heading to. The IRS routinely sends undercover agents to businesses that are for sale. Here's an example of something you definitely shouldn't try at home.

In July 2008, AJ's Green Dry Cleaners in Palo Alto, California, went up for sale. Sung Ho Choi managed the business for his parents. An IRS undercover criminal investigator approached Choi and he provided the investigator with sales data. The sales exceeded what was reported on the tax return for the business. It turned out that Choi only provided the bank records and not the complete sales records to his tax preparer. He pleaded guilty to four counts of preparing or aiding in preparing false tax returns. He was sentenced to two months' community confinement, eight months' home confinement, full restitution of $60,537, and a $5,000 fine.

How Long Should You Keep Your Records?

The IRS gives recommendations for the amount of time to keep records in Publication 583.[5] I believe the IRS recommendations are too short. In Table 3-1, I present my recommendations for the length of time to keep various records.

The IRS recommends keeping income and expense records for three years. Note that this length of time is from *the due date of the return or the date of filing, whichever is later.* I recommend eight years, a much longer period of time.

The reason I recommend this extended timeframe is that the IRS can attempt to assess a gross understatement of income penalty for six years from the due date of the return or date of filing (whichever is later). Most states give their tax agencies extra time to challenge returns; eight years is typical for many states. Of course, if you do not have a state filing requirement (for example, you are in Nevada), then six years is likely long enough. You should check with your state and/or local tax agency for their period of limitations (the amount of time they have to challenge your return).

Table 3-1. Suggested Record Keeping Times

Type of Record	How Long to Keep Record
Tax returns	Forever
Income and expense backup records	8 Years
Payroll records	Forever
Corporate minutes	Forever
Worthless security/bad debt	7 Years
Records for fraudulent return	Forever
Records if you do not file a return	Forever

[5] See IRS, Publication 583: Starting a Business and Keeping Records, www.irs.gov/pub/irs-pdf/p583.pdf, page 15.

I'm hopeful that no one reading this book would ever consider filing a fraudulent return or not filing their tax return. That said, if you don't file a return when you're required to, the statute of limitations doesn't begin to run. In theory, the IRS has forever to come after you if you don't file a return.

Finally, I strongly advise that you keep copies of your tax returns forever. The returns have information you will find useful in future years. Additionally, make sure you retain proof of filing: either the receipt from the postal service (if you mail the return, *always* mail it using certified mail, return receipt requested) or the proof of electronic filing.

Day-to-Day Expenses

It's time to examine the deductions you are allowed to take on a tax return. We begin by reviewing what's an allowable expense and what's not. We then look at each category of expenses: cost of goods sold, the office, the car, travel, meals and entertainment, fixed assets and depreciation, and everything else. (Employees, payroll taxes, and benefits are covered in Part III.)

The Basics of Expenses

The hardest thing in the world to understand is the income tax.

—Albert Einstein

What can I deduct as a business expense? How far can I stretch the envelope? What records do I need? What about expenditures that are part personal and part business? Are there business expenses that I can't deduct on my tax return?

Expenses are frequently a trouble spot for business owners. We begin by looking at what an expense is and some of the more common (and uncommon) expenses. Next, we examine the two standards that all expenses must meet: the *ordinary* standard and the *necessary* standard. The chapter concludes by looking at nondeductible expenses.

Overview of Expenses

Section 162(a) of the Tax Code begins, "There shall be allowed as a deduction all the ordinary and necessary expenses paid or incurred during the taxable year in carrying on any trade or business."

As noted in Chapter 2, nothing is deductible unless Congress allows it. That said, if you can demonstrate that the expenditure is both necessary and ordinary for your business (both terms will be discussed in depth later in this chapter), and you have proper documentation for your expense, the IRS (or the courts) will generally allow it.

Once again, the documentation is what ends up being the issue for most people. You need *proof* that you spent the money. Document, document, document! If you can show you spent the money on a legitimate business activity, you will likely prevail.

▨ **Note** **Breast implants deductible for exotic entertainer?** Most tax court cases feature mundane matters of taxation. However, every so often something unusual hits the court. So it was in 1994 when Cynthia Hess faced down the IRS over $699 of self-employment tax. Hess claimed that her breast implants were depreciable; the IRS challenged it as a personal expense.

Hess's agent urged her to increase the size of her breasts to increase her income. Her custom-made implants were size 56N. She truly earned her stage name of "Chesty Love." Her income increased but at the cost of serious medical problems. Hess considered the implants a necessary stage prop. The court agreed, noting that her implants were similar to special clothing that's essential for a business and not suitable for general or personal wear. "Petitioner's line of business, that of a professional exotic dancer, was such that part of her 'costume' was her freakishly large breasts." Hess prevailed at Tax Court and didn't owe the $699.

For the most part, your expense deduction is whatever you spend. Let's say you buy some paper for $30 for your business and are charged $2 of sales tax. The sales tax is included in your deductible expense. If you pay shipping or handling on your purchase, that is also deductible.

▨ **Tip** Sales tax and shipping and handling are includable as an expense in the cost of a purchase.

There is one expense item where you do *not* get the full cost. Congress limited *meals and entertainment* expenses to 50% of the actual cost. These expenses are discussed in depth in Chapter 9.

Documentation Requirements

In Chapter 3, I noted that you need to have proof of your business expenses. This doesn't mean just the receipt or invoice; you have to be able to show that there's a business purpose to the expense. Let's look at some examples of what's required.

Example 1. Suppose you purchase a stapler for use in your business. You save or scan the receipt. That should be sufficient to satisfy the IRS, because the use of a stapler is normal for almost any business.

Example 2. You are developing a line of cosmetics. You purchase some of your competitor's cosmetics to see what they have recently developed. This purchase meets both the ordinary and necessary standards (discussed later). However, the IRS might wonder if you're purchasing cosmetics for personal use rather than business use. Thus, you should note on the receipt the *business purpose* of the purchase. This should be done for any purchase that could be used for personal use but is being used for a business purpose.

▓ **Caution   More stringent requirements for travel, gifts, meals and entertainment, and listed property.** Section 274(d) of the Tax Code requires that there be adequate records or sufficient evidence for these categories of expenses. (*Listed equipment* relates to certain depreciable items and is discussed in Chapter 10.) As discussed in Chapter 17, you *must* have documentation for these expenses.

Keep good records of your business expenses, and make sure you know where important documents are stored. Back up all computer records (your computer can and will crash at the least opportune moment). Additionally, make sure you test your backups and that you can restore from them. If you follow good backup procedures, you will be far better off than most business owners.

The Ordinary Standard

To deduct a business expense, it must be both *ordinary* and *necessary*. The IRS notes that an *ordinary expense* is: "[O]ne that is common and accepted in your trade or business."[1] *Ordinary* also means exactly what common sense dictates: An expense cannot be extraordinary to be deductible.

This is a relatively easy standard to meet. Because you hopefully want to turn a profit, all of your expenses should be on items that are typically used in your business. Where problems arise are for lavish expenses or for unusual businesses.

Let's say you are traveling for business, and you have breakfast in the hotel coffee shop. That expense will almost certainly be considered ordinary. After all, you have to eat breakfast. You then decide to celebrate signing a huge contract with a client by eating dinner in the fanciest restaurant in town. You spend $200 a person before even considering the $500 bottle of wine. If your return is examined, you will be sitting across from an IRS auditor. When

---

[1] See IRS, "Deducting Business Expenses," www.irs.gov/Businesses/Small-Businesses-&-Self-Employed/Deducting-Business-Expenses.

government employees travel, they must live within their means; the per diem meal standard for the most expensive metropolitan areas in the United States is $71 a day. Attempting to fully deduct this dinner as an ordinary expense won't work.

If you are in an unusual business, you will likely have to help the IRS examiner if your return is audited. Although the IRS has audit manuals to help their examiners, these materials are not all-inclusive. Thus, if your business is unusual you will have to be able to explain why your expenses are used in your business. If you can show that such expenses are used by your competitors or how the expense helps your business, you should prevail at audit.

The Necessary Standard

What is a *necessary expense?* In Publication 535 (Business Expenses), the IRS states: "A necessary expense is one that is helpful and appropriate for your trade or business. An expense does not have to be indispensable to be considered necessary."[2] *Necessary* means what common sense would tell us: An expense is necessary if it helps our business.

A few years ago, I was preparing an Estate Tax return. The decedent had owned a few US silver coins from the early twentieth century. I purchased a reference book on antique coins to obtain a rough idea of their value. I needed to know if the coins were worth $100 or $10,000; if they were worth the latter, I would need to hire an appraiser to obtain an exact valuation. (The coins were worth less than $100.) Normally, a reference book on US coins would not be considered a *necessary* expense for a tax preparation business. However, I could show that I needed the book, so it became a legitimate business expense.

In general, the IRS won't deny an expense as necessary as long as you can reasonably show it is related to your business.

For the Business

Business expenses must be just that—for the *business*. They *cannot* be personal expenses. You are not allowed to deduct personal expenses on a business return. Section 262 of the Tax Code specifically disallows deductions for personal, living, and family expenses. Doing so and getting caught is a good way to find yourself heading to prison.

---

[2] See IRS, Publication 535: Business Expenses (for 2011 returns), www.irs.gov/pub/irs-pdf/p535.pdf.

▒ **Note   Personal expenses on the corporate return lead to prison.** Michael Fisher is a former co-owner of a sand and gravel business. Fisher decided to go on an African safari and renovate a truck stop he owned. There's nothing wrong with that. The problem was that these expenses were both decidedly personal in nature and had nothing to do with the sand and gravel business.

Unfortunately for Fisher, these expenses were deducted on his corporate tax return. More unfortunately, the IRS discovered these issues (plus he didn't include all of his income on his personal tax returns). Fisher pleaded guilty to nine counts of tax fraud. He was sentenced to thirty-seven months in prison, assessed a $90,000 fine, and was required to make restitution of $308,069.[3]

One obvious issue is what to do with expenses that are partially business and partially personal. Such expenses generally come in to play with sole proprietors. Let's look at a typical example of such an expense.

An individual operates a consulting practice as a sole proprietorship. He purchases a new computer that he will use both for his business and for personal use. He pays $1,000 for the computer. What amount should he base his depreciation deduction on?

(Note that a computer is *listed equipment,* so it must be depreciated. Listed equipment, depreciation, and capital assets are discussed in Chapter 10.)

First, it's clear that the computer is an ordinary and necessary business expense. However, because the computer will not be used 100% for business, the basis for the depreciation cannot be 100% of the purchase price.

What must be determined is the business use percentage of the computer. Assume that the consultant keeps a time log and can show that he uses the computer 80% for business and 20% for personal usage. Then he would be able to base his depreciation on 80% of the purchase price, or $800.

▒ **Tip   Backup required for mixed-use items.** If you have an expense item that is used for both business and personal use, you will need records to show what portion of the usage is business and what portion is personal.

There are two other expense items that can be used for both business and personal use: the car and the home. Home office expenses are discussed in

---

[3] See US Department of Justice, Tax Division, "North Dakota Executive Sentenced to Prison for Tax Fraud," www.justice.gov/opa/pr/2009/December/09-tax-1337.html, December 2009.

depth in Chapter 6; automobile expense deductions are discussed in Chapter 7.

Nondeductible Items

Besides personal expenses, some other expenses are also not deductible. Part IX of the Tax Code (sections 261–280H) notes those items that cannot be deducted on a tax return.

Most of these items will seem obvious. As already mentioned, you can't deduct personal, living, or family expenses. Items that are capital expenses cannot be deducted (although you do get to depreciate these items; §263 of the Tax Code). Many of the other items in the list cover very specific situations.

One category of nondeductible expenses includes items related to tax-exempt income. A basic principle in accounting is that you match expenses to income. If an item of income isn't taxable, it follows that the associated expenses are not deductible. Section 265 of the Tax Code notes this.

Various Tax Code sections prohibit expenses related to evading or avoiding income tax (sections 269–269A). Expenses related to illegal sales of narcotics are disallowed (section 280E). Expenses that Congress doesn't like have also been ruled as nondeductible; these include golden parachutes (section 280G) and costs associated with disposing of coal or iron ore (section 272). Although federal income tax is clearly an ordinary and necessary expense, section 275 states that you can't deduct it on your federal income tax.

Finally, penalties are not deductible. This includes penalties issued by a federal, state, or local tax agency.

Cost of Goods Sold

Whatever you tax, you get less of.

—Alan Greenspan

If you look at any business tax form, the first section after gross receipts is for cost of goods sold. Can all businesses use cost of goods sold? What part does inventory play within cost of goods sold? What other expenses, if any, are taken within this category?

As will be seen in the first section of this chapter, cost of goods sold applies when there are tangible goods being handled by the business—something that can be touched, held, or moved. Many business owners never deal with this category of expenditures.

Can All Businesses Use Cost of Goods Sold?

"If it's on a tax return form, it can be used." That's what some of my clients have told me. Sadly, that's just not true in every case. The very phrase *cost of goods sold* implies merchandise. That's what a good is—a physical item.

The Tax Court also held this. In *Perry v. Commissioner,* the court noted:[1]

---

[1] US Tax Court, *T.C. Memo 2012-237,* http://ustaxcourt.gov/InOpHistoric/PerryMemo.TCM. WPD.pdf, p. 10.

> *Cost of goods sold may be subtracted from gross receipts to compute gross income in a taxpayer's manufacturing, merchandising or mining business. See sec. 1.61-3(a), Income Tax Regs. We have held that a business must involve the sale of a material product to which direct cost may be allocated to reduce gross receipts by the costs of goods sold in computing gross income. More generally, we have held that gross receipts equal gross income where a business is primarily engaged in providing services; i.e., ability, know-how and experience.* [citations and note omitted]

This passage makes it clear that if your business is a service business—you are selling yourself or providing services to others—you *cannot* have cost of goods sold. If you're in a service business the rest of this chapter will *not* apply to you. Do note that if your business provides services *and* sells a product, you will have cost of goods sold for the portion of your business that sells a product.

Inventory: The Basics

Inventory is part of the accrual method of accounting. Some businesses don't have to use the accrual method. As noted in Chapter 2, businesses with annual revenues of $1 million or less can use the cash method.[2] Additionally, businesses that are not mining, manufacturing, wholesale or retail trade, or in the information industry and have annual revenues of $10 million or less can use the cash method.[3]

All other businesses that sell products have inventory. The idea of inventory from a tax point of view is that you clearly show your expenses as they relate to your sales. One of the fundamental principles of accounting is that expenses should be matched to revenues.

Let's say that your business manufactures a machine. The costs of manufacturing the machine will include the materials used to make it and the cost of labor used in making it. Related expenses will include the packaging used for the machine, supplies used with the machine, and inbound shipping and handling costs.

The problem in tying the expenditures to the sale is that the expenses are incurred over time. It's also nearly impossible to match specific raw materials

---

[2] Specifically, if the average annual gross receipts over the past three years is $1 million or less. The business must also not be a tax shelter.

[3] Specifically, the average annual gross receipts over the past three years is $10 million or less. The business must not be a tax shelter. The specific NAICS codes prohibited from using the cash method under this exception are given in IRS, Revenue Procedure 2002-28, *Internal Revenue Bulletin* 2002-18 (2002), www.irs.gov/pub/irs-irbs/irb02-18.pdf, p. 815.

with the cost of a specific product. You may know that you use four half-inch brass screws in your machine, but did you use the brass screws you bought in June or the ones you purchased in July that cost 10% more? You don't know which screws were used, of course. That's why inventories are used.

This whole area of accounting is called *cost accounting* and is the subject of a semester-long course in colleges. The nuances are generally beyond the scope of this book. What you need to know for purposes of taxation is that your inventory allows you to match your expenses to your income. You also need to know the methods of inventory that are allowed, how you value that inventory, and what happens if you're a cash-basis business that sells goods.

What's in Inventory?

Inventory normally includes the merchandise you sell, the raw materials you use to manufacture the merchandise (if applicable), work in progress (if applicable), finished goods, and supplies that become part of the goods you sell.

Cost of Goods Sold for the Year

If you look at a tax form where cost of goods sold is calculated (such as Part III of a Schedule C,—Sole Proprietorship), you will see the basic calculation used in determining your cost of goods sold. Part III of Schedule C is shown in Figure 5-1.

Schedule C (Form 1040) 2011			Page 2
Part III	**Cost of Goods Sold** (see instructions)		
33	Method(s) used to value closing inventory: a ☐ Cost b ☐ Lower of cost or market c ☐ Other (attach explanation)		
34	Was there any change in determining quantities, costs, or valuations between opening and closing inventory? If "Yes," attach explanation	☐ Yes	☐ No
35	Inventory at beginning of year. If different from last year's closing inventory, attach explanation	35	
36	Purchases less cost of items withdrawn for personal use	36	
37	Cost of labor. Do not include any amounts paid to yourself	37	
38	Materials and supplies	38	
39	Other costs	39	
40	Add lines 35 through 39	40	
41	Inventory at end of year	41	
42	**Cost of goods sold.** Subtract line 41 from line 40. Enter the result here and on line 4	42	

Figure 5-1. Cost of goods sold calculation

The cost of goods sold for the year is the beginning inventory, minus the ending inventory, plus any related expenses. Some of this appears obvious (and is), but there are many facets to cost of goods sold that you should know.

How Inventory Is Expensed

If you look at Figure 5-1, you will notice that there are various choices you have in how you value inventory. These choices matter, and the method you use influences whether you are considered profitable for tax purposes. Note that it is quite possible to have a profit (or loss) for tax purposes but a loss (or profit) based on cash flow. There are two major methods used for inventory valuation: *cost* and *lower of cost or market*.

Cost

Valuing your inventory at cost means that you generally use the price you pay for goods. You adjust the price for shipping and handling costs and for cash discounts you receive on purchases.

When you value your inventory (see the "Inventory Valuation and the Physical Inventory" section later), you identify the specific pieces of inventory and use the price you paid for each item. Most businesses can't do this: How can you tell one widget from another?

IRS regulations allow for two methods around this problem: last-in, first-out (LIFO) and first-in, first-out (FIFO). These have important tax consequences.

Under both methods you value inventory based on the purchase price of goods. Where the methods differ is on which goods are considered sold: the last goods purchased or the first goods purchased.

LIFO

LIFO assumes that the *last* product purchased is what is sold from your inventory. Using LIFO lessens the impact of price changes. If you are selling the most recently purchased inventory, most of what you sell will be those recently purchased items. If your inventory turns a lot, the value of the inventory could be based on prices from years ago. (Inventory *turnover* or *turns* is a measure of the number of times inventory is sold or used in a time period, typically one year. A higher number of turns means your inventory moves quickly; a low number of turns means your inventory might be on your shelves for some time.)

Under LIFO, your most recently purchased inventory will be "used" first. If prices are changing, your income tax statement will tend to show current costs. With LIFO, your tax returns will be closer to reality than they would with FIFO. You will tend to have older costs in your inventory; this can have the benefit of reducing personal property taxes on inventory (if prices are increasing). Finally, when inventory costs increase, the taxable income will decrease. This is because more recent costs are shown in cost of goods sold. An increase in cost of goods sold *decreases* income.

▨ **Note   Purchases directly impact cost of goods sold.** If you look at Figure 5-1, you will see that purchases made are part of cost of goods sold. In an environment of rising prices, those purchases will have a direct impact on cost of goods sold, likely increasing cost of goods sold and decreasing profit.

There are drawbacks to using LIFO. First, if costs are falling LIFO will tend to increase taxable income. If an old inventory layer begins to get used (in calculating cost of goods sold), this also tends to increase income. There is also a LIFO recapture tax on a C corporation that elects to become an S corporation (if the business uses LIFO).

▨ **Note   What is an inventory layer?** A *layer* of inventory refers to a group of inventory purchased at one price. In an environment of rising prices, those purchases will have a direct impact on cost of goods sold, likely increasing cost of goods sold and decreasing profit.

Overall, LIFO leads to an increase in cost of goods sold and a decrease in tax profit when prices are increasing. When prices are decreasing, LIFO leads to a decrease in cost of goods sold and an increase in tax profit.

FIFO

FIFO means that the oldest inventory on the books is what is considered sold. This mimics what most businesses actually do: They use the oldest stock first to avoid spoilage. FIFO has its own advantages and disadvantages for tax purposes.

First, FIFO is far simpler to understand than LIFO. FIFO is what we do in our lives. If we're going to heat a can of soup, we usually use the oldest can first. This is the normal procedure for businesses; almost everyone uses the oldest materials first.

FIFO leads to an *increase* in cost of goods sold and a *decrease* in taxable income when prices are decreasing. Many technology products see a decrease in costs over time; thus, FIFO can be advantageous for high-technology businesses.

There is a major disadvantage to FIFO as well. When prices are increasing, FIFO will not reflect the current (market) price of goods. Thus, in this situation, FIFO leads to a lower cost of goods sold than with LIFO, and a higher tax profit.

Businesses with inventory using the cost method should carefully weigh the advantages and disadvantages of LIFO versus FIFO in choosing a method for their business. Like most everything in tax, there is no one-size-fits-all choice.

Lower of Cost or Market

The second major method used in valuing inventory is the *lower of cost or market*. Here, inventory is valued at either its cost or the market price if the price has gone down. Businesses using LIFO *cannot* use lower of cost or market.

Lower of cost or market allows a write-down of inventory when prices fall. Say your inventory has some microprocessors valued at $100 each. A new microprocessor is introduced with double the speed at the same price; the microprocessors you have in stock are now on sale for just $50 each. In such a situation, if you are using lower of cost or market you can take a write-down of $50 per microprocessor on hand. This will *increase* your cost of goods sold and *decrease* your tax profit.

Inventory write-downs are normally taken in conjunction with the year-end physical inventory (see the section on "Inventory Valuation and the Physical Inventory," later). Assume that in the example above that the business has 100 of the old microprocessors in stock at year-end. They are on the company's books at a value of $10,000; however, they are now worth only $5,000. The company can take a $5,000 write-down of inventory based on the new lower price for the microprocessor.

▧ **Caution   Estimates don't work for write-downs.** If you're going to take a write-down of inventory, you need objective evidence, not subjective estimates. In *Best Auto Sales, Inc. v. Commissioner,* the Tax Court noted that "The testimony of [the] president that at year-end he made estimates of the value of the automobiles does not provide a basis on which the claimed inventory write-downs can be allowed in this case."[4]

---

[4] *Best Auto Sales, Inc. v. Commissioner, T.C. Memo* 2002-297, p. 11 (http://ustaxcourt.gov/ InOpHistoric/BestAuto.TCM.WPD.pdf).

Other Methods

There are other methods that have been allowed for specific industries. Section 1.471-2(b) of Income Tax Regulations states, "It follows, therefore, that inventory rules cannot be uniform but must give effect to trade customs which come within the scope of the best accounting practice in the particular trade or business."

Most of these other methods are used in specific industries. For example, when I worked in the citrus industry, the orange juice plant my employer owned used a hybrid average cost method that was standard for citrus juice plants.

Inventory Valuation and the Physical Inventory

Almost all businesses with significant inventory conduct an annual *physical inventory*. A physical inventory is usually conducted at year-end. You are required to include an accurate valuation of your year-end inventory on your tax return.

The main reason physical inventories are conducted is to verify that your inventory records are accurate. Additionally, expired merchandise should be disposed of. Physical inventories are also a check for employee malfeasance.

The most important part of a physical inventory is the preparation. Count sheets, cards, or bar-code scanners are prepared, and personnel are assigned (where applicable) to handle the count. If you have a single retail store, you may be the only individual involved in the physical inventory.

Prior to the inventory, it's a good idea to straighten everything out. Cleaning up the location of the physical inventory will make the process go faster and increase its accuracy.

Once the inventory is complete, you enter the corrected quantities (where applicable) into your computer system. If you are using lower of cost or market, this is also the time to adjust prices downward. At the conclusion of your data entry, you will have your year-end inventory valuation.

▨ **Tip   Counting by weight.** Suppose your inventory contains tens, hundreds, or thousands of resistors, capacitors, screws, or other small objects with a low per-piece value. Instead of counting each small item, you can count these items by weight. Suppose ten 100-ohm resistors weigh 3.0 ounces. You weigh your bin of 100-ohm resistors and find that it weighs 15.0 ounces (excluding the weight of the bin). You can conclude that you have fifty 100-ohm resistors in your inventory.

If you determine that adjustments need to be made to your inventory for reasons other than change in quantity and/or lower of cost or market, adjustments are also made at this time. These changes might include theft and spoilage adjustments.

▓ **Note   Goods on consignment.** If you have goods out on consignment—products for which you still have title but that are in the possession of others—those goods *are* includable in your inventory. Similarly, if you have possession of goods belonging to others on consignment to you, those items should *not* be included in your inventory.

Cash Basis Inventory

If a business sells merchandise but uses the cash basis, what does it do for inventory? First, such a business does *not* record inventory on its tax return. There is no such thing as inventory for a cash basis business.

However, that does not mean there isn't a cost of goods sold. All of the other expenditures used in cost of goods sold are still recorded. This business will have purchases, shipping, labor, and other related costs.

Other Expenses Included in Cost of Goods Sold

There are other items in addition to inventory that impact cost of goods sold. Although some directly relate to inventory, others do not.

Purchases

Purchases are exactly what it sounds like: the expenditures made to acquire raw materials and goods for sale or resale. These are the purchases of goods that make up your inventory. This is very straightforward in that this should exactly match your cost of the items purchased.

Do note that if you remove any items for your personal use, those items must be deducted from purchases.

Cost of Labor

Cost of labor is your expense for personnel working in the manufacturing or mining industries. Note that only direct labor costs (wages) are included; indirect costs (i.e., administrative costs and selling costs) are not part of cost of goods sold. Certain overhead costs *are* part of cost of goods sold but are noted separately.

Materials and Supplies

These costs are for items used in the manufacturing process but do not become part of finished goods. Some examples are hardware and chemicals. These items are expensed when used.

Other Costs

There are other items that are part of cost of goods sold; the "other costs" section of the tax return is where these items are listed. Following are the most likely examples.

Shipping Containers

Containers and packaging material that become part of a product are included in cost of goods sold. This also includes pallets used for stacking finished goods.

Freight In

Cost of shipping goods, materials, and supplies used in production or for sale to your facility is part of cost of goods sold.

Overhead Expenses

You are allowed to apportion overhead expenses—items such as rent, utilities, depreciation, taxes, and repairs and maintenance—so that a portion is charged to your cost of goods sold.

Depreciation of Fixed Assets Used in Manufacturing

Your depreciation expenses related to equipment used in producing goods for sale should be included in cost of goods sold.

Other Items

There can be other costs that should be included in cost of goods sold. If the expenditure directly relates to the production of goods for sale or the costs related to selling goods at wholesale or retail, it is probably includable in cost of goods sold.

The Office

I just filled out my income tax forms. Who says you can't get killed by a blank?

—Milton Berle

The single largest investment for most Americans is a home. Many small businesses are conducted out of the home. This chapter focuses on the office, whether it is rented or in your home.

The first part of the chapter looks at the rented office. Certainly rent is deductible. But how are leasehold improvements handled? What's done with CAM charges?

The second part of the chapter looks at the home office: which home offices are (and are not) deductible and how the type of business entity changes the deductibility. The chapter closes by looking at how the deduction is calculated and provides an example of the calculation.

The Rented Office

Many small businesses are conducted out of rented space. This could be an executive suite or a building in a light industrial park. Obviously, rent is deductible as an ordinary and necessary business expense.

Many lease agreements come with additional charges. Generally, all of these additional charges are ordinary and necessary expenses and are thus deductible. That's because these expenditures are required for you to lease the office space.

Many commercial leases are structured as *triple-net leases* (sometimes called NNN leases). With a triple-net lease the lessee is responsible for property tax, building insurance, and maintenance (the three *nets* referred to in the name). Almost all leases are written so that the lessee is responsible for a proportionate amount of the costs of any common areas. These are sometimes referred to as common area maintenance (CAM) charges, which are deductible business expenses.

In an audit situation, the IRS will usually ask to see a copy of your lease. The lease document and copies of any invoices for triple-net and CAM charges (along with canceled checks noting the payments of these amounts) is usually all the proof you need to show your rent expense.

Finally, if you rent an off-site storage space—for example, a ten-by-ten-foot space at a self-storage facility—that expense would also be noted as rent.

The Home Office

A great many small businesses are conducted out of the home. Until 1976 there was nothing specific in the Tax Code regarding the home office. In that year, Congress added Section 280A to the Tax Code. Today the general rules for a deductible home office are settled for the business owner.

Generally you can take a deduction for a home office if the space is used *exclusively* as a home office, solely for your business. "Exclusively" has two meanings here: The space is used exclusively as a home office, and it is used exclusively by you as a home office. Let's say you use a room in your home as your home office; your spouse also uses the room as her office. Your home office would *not* be deductible because it is not used exclusively as a home office for a single business.

IRS Publication 587 has a flowchart that shows the general rules on whether you can take a home office deduction, reproduced in Figure 6-1. Let's look at how this flowchart works. (Note that there are different rules for storage spaces within the home and for daycare facilities.)

The first question is whether you're using your home in connection with your business. You can't deduct personal expenses, so if you are not using your home for the business, you can't take the home office deduction.

▓ **Tip** **Apartments count.** You do not have to live in a house to take the home office deduction. An apartment or other rented space can be deductible if it meets the criteria for the home office deduction.

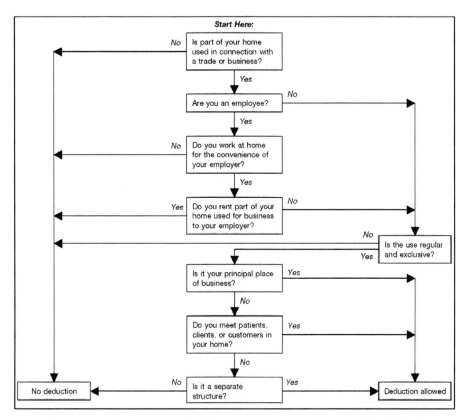

Figure 6-1. Can you deduct business use of the home expenses? (From IRS, Business Use of Your Home, Publication 587 [2011 edition], www.irs.gov/pub/irs-pdf/p587.pdf, p. 4)

This book is concerned generally with business owners and not employees. Next we look at whether the use of the home is regular and exclusive. If it's not, you can't take the home office deduction. You can then take the deduction if it's your principal place of business, if you meet with clients in your home, or if it is a separate structure.

There's another way the deduction is allowed: If you perform administrative or management functions solely in your home office even if you perform other functions elsewhere. In 1997, Congress amended the Tax Code to specifically allow for this to be a valid reason for the deduction. Here's an example.

Suppose you are an anesthesiologist performing work in a few local hospitals. None of the hospitals gives you any space for the administrative functions of your work (billing, writing reports, etc.). You use a room in your home exclusively as a home office to perform these required functions. You can take the home office deduction.

▨ **Note**   **The anesthesiologist we have to thank for an administrative home office.** Dr. Nadir Soliman, a Washington, DC–area anesthesiologist, took the home office deduction in 1983 (his use of a home office mirrored the facts in the paragraph above). His deduction was challenged by the IRS. Soliman took his case to Tax Court and won. The IRS appealed and lost in the Fourth Circuit Court of Appeals. The IRS then appealed to the Supreme Court, which took the case. In 1993 the Supreme Court ruled against Soliman (see *Commissioner v. Soliman* [91-998], 506 U.S. 168 [1993]). The uproar against this decision was a major factor in persuading Congress to change the law in 1997. As noted, Soliman's deduction would be allowed today.

What If You Use the Home Office for Two Activities?

Assume you use your home office for two activities. If you use it for two businesses, and you meet the criteria for the home office deduction for *both* businesses, you can take the deduction. If not, you cannot take the deduction for *either business*. This rule also holds if you use your home office for a business and as an employee: You must meet the criteria for a deductible home office for both activities to take the deduction for either activity.

Deducting a home office as an employee is more difficult: You must meet the *convenience of the employer* test.[1] If you think you won't meet the test but would still like to deduct your home office for your business, you may want to not use your home office for the employer work. Set up a desk in a different room of your home for telecommuting. Your home office will now be used exclusively for your business, so you should be able to take the home office deduction.

What Can You Deduct?

If you have a home office, you are allowed to deduct both direct and indirect costs of the office. *Direct expenses* directly relate to your office. These include repainting and repairs made to your office. *Indirect expenses* are for your entire home. These include your mortgage interest (or rent), utilities, insurance, repairs on your entire house, and property tax. You cannot deduct direct expenses that are unrelated to your home office. If you repair a gazebo in your back yard or paint a bedroom, those expenses are not deductible for your home office.

---

[1] If your employer provides you with an office at their facility, you will generally *not* meet this test.

How the Deduction Is Figured

The deduction is calculated differently depending on your business structure. A sole proprietor uses Form 8829 (see Figure 6-2). A partner (or a member of an LLC that files as a partnership) uses a worksheet to determine the

Form **8829**	**Expenses for Business Use of Your Home**	OMB No. 1545-0074
Department of the Treasury Internal Revenue Service (99)	► File only with Schedule C (Form 1040). Use a separate Form 8829 for each home you used for business during the year. ► See separate instructions.	20**11** Attachment Sequence No. **176**
Name(s) of proprietor(s)		Your social security number

Part I Part of Your Home Used for Business

1	Area used regularly and exclusively for business, regularly for daycare, or for storage of inventory or product samples (see instructions)	**1**	
2	Total area of home	**2**	
3	Divide line 1 by line 2. Enter the result as a percentage	**3**	%
	For daycare facilities not used exclusively for business, go to line 4. All others go to line 7.		

4	Multiply days used for daycare during year by hours used per day	**4**		hr.	
5	Total hours available for use during the year (365 days x 24 hours) (see instructions)	**5**	8,760 hr.	
6	Divide line 4 by line 5. Enter the result as a decimal amount . . .	**6**	.	
7	Business percentage. For daycare facilities not used exclusively for business, multiply line 6 by line 3 (enter the result as a percentage). All others, enter the amount from line 3 . . . . ►	**7**		%

Part II Figure Your Allowable Deduction

8	Enter the amount from Schedule C, line 29, **plus** any gain derived from the business use of your home and shown on Schedule D or Form 4797, minus any loss from the trade or business not derived from the business use of your home and shown on Schedule D or Form 4797. See instructions . .			**8**	
	See instructions for columns (a) and (b) before completing lines 9–21.		**(a)** Direct expenses	**(b)** Indirect expenses	
9	Casualty losses (see instructions)	**9**			
10	Deductible mortgage interest (see instructions)	**10**			
11	Real estate taxes (see instructions)	**11**			
12	Add lines 9, 10, and 11	**12**			
13	Multiply line 12, column (b) by line 7		**13**		
14	Add line 12, column (a) and line 13			**14**	
15	Subtract line 14 from line 8. If zero or less, enter -0-			**15**	
16	Excess mortgage interest (see instructions) .	**16**			
17	Insurance	**17**			
18	Rent	**18**			
19	Repairs and maintenance	**19**			
20	Utilities	**20**			
21	Other expenses (see instructions).	**21**			
22	Add lines 16 through 21	**22**			
23	Multiply line 22, column (b) by line 7		**23**		
24	Carryover of operating expenses from 2010 Form 8829, line 42 . .		**24**		
25	Add line 22 column (a), line 23, and line 24			**25**	
26	Allowable operating expenses. Enter the **smaller** of line 15 or line 25			**26**	
27	Limit on excess casualty losses and depreciation. Subtract line 26 from line 15			**27**	
28	Excess casualty losses (see instructions)	**28**			
29	Depreciation of your home from line 41 below	**29**			
30	Carryover of excess casualty losses and depreciation from 2010 Form 8829, line 43	**30**			
31	Add lines 28 through 30.			**31**	
32	Allowable excess casualty losses and depreciation. Enter the **smaller** of line 27 or line 31 . .			**32**	
33	Add lines 14, 26, and 32.			**33**	
34	Casualty loss portion, if any, from lines 14 and 32. Carry amount to **Form 4684** (see instructions)			**34**	
35	**Allowable expenses for business use of your home.** Subtract line 34 from line 33. Enter here and on Schedule C, line 30. If your home was used for more than one business, see instructions ►			**35**	

Part III Depreciation of Your Home

36	Enter the **smaller** of your home's adjusted basis or its fair market value (see instructions) . .		**36**	
37	Value of land included on line 36		**37**	
38	Basis of building. Subtract line 37 from line 36		**38**	
39	Business basis of building. Multiply line 38 by line 7.		**39**	
40	Depreciation percentage (see instructions).		**40**	%
41	Depreciation allowable (see instructions). Multiply line 39 by line 40. Enter here and on line 29 above		**41**	

Part IV Carryover of Unallowed Expenses to 2012

42	Operating expenses. Subtract line 26 from line 25. If less than zero, enter -0-	**42**	
43	Excess casualty losses and depreciation. Subtract line 32 from line 31. If less than zero, enter -0-	**43**	

For Paperwork Reduction Act Notice, see your tax return instructions.	Cat. No. 13232M	Form **8829** (2011)

Figure 6-2. Form 8829 (2011 version)

deduction (see the "Deducting the Home Office as a Partner" section). The home office for a corporation is discussed later in this chapter (see "S Corporations and C Corporations").

You must first determine the percentage of your home used as a home office. Most business owners take the ratio of the square footage of their home office to the square footage of their whole home.

However, you are allowed to use other methods if they accurately show the portion used as a home office. If you rent an apartment and all the rooms are approximately the same size, you can take the ratio of room(s) used as a home office to the total number of rooms in your apartment.

After you compute the business percentage, you enter all of your direct and indirect expenses. The trickiest calculations relate to mortgage interest and including certain indirect expenses.

Mortgage Interest

Only allowable mortgage interest can be deducted; the fact that you are taking the deduction on Form 8829 rather than on Schedule A (itemized deductions) does not change whether the interest is deductible. Thus, you must first determine the amount of your deductible mortgage interest.

You are only allowed to deduct mortgage interest based on $1.1 million of home acquisition debt.[2] You can also deduct all points paid on the acquisition of your main home.[3] (Points are fees charged by your mortgage lender for your loan; generally, the more points you pay, the lower the interest rate. Points are also called loan origination fees, maximum loan charges, loan discount, or discount points.) However, you must deduct points paid on refinancing over the *life of the loan*. Again, taking the deduction on Form 8829 rather than Schedule A does not change this rule. Let's look at an example of how this works for a refinancing.

You refinance the $200,000 of principal left on your mortgage, and obtain a new 4% 30-year loan. You pay *one point,* or 1% of the loan amount ($2,000). Your loan closes on July 1. What portion of the points can be deducted?

The points must be amortized over the life of the loan, or over 360 months. The deduction will be based on $2,000 ÷ 360 × 6 = $33. The $33 of deductible

---

[2] You are allowed to deduct up to $1 million of home acquisition debt between your first and second home ($500,000 if married filing separately). However, you can also deduct up to $100,000 of home equity debt. Generally, this allows you to deduct up to $1.1 million of home acquisition debt.

[3] There are specific rules detailing this given in IRS Publication 936.

points for the current year will be split between the home office deduction and the mortgage interest deduction (taken on Schedule A).

The allowable mortgage interest that is not deductible on Form 8829 is taken on Schedule A. Most tax software automatically flows the nonbusiness portion of mortgage interest directly to Schedule A. However, you may need to confirm that the points taken on Schedule A are correct, especially if you are deducting points paid on a refinanced mortgage.

Indirect Expenses

Make sure you include all allowable indirect expenses you have incurred. Some common expenditures that are frequently forgotten include burglar alarm monitoring fees, pest control, *all* utilities (including water and sewer), janitorial service, and homeowners association fees.

Depreciation

If you own your home, you can recover a portion of the costs through *depreciation*. As noted on line 36 of Form 8829, you depreciate based on the *lesser* of your adjusted basis or its fair market value. Most fixed assets and depreciation of those assets are covered in Chapter 10. Here we focus only on the depreciation of a home.

Basis is generally (but not always) your cost. For a home, basis is adjusted by any improvements made to the home and any costs of acquiring the home that could not be expensed at the time of purchase.

Land *never* depreciates. Although Dust Bowl farmers of the 1930s might disagree, land is there forever, so it can't depreciate. You must subtract the value of the land (as shown on line 37) to determine the basis of the building. Usually, the property tax assessment has a breakout of the value of the land and buildings on your property.

You multiply the business percentage use of your home by the basis of the building to determine the business basis of the building. The depreciation percentage (line 40) is given in the instructions to Form 8829.[4]

---

[4] See IRS, Instructions to Form 8829, 2011 edition, www.irs.gov/pub/irs-pdf/i8829.pdf, instructions to line 40.

▓ **Caution** One drawback of depreciation for a home office is that this depreciation is *recaptured* **when you sell your home.** At that time, any depreciation you have is generally income. You cannot avoid this by electing to not take depreciation when you have a home office, though. Depreciation is required to be taken if you have ownership of your home (and are taking the home office deduction). If you don't take it, the IRS can impute it, and you could have depreciation recapture when you never took the depreciation expense!

Allowable Home Office Expenses

One rule for home office expenditures is that these expenses cannot force your business into a loss. If your expenses are large enough that taking all of them would cause a loss, any expenditures that would cause a loss are carried forward to the following year. You can take these expenses in the following year (subject to that year's limitation) even if you reside in a different home.

Home Office Deduction for Partners and LLC Members

Partners and members of LLCs that are taxed as partnerships can also take the home office deduction. This deduction is *not* taken on Form 8829; instead, a worksheet is prepared that is not submitted with the tax return. That worksheet is shown on Figure 6-3.

Note that the calculations done are basically identical to that of Form 8829. The difference is that the calculations are not shown when filing the return. You need to keep the worksheet; if your return is examined (audited), you will need to provide the auditor with the worksheet and the backup information.

▓ **Caution** Having a deductible home office is *not* enough for a partner (member). To deduct unreimbursed partnership expenses, the partnership agreement (or LLC operating agreement) must require that the partners (members) pay these expenses. Otherwise, the partners must submit the expenses to the partnership (or LLC) and be reimbursed by the partnership. In that case, the partnership (or LLC) would take the expenses on its books.

Worksheet To Figure the Deduction for Business Use of Your Home
Use this worksheet if you file Schedule F (Form 1040) or you are an
employee or a partner.   *Keep for Your Records*

PART 1—Part of Your Home Used for Business:
1) Area of home used for business . . . .   1) _____
2) Total area of home . . . .   2) _____
3) Percentage of home used for business (divide line 1 by line 2 and show result as percentage) . . . . .   3) _____ %

PART 2—Figure Your Allowable Deduction
4) Gross income from business (see instructions) . . . .   4) _____

	(a) Direct Expenses	(b) Indirect Expenses
5) Casualty losses . . . . 5)		
6) Deductible mortgage interest and qualified mortgage insurance premiums . . . . 6)	_____	_____
7) Real estate taxes . . . . 7)	_____	_____
8) Total of lines 5 through 7 . . . . 8)	_____	_____

9) Multiply line 8, column (b), by line 3 . . . .   9) _____
10) Add line 8, column (a), and line 9 . . . .   10) _____
11) Business expenses not from business use of home (see instructions) . . . .   11) _____
12) Add lines 10 and 11 . . . .   12) _____
13) Deduction limit. Subtract line 12 from line 4 . . . .   13) _____

14) Excess mortgage interest and qualified mortgage insurance premiums . . . . 14)	_____	_____
15) Insurance . . . . 15)	_____	_____
16) Rent . . . . 16)	_____	_____
17) Repairs and maintenance . . . . 17)	_____	_____
18) Utilities . . . . 18)	_____	_____
19) Other expenses . . . . 19)	_____	_____
20) Add lines 14 through 19 . . . . 20)	_____	_____

21) Multiply line 20, column (b) by line 3 . . . .   21) _____
22) Carryover of operating expenses from prior year (see instructions) . . . .   22) _____
23) Add line 20, column (a), line 21, and line 22 . . . .   23) _____
24) Allowable operating expenses. Enter the **smaller** of line 13 or line 23 . . . .   24) _____
25) Limit on excess casualty losses and depreciation. Subtract line 24 from line 13 . . . . .   25) _____
26) Excess casualty losses (see instructions) . . . . 26) _____
27) Depreciation of your home from line 39 below . . . . 27) _____
28) Carryover of excess casualty losses and depreciation from prior year (see instructions) . . . . 28) _____
29) Add lines 26 through 28 . . . .   29) _____
30) Allowable excess casualty losses and depreciation. Enter the **smaller** of line 25 or line 29 . . . .   30) _____
31) Add lines 10, 24, and 30 . . . .   31) _____
32) Casualty losses included on lines 10 and 30 (see instructions) . . . .   32) _____
33) Allowable expenses for business use of your home. (Subtract line 32 from line 31.) See instructions for where to enter on your return . . . .   33) _____

PART 3—Depreciation of Your Home
34) Smaller of adjusted basis or fair market value of home (see instructions) . . . .   34) _____
35) Basis of land . . . .   35) _____
36) Basis of building (subtract line 35 from line 34) . . . .   36) _____
37) Business basis of building (multiply line 36 by line 3) . . . .   37) _____
38) Depreciation percentage (from applicable table or method) . . . .   38) _____ %
39) Depreciation allowable (multiply line 37 by line 38) . . . .   39) _____

PART 4—Carryover of Unallowed Expenses to Next Year
40) Operating expenses. Subtract line 24 from line 23. If less than zero, enter -0- . . . .   40) _____
41) Excess casualty losses and depreciation. Subtract line 30 from line 29. If less than zero, enter -0- . .   41) _____

Figure 6-3. Worksheet for business use of home for partners

The unreimbursed partnership expenses, including the home office deduction, are shown on Part II of Schedule E (page 2). A sample deduction is shown in Figure 6-4.

Schedule E (Form 1040) 2011			Attachment Sequence No. **13**		Page **2**

Name(s) shown on return. Do not enter name and social security number if shown on other side.

George & Jane Jetson

Your social security number
123-45-6789

Caution. The IRS compares amounts reported on your tax return with amounts shown on Schedule(s) K-1.

Part II **Income or Loss From Partnerships and S Corporations** Note. If you report a loss from an at-risk activity for which any amount is **not** at risk, you must check the box in column (e) on line 28 and attach **Form 6198.** See instructions.

27 Are you reporting any loss not allowed in a prior year due to the at-risk or basis limitations, a prior year unallowed loss from a passive activity (if that loss was not reported on Form 8582), or unreimbursed partnership expenses? If you answered "Yes," see instructions before completing this section. ☐ **Yes** ☐ **No**

28 (a) Name		**(b)** Enter P for partnership; S for S corporation	**(c)** Check if foreign partnership	**(d)** Employer identification number	**(e)** Check if any amount is not at risk
A	Acme LLC	P	☐	00-1234567	☐
B	UPE	P	☐	00-1234567	☐
C			☐		☐
D			☐		☐

	Passive Income and Loss			Nonpassive Income and Loss	
	(f) Passive loss allowed (attach **Form 8582** if required)	**(g)** Passive income from **Schedule K–1**	**(h)** Nonpassive loss from **Schedule K–1**	**(i)** Section 179 expense deduction from **Form 4562**	**(j)** Nonpassive income from **Schedule K–1**
A					12,345
B			2,020		
C					
D					

29a	Totals					
b	Totals					
30	Add columns (g) and (j) of line 29a				**30**	12,345
31	Add columns (f), (h), and (i) of line 29b				**31** (	2,020)
32	**Total partnership and S corporation income or (loss).** Combine lines 30 and 31. Enter the result here and include in the total on line 41 below				**32**	10,325

Figure 6-4. Sample deduction of unreimbursed partnership expenses in Part II of Section E

S Corporations and C Corporations

The rules are far trickier for the owner of an S corporation or C corporation who works from his or her home. Although there are other methods available, the best means to recover the expenses is through an *accountable plan*. This plan, which is typically noted through a corporate resolution, states that the business portion of expenses (utilities, insurance, maintenance, etc.) will be reimbursed by the corporation.

The other methods—using unreimbursed employee business expenses (Form 2106) and renting—have potential issues. With unreimbursed expenses, the deduction is subject to a limitation of 2% of your adjusted gross income. Rent paid by the corporation would be income to you, so there are not huge tax savings. Additionally, the requirements of Section 280 of the Tax Code lessen the practicality of this method.[5]

The major benefit of an accountable plan is that the reimbursements are *not* income to the shareholder. This makes an accountable plan an excellent means to get money out of a closely held corporation.

---

[5] Section 280A of the Tax Code does not disallow a corporation from paying rent to an employee. However, it specifically limits the expenses that are deductible to mortgage interest and property tax (both of these are deductible on Schedule A); there is no deduction available for all of the other indirect expenses such as utilities, insurance, etc.

Note that if you are reimbursed by your corporation for $1,000 of property tax out of a total of $5,000, you can only take a deduction for $4,000 of property tax on your Schedule A. The S corporation will be deducting the other $1,000—a single expense can only be deducted once.

Note **What is an accountable plan?** An *accountable plan* is a written plan for reimbursing expenses. The plan can only cover job-related expenses. The business must approve the plan; for a corporation, this should be through a corporate resolution.

To be reimbursed under an accountable plan, the owner (whether a shareholder/employee of an S corporation or C corporation, or a member of an LLC) completes an expense report detailing all of the expenses and provides receipts for them. The expense report should be processed as is any other expense report handled by the business.

An accountable plan has one other benefit. Let's assume that your business rents office space, which is where most of your work is done. You also maintain a home office that is used solely for your business. Expenses for the home office can be reimbursed under an accountable plan. The business expenses meet the ordinary and necessary criteria (if it's a home office used exclusively for the business). Assuming the accountable plan allows for reimbursement in this situation, the expenses can be reimbursed.

The Car

The avoidance of taxes is the only intellectual pursuit that carries any reward.

—John Maynard Keynes

The second largest investment for most Americans is a car. For most business owners, an automobile is an essential investment; it's used to meet potential clients, deliver products, and for business errands (going to the bank or the post office).

This chapter focuses on what can and cannot be deducted in relation to automobile expenses. There are very specific rules on recordkeeping that *must* be followed if you want to deduct the business use of your car.

Automobile Expenses: The Basics

Like any other expense, you are allowed to deduct the ordinary and necessary use of your car. Long ago, the IRS grappled with how this should be handled. How should the business use of an automobile be calculated? If I drive my car 15,000 miles this year and I say I drove 10,000 miles for business use, is that enough to justify taking two-thirds of my automobile expenditures as a business expense?

Both Congress (through Section 6001 of the Tax Code) and the IRS (through Section 1.6001-1(a) of Income Tax Regulations) mandate that you keep sufficient records to justify the deductions. The Tax Court does have the ability to approximate a business deduction; this is called the *Cohan rule*.[1] The Cohan rule does not apply for certain business expenses: travel, gifts, meals

---

[1] This rule was named after playwright George M. Cohan of *Give My Regards to Broadway* and *Yankee Doodle Dandy* fame. The Cohan rule is covered in depth in Chapter 17.

and entertainment, and "listed property." Section 274(d) of the Tax Code requires that a taxpayer substantiate these expenses with adequate records or sufficient evidence corroborating the taxpayer's statement.

Automobiles are a type of listed property; thus, you are required to maintain proper records to deduct car expenses. The easiest method of complying with the regulations adopted by the IRS under this section of the Tax Code[2] is to maintain a contemporaneous, written mileage log. Although other methods of proving the deduction exist,[3] they are much more difficult and result in smaller deductions.

Recordkeeping Requirements

There are two methods allowed for deducting automobile expenses: standard mileage and actual expenses. Both methods require that you keep a contemporaneous, written mileage log.

The mileage log should note the date, starting mileage, ending mileage, where you went, and the business purpose of each trip. Only your business-related automobile expenses are deductible. The mileage log should note your business-related mileage. It should also note the odometer reading on January 1 and December 31 (the beginning and end of the calendar year). Most mileage logs include only the business-related trips.

Figure 7-1 is a portion of my own mileage log. I use a small spiral notebook that I keep in the center console of my car. Every business trip and the business purpose are recorded. The log is in ink, not pencil. You can create a log using a small notebook or purchase a mileage logbook at most office supply stores.

I had a client who had two cars: He used one for business and used the other for nonbusiness driving. I told him to keep a written mileage log; he told me that it wasn't needed because "all the mileage in the business car is for business." I warned him that wasn't the case, and if he were audited the IRS wouldn't accept it. He was audited, and his invoices and other backup records could only substantiate about 70% of his actual business mileage. He lost the auto expense deduction for his meetings with potential clients, and much of the day-to-day driving that he did that was business-related.

---

[2] Sections 1.274-5(c)(2)(iii) and 1.274-5T(c)(2) of Income Tax Regulations.
[3] Section 1.274-5T(c)(3) of Income Tax Regulations and Temporary Income Tax Regulations, *50 Fed. Reg.* 46020 (Nov. 6, 1985) specify that substantiation by other sufficient evidence requires the production of corroborative evidence in support of a taxpayer's statement specifically detailing how he or she met the requirements.

1/1 2012 Beg. Mileage 30,112.0

1/3 30,116.5 -> 30,140.3
Home - Post Office (Red Rock
Vista Stn) - Home; Mail letters

1/5 30,169.5 -> 30,215.9
H - Law office of James Smith,
2137 E Warm Springs, LV (Mtg
on H. Jones issue) - Red Rock
Vista Post Office (mail certified
letter) - H

1/5 30,215.9 -> 30,219.6
H - Office Supply Co/Rainbow &
Lake Mead - H
Buy envelopes

Figure 7-1. Sample mileage log

▨ **Caution** **Spreadsheets and smart phone apps might not be accepted by the IRS.** We're in the computer age, and my smart phone has more power than most computers from the 1970s. Unfortunately, that does *not* mean that the IRS will accept a mileage log from a smart phone or a spreadsheet showing your mileage. The problem is that it is far easier to falsify a computer spreadsheet or a smart phone app than it is to falsify a written mileage log. The institutional mentality of the IRS is such that a nonwritten mileage log has less credibility than a written one.

This does *not* mean that a log maintained on a smart phone will not be accepted by the IRS. One strategy that would likely validate a smart phone–based log is to keep monthly or weekly backups of your log. If the IRS were to question the log, you would be able to show that the log was contemporaneous through the backup copies.

Bad things can happen if you don't keep adequate records. Consider the case of Jessica Solomon. She went to Tax Court, and one of the issues was her mileage log.[4]

> *Petitioner kept track of her automobile mileage using a daily mileage log. However, there are several problems with the mileage log. First, the mileage log simply notes the odometer reading on petitioner's car at the beginning and end of each day and includes no information regarding where petitioner drove, the purpose of the trip, or petitioner's business relationship to the persons she visited. Second, petitioner included in the mileage log the roughly 27 miles she drove each workday commuting to and from MV Marketing's office. Finally, petitioner conceded that she may have included some personal trips in the mileage log. Petitioner did not present any evidence at trial, such as appointment books, calendars, or maps of her sales territories, to corroborate the bare information contained in the mileage log, nor did she testify with any specificity regarding her vehicle expenses in 2006.* (notes omitted)

The Tax Court concluded that although she undoubtedly had business mileage in the year in question, she did not satisfy the adequate record requirement of Section 274(d). She also didn't present any corroborating evidence that could have bolstered her claimed mileage.

The Standard Mileage Rate

The simplest method of deducting business mileage is to take the number of business miles driven and multiply that by a rate. That's exactly what the *standard mileage* method is. Every year the IRS commissions a study that determines the rate for the coming year. The announcement is usually made in early December in a press release and in a notice released on the IRS website.[5]

The standard mileage rate is not allowed in certain situations:

- You must not be operating five or more cars at the same time.

- You must not have used "bonus" depreciation, taken a Section 179 depreciation deduction, or used MACRS (Modified Accelerated Cost Recovery System) depreciation on the car.

---

[4] See US Tax Court, *Solomon v. Commissioner*, T.C. Memo 2011-91, http://ustaxcourt.gov/InOpHistoric/SOLOMON2.TCM.WPD.pdf, pp. 8–9.

[5] IRS Notice 2012-1 (available at www.irs.gov/pub/irs-drop/n-12-01.pdf) lists the 2012 standard mileage rates.

- You must not have leased the car and have taken actual expenses for the car in a prior year.

- You must not be a rural mail carrier who received a qualified reimbursement.

The only item that needs an explanation relates to the depreciation issues. As will be discussed in the "Actual Expenses" section, a major reason to use actual expenses is accelerated depreciation. When you acquire a car, you can take a combination of "bonus" depreciation, Section 179 deprecation, and MACRS to obtain a larger deduction than if you were to use the standard mileage deduction.

▓ **Tip**   Once you use actual expenses for a vehicle, you will almost always use actual expenses for the life of that vehicle.

One other note on this: Once you use actual expenses for a vehicle lease, you *must* use actual expenses for all future years of that lease *and any renewals*.

Using the standard mileage method does *not* relieve you from the requirement of maintaining a mileage log. It does relieve you from keeping track of all your expenses for your car (gasoline, maintenance, etc.) because those are not needed to calculate the deduction.

Actual Expenses

The alternate method of deducting automobile expenses is to deduct your *actual expenses*. To do this, multiply the total of your expenses for the year by the ratio of your business miles to your total miles driven for the year.

Your actual expenses are all of the expenses for driving the vehicle. These include:

- Gasoline

- Oil

- Maintenance and repairs

- Tires

- Vehicle license and registration fees

- Insurance

- Lease payments

- Interest expense on car payments
- Depreciation

Like all business expenses, you need to have proof of your expenditures. This means you need to keep your receipts if you're using actual expenses.

Note that lease payments are considered an ordinary and necessary business expense. However, the principal portion of a car (loan) payment is not deductible. That's because you get to depreciate the car over its useful life.

Depreciation

As mentioned earlier, automobiles are listed equipment. Cars last more than one year, so to recover the cost of the car—including sales tax and any options, handling fees, and so on—the car is depreciated. This recovers the expenditure over the life of the asset. (Depreciation is covered in Chapter 10.)

Years ago, depreciating an asset was simple because the only kind of depreciation allowed was *straight-line depreciation*. You took the cost of the asset, divided it by the useful life of the asset in years, and the result was the depreciation. Today, you basically need a computer to calculate the depreciation for a car. Between MACRS, Section 179, and bonus depreciation, it's extremely difficult to calculate depreciation by hand. For cars, there are some simple rules that apply.

The More Than 50% Rule

This rule requires that you *use your car more than 50% for business* to take any Section 179 depreciation. Let's say you drive your car 18,123 miles this year, and 5,892 of those miles are for business. You cannot take a Section 179 depreciation deduction.

Limits on Section 179 Depreciation

Congress has imposed limits on Section 179 depreciation. The overall limit for 2012 is $500,000.[6] The maximum first-year depreciation is $11,160 (except for certain "heavy" vehicles, as discussed next). Note that the maximum allowable depreciation decreases to $5,100 in the second year, $3,050 for the third year, and $1,875 in the fourth and all other years.[7]

---

[6] This limit decreases to $139,000 once expenditures exceed $560,000 (2012 limits).

[7] See IRS, Part III, Administrative, Procedural, and Miscellaneous, Rev. Proc. 2012-23, www.irs.gov/pub/irs-drop/rp-12-23.pdf.

Heavy Vehicles

Automakers have had good lobbyists. They have been able to get special rules for heavy sport utility vehicles (SUVs) (rated at more than 6,000 pounds gross vehicular weight) written into the Tax Code. In some years (e.g., 2011) you could write off 100% of the purchase price for these autos. For 2012, the limit is 50% of the purchase price through bonus depreciation.

Benefit of Actual Expenses

The reason that many business owners use actual expenses for automobile deductions is that they get a larger deduction sooner; this directly lowers their taxes. Most of this deduction comes from depreciation.

I have been representing taxpayers in audits (examinations) for more than thirteen years. Almost every one of these audits has looked at automobile expenses (if car expenses were taken on the tax return being examined). My clients with good records and a contemporaneous, written mileage log rarely had problems with automobile expenses in these audits.

Tip   If you're taking actual expenses, you *must* have a contemporaneous mileage log.

Changing from Actual Expenses to Standard Mileage (or Vice Versa)

The Tax Code allows for you to change from standard mileage to actual expenses (or vice versa). In practice, you can easily move from the standard mileage deduction to actual expenses. However, it's almost impossible to move from actual expenses to the standard mileage deduction. This is because one of the major benefits of actual expenses is accelerated depreciation. The Tax Code specifically disallows moving from actual expenses to the standard mileage deduction if you have taken accelerated depreciation in any form.

Commuting Mileage

Section 262 of the Tax Code and Revenue Ruling 90-23[8] govern commuting mileage. If you commute from your home to your office, that mileage is *not* deductible. Personal expenses are not deductible; commuting to and from your office is considered a personal expense.

---

[8] See, for example, www.bradfordtaxinstitute.com/Endnotes/Rev_Rul_90-23.pdf.

Now consider a business owner with his office in his home (whether it is a deductible home office is *not* relevant here). He or she doesn't have commuting mileage because his commute is footsteps from his or her bedroom to the office.

The trickier situation is when there are two or more offices. Another ruling (Revenue Ruling 99-7[9]) addresses this case. Generally, as long as your home office is a "principal place of business" you *can* deduct your mileage driving from one office to another. Note that each case would be judged on its facts and circumstances. See Chapter 6 to see whether your home office qualifies as a principal place of business.

Mixed Trips

What if you drive from your office to the bank, and on the way back stop at the market to purchase something for your personal use? Is the trip deductible?

The answer to this lies in that business mileage is deductible, but personal mileage is not. Say you drive three miles to the bank to make a business deposit. Clearly, that's an ordinary and necessary business expense. On the way back to your office, you stop at a supermarket to pick up dinner. That's personal and not deductible. However, assume that you did not drive out of the way—the market was located on your drive back. Because the number of miles driven did not change, there's no problem—there are no excess miles.

Consider a slightly different itinerary. You drive three miles to the supermarket to purchase your dinner. On the drive home, you stop at the bank (one-half mile from the market on the direct drive back to the office) to make that business deposit. You cannot deduct the one mile of excess mileage, as that mile is personal.

Ancillary Expenses

Certain car-related expenditures can be deducted no matter if you take actual expenses or the standard mileage deduction. These include parking fees and tolls that relate to business use of the car.

Reporting Car Expenses

For the most part, car expenses are reported on the specific line for these expenses. For a sole proprietorship, that's on Schedule C (line 9 for 2011).

---

[9] See *Internal Revenue Bulletin* 1999-5, p. 4 at www.irs.gov/pub/irs-irbs/irb99-05.pdf.

For partnerships and corporations, automobile expenses are reported as an "other expense" item.

Additional information is required to be listed on a Schedule C where automobile expenses are taken. Part IV of Schedule C requires you to list out information on your car (unless you have to file Form 4562, Depreciation). Most sole proprietors will not file Form 4562 for their car, so they will end up completing Part IV of Schedule C. This portion of Schedule C is illustrated in Figure 7-2.

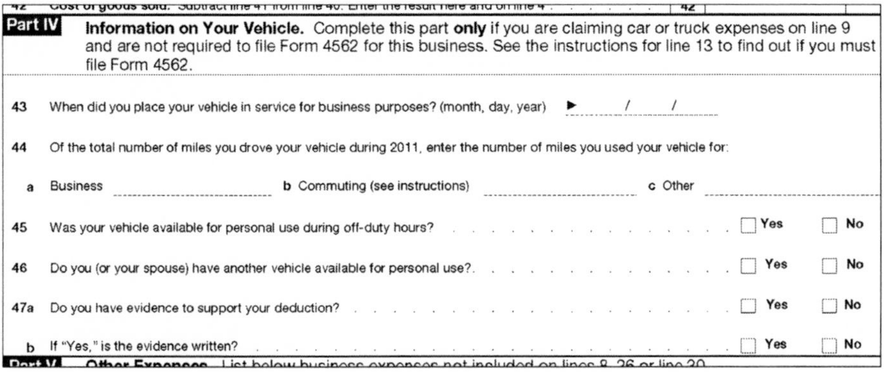

Part IV **Information on Your Vehicle.** Complete this part **only** if you are claiming car or truck expenses on line 9 and are not required to file Form 4562 for this business. See the instructions for line 13 to find out if you must file Form 4562.

43 When did you place your vehicle in service for business purposes? (month, day, year) ▶ / /

44 Of the total number of miles you drove your vehicle during 2011, enter the number of miles you used your vehicle for:

a Business b Commuting (see instructions) c Other

45 Was your vehicle available for personal use during off-duty hours? ☐ Yes ☐ No

46 Do you (or your spouse) have another vehicle available for personal use? ☐ Yes ☐ No

47a Do you have evidence to support your deduction? ☐ Yes ☐ No

b If "Yes," is the evidence written? ☐ Yes ☐ No

Figure 7-2. Part IV of Schedule C (Information on Your Vehicle)

Note that you are required to answer whether you have *written* evidence to support your deduction. Checking "no" on this question and taking a significant car expense deduction is a red flag for an audit. Checking "yes" on this question when you do not have written evidence opens you up for a host of problems. Deliberately lying on a tax return is perjury.

Company Cars

A company car is a vehicle owned (titled) or leased in the name of the business. This won't apply for sole proprietors (the business name is just another name for you, the proprietor), but it is a fairly common situation in the corporate world. The major issue to be aware of is the difference between personal and business miles.

Business miles are a business expense; personal miles are not. If the company is paying for the car, how do the personal miles get off the company's books? This is done by adding in the dollar value of the personal miles to the driver's wages. The driver owes taxes (including Social Security and Medicare taxes) on the value of those personal miles.

Calculating the value of those miles can be difficult. If the vehicle is leased, an IRS table can be used.[10] If the vehicle is owned, the actual expenses must be calculated to determine the value of those miles. (An exception to this is available if the vehicle's personal use is limited to commuting to and from work and *de minimis* personal use.[11]) Obviously, excellent record keeping is a must with company vehicles.

Other Kinds of Vehicles

There are other kinds of vehicles used by businesses besides cars, light-duty trucks, SUVs, and passenger vans. Panel trucks, large trucks, vans, and motorcycles are also listed equipment. You *must* use actual expenses for the business mileage of these vehicles.

---

[10] See IRS, Employer's Tax Guide to Fringe Benefits (2011), Publication 15-B, www.irs.gov/pub/irs-pdf/p15b_11.pdf, "Lease Value Rule."

[11] There are other rules regarding this exception; generally, the vehicle cannot be driven by a "control employee"—for example, someone who earns $195,000 or more who owns 1% or more of the stock of the company.

Travel

You got to be careful if you don't know where you're going, because you might not get there.

—Yogi Berra

One of the perks I enjoyed in my younger years was traveling. I used to travel to glamorous locations (like Las Vegas) and the not so glamorous ones (such as Bakersfield, California).

When you travel on business, the business-related expenses are deductible. This chapter focuses on these expenses, what can and can't be deducted, and how to report these expenses on a tax return. We also examine the rules covering trips where you combine business with a vacation.

Business Travel

Clearly, business travel is deductible: It's an ordinary and necessary expense. However, personal travel is *not* deductible. If you bring your spouse on a trip with you, his or her airfare is not deductible as a business expense (it's not necessary).

When you travel for business, all the expenses from the time you leave your home to the time you return are deductible. This includes ground transportation to the airport, airfare, ground transportation at the destination or a rental car, your hotel, and all the expenses of the return trip.

As noted in Chapter 4, Section 274(d) of the Tax Code makes travel deductions subject to more stringent backup requirements than other deductions. You cannot use the Cohan rule to estimate travel expenses. You need receipts or other proof of your expenses.

Tax Home

A key concept in travel is your *tax home*. The IRS defines tax home as your regular place of business, not necessarily your personal home. If you live and work in the same metropolitan area, your tax home is the same as your family home.

There are three factors used to determine your tax home:[1]

1. You perform part of your business in the same local area as your main home and use that home for lodging while doing business in the area. For example, you are a consultant living in New York City. You take a consulting assignment in Stamford, Connecticut and commute to and from your residence each day.

2. You have living expenses at your main home that you duplicate because your business requires you to be away from home. An example is: Assume you are a consultant residing in New York City. You take a long-term assignment in Chicago. You rent an apartment in Chicago, duplicating a portion of your living costs in New York.

3. You have not abandoned the area where you have resided and called your main home; you have one or more members of your family living in your main home; or you often stay at your main home. Again, assume you are a consultant in New York who has taken a long-term assignment in Chicago. You've rented an apartment in Chicago. However, your spouse and children continue to reside in your New York home.

It is possible to have *no* tax home. Imagine you are a salesperson covering a large region in the western United States. You live with your brother and his family rent-free in San Francisco, but each month you are on the road for twenty-five days. You would not have a tax home. If you have no tax home, you cannot deduct travel expenses.

What Can Be Deducted

Though most of the travel expenses that are deductible are obvious, some are not. Here's a list of the expense types that you are allowed to deduct.

---

[1] These rules are taken from IRS, Travel, Entertainment, Gift, and Car Expenses, Publication 463 (2011 edition), available at www.irs.gov/pub/irs-pdf/p463.pdf. Revenue Ruling 73-529 has a more thorough description of the same test.

Transportation

Your costs to travel by plane, train, bus, or car from your home to your business destination are deductible. There are special rules for cruise ship travel (covered in the "What Can't be Deducted" section).

Ground Transportation

Your ground transportation between your home and the airport/terminal and from your hotel to and from the airport/terminal is deductible. This includes public transportation, a taxi, or a rental car. Ground transportation in your destination city is also deductible as long as it is business-related.

Baggage and Shipping

Costs of shipping bags and materials from your regular work location to your other work locations are an ordinary and necessary business expense and are deductible.

Car

Your business-related car expenses while traveling are deductible. If you use your own car, this deduction is taken as an automobile expense, not a travel expense. If you use a rental car, the expense is taken as a travel expense. Note that only the business-related portion of your rental car expense is deductible.

Lodging

You business-related lodging is a deductible travel expense.

Meals

Your meals while traveling away from home on business are deductible. Note that meals are deducted as *meals and entertainment,* not as a travel expense. The specifics of how meals are deducted and the rules for meal deductions are covered in Chapter 9.

Cleaning

Dry cleaning and laundry expenses while traveling are deductible. Additionally, you can deduct dry cleaning and laundry of clothes worn while traveling once you return home. Note that this should be deducted as a travel expense.

Tips

Any gratuities you pay for any of the items already noted are deductible.

Other Expenses

Any other expense you have while traveling, as long as it is both ordinary and necessary (and you have records to support it), will be deductible.

What Can't Be Deducted

Though most travel expenses can be deducted, there are some expenses that are exceptions. The most common of these are personal expenses: you can't deduct a vacation as a business expense.

Most issues arise when business and pleasure are mixed. The general rule is *if the primary purpose of the trip is business, your travel expenses are deductible; if the primary purpose of the trip is personal, your travel expenses are not deductible.* Let's look at some examples.

Example 1. You fly to Chicago to attend a friend's wedding. While there, you need to fax documents to a client. The costs directly related to faxing the documents are deductible. Your transportation, hotel, meals, and so on, are not deductible.

Example 2. You and your family fly to Orlando to spend a week at Walt Disney World. While there, you use a rental car and spend a day with a client in nearby Kissimmee. You cannot deduct your travel expenses to Orlando or your hotel. You can deduct one day of your rental car expenses. If you take your client out to lunch, that would be a deductible business meal.

Example 3. You fly to Las Vegas for the annual convention of your industry on a Sunday (the convention runs Monday to Thursday). Your spouse flies to Las Vegas on Friday after the convention, and you spend the weekend together taking in shows and gambling before flying home on Sunday. Your travel expenses are deductible; your spouse's travel expenses are not deductible. Your hotel room is deductible from Sunday through Thursday night (from the day before the convention to the day the convention ends). If the hotel charged you a double rate that was more expensive than the single rate, you can only deduct the single rate. Your meals from Sunday through Thursday are deductible. Your ground transportation costs in Las Vegas are deductible except for Friday and Saturday. Note that the cost for you to return to the airport in Las Vegas is deductible.

Travel Outside of the United States

There are special rules for travel outside of the United States. Generally, you can deduct all of the travel expenses if the trip is entirely for business. If the trip is partially for business and partially for personal matters, you must allocate expenses based on the number of business days and personal days unless an exception exists (see the following list). As a rule, business days are the days you spend on business activities. If you are outside of the United States and have a business activity on both a Friday and a Monday, the weekend days in between will count as business days. However, if you have business on a Friday and choose to spend the weekend on personal matters and fly home on Monday, the weekend days do *not* count as business days. Travel days (days you are flying on business) count as business days.

There are four exceptions to these rules.

1. *No substantial control.* If you are an employee and have no control over the travel, your trip is considered entirely business-related. Self-employed individuals are always considered to have substantial control.

2. *The trip lasts one business week or less.* If you are outside of the United States for one week or less, your trip is considered entirely business *for transportation expenses to and from the United States.* Note that you do not count the day you travel from the United States as a day; however, the day you return is counted.

3. *You spend less than 25% of the time on personal activities.* If you spend more than a week outside of the United States, but less than 25% of your time is spent on personal activities, you can deduct 100% of your transportation expenses. You can only deduct the business portion of your other expenses (lodging, meals, etc.).

4. *Vacation was not a major consideration.* If you can show that a vacation was *not* a major consideration (even when you arrange the trip), your trip will be considered entirely business-related. This is determined based on the facts and circumstances.

If you travel outside of the United States for personal reasons but have direct business expenses, those expenses can be deducted. Suppose you travel to Paris for a vacation, but you spend a day visiting a customer in France. The costs directly related to visiting the customer are deductible.

Luxury Water Travel

There are specific limits to travel expenses if you take a trip on a cruise line or other luxury water transportation. You are allowed as a daily limit *twice the maximum federal per diem rate* at the dates of travel. You can find this rate in IRS Publication 463.

Let's say you took a business-related ten-day cruise in June 2011 at a cost of $7,000. The maximum federal per diem during that time was $304 per day. Thus, the maximum deductible per-day expense was $608, or $6,080 for your cruise. You can only deduct $6,080 rather than the $7,000 you actually spent.

If your cost of meals is separately stated, you must apply the 50% limit on meals and entertainment expenses (discussed in the next chapter) before applying the daily limit. Assume the same facts as before, except that meals represent $2,000 of the $7,000 that was spent. To determine the allowable deduction, you multiply the meal cost of $2,000 by 50% to obtain $1,000. You then add to that the $5,000 of other costs for the cruise to obtain $6,000. This is compared to the daily limit of $6,080. You are allowed the *lesser* of the daily limit or your expenses, so you take a $1,000 meal deduction and a $5,000 travel expense.

■ **Note** **Convention exception to luxury water travel.** It wouldn't be tax without exceptions to exceptions. If you attend a business-related convention, seminar, or meeting on a cruise ship, the daily limit does not apply.

However, there is a maximum allowable deduction of $2,000 per year on cruise ships. Additionally, there are very specific rules that must be met: The trip must be business-related; the cruise ship must be registered in the United States; all of the ports of call must be in the United States or be U.S. possessions; you must attach a written statement to your return that includes information on the total days of the trip, the hours each day spent on business activities, and a program of the business activities; you must attach a written statement signed by an organizer of the meeting that includes a schedule of the business activities and the number of hours you spent attending the scheduled business activities.

In practice, there are very few cruise ships with U.S. registry (these mainly cruise between Hawaii and California or on the Mississippi River). Thus, the ability to actually deduct a business meeting on a cruise ship is very limited.

Conventions Outside of North America

Attending a business-related convention, seminar, or meeting outside of North America is generally deductible. However, it must be reasonable that the convention is held outside of North America rather than inside North America. The reasonableness test is based on the facts and circumstances of the event. Generally, the IRS can disallow seminars and meetings outside of the United States when you could have attended a similar meeting within the United States. Let's look at an example.

You need to attend a specific continuing education conference on your field. The identical week-long seminar is being offered in Miami and Macau. Unless you can show there is a conflict with the seminar in Miami, the IRS could disallow travel expenses for attending the seminar in Macau.

Note   Congress has an unusual view of North America. The rule on conventions outside of North America brings up an obvious question: What countries are within North America? Congress has decided which countries are and are not within North America *for this purpose*.

Consider the island of Hispaniola. There are two countries on this island: Haiti and the Dominican Republic. The Dominican Republic is included within North America, but Haiti is not.

There are numerous other oddities. Most of the islands of the Caribbean are included, but the Cayman Islands are not. Honduras in Central America is included, but Panama, Nicaragua, El Salvador, and Belize are not. Guyana, which is in South America, is included in North America for this purpose. The countries that border the United States, Canada and Mexico, are both considered to be in North America.

You can find the full list of countries in the North American area in IRS Publication 463.

Reporting Travel Expenses

Where and how travel expenses are reported depends on the type of business entity you have. The amount that is a deductible business expense does *not* change; however, where the deduction is taken will vary.

Sole Proprietor

This is the simplest situation. A sole proprietor reports his or her travel expenses on Schedule C. Remember, meal expenses are reported separately from travel expenses.

Partnerships (and LLCs Filing as Partnerships)

The travel expenses of the partnership are included in other deductions for the partnership. This leads to the obvious question: how does a partner either get reimbursed or take a tax deduction for the expenses?

Most partnerships will have an accountable plan for reimbursing partners and employees of the partnership for business expenses (see Chapter 6). The partner completes an expense report noting his or travel expenses and receives reimbursement from the partnership. The partnership deducts the travel expenses as an ordinary and necessary expense.

If there is no accountable plan but the partnership agreement (or LLC operating agreement) allows for unreimbursed partnership expenses, then the partner will deduct the travel expenses as an unreimbursed partnership expense. This deduction is taken in Part II of Schedule E (see Figure 6-4 for an example).

If the partnership agreement (or LLC operating agreement) does *not* allow for unreimbursed partnership expenses and there is no accountable plan, then neither the partner nor the partnership can take a deduction for travel expenses.

Corporations

Travel expenses can be reimbursed through an accountable plan (as discussed in Chapter 6). If there is no accountable plan, the expense must be taken as an unreimbursed business expense. That deduction is taken on Form 2106 (or Form 2106-EZ) but is reduced by 2% of your adjusted gross income.

Meals and Entertainment

Look, we play the Star Spangled Banner before every game. You want us to pay income taxes, too?

—Bill Veeck

As discussed in Chapter 8, your meal expenses while traveling for business are deductible. Are other meal expenses deductible? What about entertainment expenses, such as taking a client to a show or a baseball game?

In this chapter we look at meal and entertainment expenses: what can be deducted and how. Some meal and entertainment expenses are not deductible; we let you know about those so you don't take the nondeductible expenses.

Meal Expenses

You are allowed to deduct your meals while away from home on business. Can you deduct meal expenses while you are out of your office but still near it? Can you deduct a meal when you're discussing business with a client?

As with all business expenses, meal expenses that are both ordinary and necessary are deductible. As noted in Chapter 4, meal expenses are subject to the stringent backup requirements of Section 274(d) of the Tax Code. If you are not taking the per diem meal deduction (discussed later in this chapter), you must have receipts to justify your deduction.

Meal expenses cannot be lavish or extraordinary. This doesn't mean you can't eat at a fancy restaurant; however, it does mean if the *facts and circumstances* don't justify the deduction, it will be disallowed.

In an examination (audit), you will be sitting across from an Internal Revenue Service (IRS) auditor. When traveling, this auditor is subject to the government rules on expenses. As noted in Chapter 4, the meal allowance is currently $71 a day in the most expensive cities in the country, such as New York City. If you attempt to justify a $710 per person meal in front of an auditor who must eat on $71 a day, I wish you good luck (you'll need it). What this means is your expenses need to be normal for the situation. If you're taking a potential client to lunch, eating at an upscale restaurant is normal for that situation and should be acceptable.

In addition to meals while traveling, meals when you meet with clients, vendors, business partners, and similar individuals will be deductible. However, you need to mark on the receipt whom you met with and the business purpose of the meeting. Figure 9-1 shows a sample receipt with this information.

The amount you can claim for meal and entertainment expenses is reduced by 50%.[1] If your actual meal and entertainment expenses total $3,500, you are allowed a $1,750 deduction.

■ **Note** **What are *facts and circumstances?*** You have probably noticed the phrase "facts and circumstances" in the text and may be wondering why that phrase keeps recurring. The reason is that both the Tax Code and IRS regulations frequently use this phrase.

The idea behind this phrase is to note that the subjective issues of each individual's (or business's) facts and circumstances in regard to the subject at hand should be weighed in the decision of whether an expense is deductible. For example, large air conditioning expenses where I reside (Las Vegas, Nevada) are normal. However, an individual living in Seattle is unlikely to need to spend the same amount of money on air conditioning. What is normal for one set of facts and circumstances might not be normal for another.

---

[1] Section 274(n) of the Tax Code limits the deduction for meals and entertainment to 50% of the actual expense.

```
        FOUNTAINBLUE COFFEEHOUSE
            3456 LAS VEGAS BLVD S
            LAS VEGAS, NV 89199


CHK 715847 05/24/2012 3:30PM

VT ICD BL TEA SHK       2.45
  NO SYRUP
  RASPBERRY SYR


CASH TENDERED           3.00


SUBTOTAL                2.45
8.1% CLARK CTY TAX      0.20
TOTAL                   2.65

Change Due             $0.35

Meeting w/John Smith,
Potential Client; Tax
Issues with his business
```

Figure 9-1. Sample receipt with meeting information

Let's examine another common situation. You drive to a business meeting at a potential client's office (about an hour from your office). When the meeting concludes, it's nearly noon, so you stop at a restaurant to eat lunch. Is that meal a deductible business expense?

Generally, that meal will *not* be deductible. If you are eating a meal in your tax home—generally considered for this purpose to be the metropolitan area in which you work—you cannot deduct the meal. The theory is you would have had to eat anyway.

If the area where you work is large (based on geography), this can be an issue. A literal reading of the law would say that even if you're two hours from your office, you can't take a meal deduction. However, this is an area where facts and circumstances might help you. Most IRS personnel understand that, given these facts, eating at a restaurant would be justified. However, if you are within an hour's drive of your office (and are in the same metropolitan area), the meal will *not* be deductible.

Entertainment Expenses

You are allowed to deduct business-related entertainment expenses. There are very specific rules about what entertainment expenses can be deducted. Generally, the expense must meet one of two tests: the *directly-related test* or the *associated test*.

Directly-Related Test

The *directly–related test* allows an entertainment expense to be deductible if it's directly related to your business. There are two means of meeting this test. First, the entertainment can take place in a *clear business setting*. Examples of this include:

- Entertainment in a hospitality suite at a business meeting or convention. Goodwill (for your business) is created through your products being on display and/or possible discussion of selling your products to customers, and so on.

- Entertainment at the grand opening of your business. Here, the goal of the entertainment is obtaining good publicity for your business. This meets the directly-related test.

The directly-related test will not be met if you (or an employee) are not present. Additionally, if there are substantial distractions, the directly-related test will also not be met.

The IRS considers meetings at nightclubs, discos, cocktail parties, theaters, baseball games, and other sporting events to have substantial distractions. Additionally, meetings of a purely social nature where you are not meeting for a business purpose do not meet the directly-related test. This would include golfing with strangers, meeting with random people at a resort, and talking with people at the health club.

Associated Test

You can still deduct entertainment expenses if you meet the *associated test*. To pass this test, the expense must be:

1. Associated with the active conduct of your business, and

2. Directly before or after a substantial business discussion.

Let's consider an example. You invite your client to a baseball game. He meets you at the ballpark. During the breaks in the game, you discuss your new products. Immediately after the game, you go off your separate ways.

The entertainment expense in this example would *not* be deductible. Though it clearly meets the first part of the associated test (it's related to your business), it does *not* meet the second part of the test. Your discussion occurred during the game, not before or after. Because there are substantial distractions during the event, you would need to have talked with the client either before or after the game.

Let's modify this example. You take your client out to dinner two hours before the baseball game. At dinner, you engage in a discussion of your new business products. You then go to the baseball game. After the game, you head your separate ways. Here, the entertainment expense *would* be deductible because you engaged in a substantial business discussion before the entertainment.

You must have adequate records to deduct entertainment expenses. You need to note the date, place, amount spent, the business purpose and benefit to be gained, and the relationship of the person being entertained to you (e.g., potential client). Either you or an employee *must* be present at the entertainment (the person present should be noted on the receipt or statement).

Meetings at conventions are presumed to be business-related. Note that you must have a business purpose for attending the convention. If you entertain a client following a business seminar, that entertainment generally meets the associated test.

Note that the associated test specifies that the entertainment must occur directly before or after the substantial business discussion. If it's not the same day as the entertainment, then the facts and circumstances must be examined. In Publication 463, the IRS uses the example of entertainment the day before or the day after the business discussion. For those circumstances, "the entertainment generally is considered to be held directly before or after the discussion."

▓ **Caution Make sure you note the business that was discussed.** Meal and entertainment expenses are often a point of emphasis in audits. You *will* need adequate support to justify your expenditures. For entertainment expenses, you must list the content of the "substantial business discussion." You can't just state "our businesses." That said, the IRS is not looking for a minute-by-minute rehash of what you discussed. If you talked about a new product, include a notation, "Discussed new product and potential cost savings for client." If you're entertaining a potential new client, noting that fact and that you discussed how your business can help the potential client's business should be sufficient.

As with meals, entertainment expenses are limited to 50% of the actual amount spent.

Per Diem Expenses

What if I told you there is a way to deduct meal and entertainment expenses without saving any receipts? It's true. You can either deduct actual expenses or use the *per diem method.*

Per diem expenses can be used when traveling for business. Let's say you take a seven-day business trip. You can take either your actual meal and entertainment expenses, or you can use the per diem expenses. To determine the per diem, you consult official tables of per diem rates for your destination. If the travel is within the continental United States, you consult the General Services Administration's per diem chart. For travel that is outside of the United States, you consult the State Department's per diem table. If your travel is outside of the continental United States but is not foreign (Alaska, Hawaii, Puerto Rico, the U.S. Virgin Islands, American Samoa, etc.), you use the Department of Defense's per diem table. Table 9-1 shows where to find the per diem rates.

When you look at the per diem charts, you will see columns for lodging and for meals and incidental expenses. The only per diem expenses you are allowed to use are for meals and entertainment. You *cannot* use per diem for lodging.

Table 9-1. Where to Find Per Diem Rates

Destination	Agency	Website
Within the Continental United States	GSA	www.gsa.gov/portal/category/21287
United States, but Outside the Continental United States	Dept. of Defense	www.defensetravel.dod.mil/site/perdiemCalc.cfm
Foreign Countries	Dept. of State	http://aoprals.state.gov/web920/per_diem.asp

Let's look at an example of calculating the per diem. Assume you traveled to Las Vegas in March 2012 for six days. By clicking on Nevada on the GSA per diem web page, you can see the meals and incidental expenses for the current fiscal year (October 2011–September 2012) for Las Vegas is $71 a day. However, the per diem is not $71 × 6 = $426. You are only allowed 75% of the per diem rate on your first and last days of travel.[2] So the allowed per diem is ($71 × 2 × 75%) + ($71 × 4) = $107 + $284 = $391.

▨ **Caution   The tables default to the current fiscal year.** The default for the GSA per diem table is the current fiscal year. For example, FY2013 runs from October 2012 through September 2013. If you need the per diem for a different period, remember to change the fiscal year. Similarly, the State Department's and Defense Department's per diems default to the current month, so you may need to change the month to get the right rate for your travel.

If you look at the tables, you will see that not every location is listed. Let's say you traveled to Denton, Texas. Denton is not listed in the table for Texas, so you must use the standard rate. The standard rate is used for all cities without specific rates.

Let's assume you have excellent records for all of your meals and entertainment expenses except for one business trip. So you calculate the per diem for that trip, add it to the rest of your actual meal expenses, and get your total for the year. *You are not allowed to do this.* You cannot mix per diem and actual expenses for the same year. You must use either per diem or actual expenses for the entire year.

This obviously limits the usefulness of the per diem deduction. I have found in my tax practice that the per diem method is useful for business owners with bad recordkeeping practices (at least a deduction can be taken, rather than no deduction). It is also useful for individuals whose only meal and entertainment expenses are incurred through traveling.

The per diem method is especially useful for individuals who travel outside of the United States. The per diems allowed by the GSA are not generous; the current maximum per diem is $71 a day. In an expensive location like New York City, that might not be sufficient. The State Department per diems are more reflective of actual costs.

You are allowed to switch from per diem to actual expenses each year. If your actual expenses are $5,000 and your per diem is $4,500, you would normally

---

[2] Alternatively, you can use a different proration method if you apply it consistently and it is in accordance with reasonable business practice.

choose the actual expenses. If the following year the situation is reversed, you can use the actual expenses.

Like the other meals and entertainment expenses, the per diem that you calculate must be reduced by 50% to determine the deduction you can take.

Special Situations

There are a number of special situations that can impact meal and entertainment expenses. Here are some of the more common ones.

100% Deductible Meal and Entertainment

There are certain circumstances where providing meals to the office or a group is fully (100%) deductible. These include:

- Meal expenses for occasional large group in-office meetings. This would be categorized as an office expense.

- Meal expenses for large group meetings inside or outside of the office for promotional seminars or related events. This would be categorized as an advertising expense.

- Meal expenses for group meetings while attending a conference, seminar, or training, paid directly by the company. This would be expensed with the related conference, seminar, or training.

- Meal expenses for occasional in-office working meals (breakfast, lunch, or dinner) for the convenience of the employer. This would be considered an office expense.

- Meal expenses for buffets or continental breakfasts for meetings either inside or outside of the office. This would be expensed with the related meeting costs.

- Meal and entertainment expenses for social and recreational purposes, such as an annual holiday party, company picnic, and so on for non–highly compensated employees. Only meal expenses are deductible for social and recreational purposes for highly compensated employees. These expenses are typically office expenses.

- Meal and entertainment expenses for employee recognition and mentoring programs. These are normally expensed with the underlying program.

- Tickets provided to employees on a nondiscriminatory basis for sporting and cultural events. This would be considered as an employee benefit expense.

Business Gifts

Business gifts are deductible up to $25 per person per year. If your company gives *de minimis* gifts, such as a turkey to every employee, these are 100% deductible as a gift expense. Similar gifts to customers are also deductible, as gifts, up to $25 per customer per year.

Coffee and Water Service

Food and drinks that are of *de minimis* value, such as coffee service, water service, or free soft drinks for the office, are considered office expenses and are 100% deductible.

Audiovisual and Room Charges

If you put on a seminar and have room and/or audiovisual equipment charges, these are 100% deductible. They are not meal or entertainment expenses; rather, they are expensed based on the reason for the meeting or seminar.

Dues for Professional Service Clubs

Dues for networking organizations, professional societies, and chambers of commerce are 100% deductible as dues. Note that the portion of the dues used for political or lobbying purposes (if applicable) is *not* deductible. The deductible expense is reported as dues and subscriptions.

You will notice that in all of these cases the cost is *not* reported as a meal and entertainment expense; it is reported as some other expense. Although these expenses certainly involve meals or entertainment, there is an *underlying business activity* that would make the expense fully deductible.

Section 162(a) of the Tax Code states that, "There shall be allowed as a deduction all the ordinary and necessary expenses paid or incurred during the taxable year in carrying on any trade or business."

Each of the expenses just noted meets the definition of an ordinary and necessary business expense. The list is not complete; there are other business expenses involving meals and entertainment that are fully deductible based on the activity that is occurring.

There are three other special situations worth noting.

Charitable Sporting Events

The Tax Code (Section 274(l)(1)(B)) specifically allows a 100% deduction for any ticket to a sporting event that benefits a charitable organization. All of the net proceeds of the event must benefit the charity, and volunteers must perform substantially all of the work at the event.

Skyboxes and Luxury Suites

The Tax Code (Section 274(l)(2)) specifically *limits* deductions for renting a luxury suite to see a sporting or cultural event if the rental is for more than one event. In such a situation, the allowed deduction is limited to the face value of non–luxury box seat tickets for the seats in the luxury suite.

Transportation Workers

Transportation workers are allowed to use their own special per diem rate. That rate is currently $59/day within the United States and $65 outside of the United States.

Reporting Meals and Entertainment

Meals and entertainment expenses are reported in different places depending on the type of business entity you have. The amount that is a deductible business expense does *not* change; however, where the deduction is taken will vary.

Sole Proprietor

This is the simplest situation. A sole proprietor reports his or her meal and entertainment expenses on Schedule C. The amount reported as a deduction is 50% of the total expense incurred. If you use computer software, you will likely enter in the *full* amount rather than the deductible amount. Remember, travel expenses are reported separately from meals and entertainment.

Partnerships (and LLCs Filing as Partnerships)

The situation here is the same as it is for travel expenses. Partnerships with an accountable plan will reimburse partners when they complete expense reports noting their meal and entertainment expenses. The partnership will deduct the meal and entertainment expenses (reducing the amount spent by 50%).

If there is no accountable plan, but the partnership agreement (or LLC operating agreement) allows for unreimbursed partnership expenses, the partner will deduct the travel expenses as an unreimbursed partnership expense. This deduction is taken on part II of Schedule E (see Figure 6-4 for an example).

If there is neither an accountable plan nor a partnership agreement (or LLC operating agreement) allowing for unreimbursed partnership expense, then the expenses cannot be deducted by the partner or the partnership.

Corporations

Meal and entertainment expenses can be reimbursed through an accountable plan (like for partnerships). If there is no accountable plan, the expense must be taken as an unreimbursed business expense. That deduction is taken on Form 2106 (or Form 2106-EZ) but is reduced by 2% of your adjusted gross income. Note that only the deductible portion of meal and entertainment expense is reported; the amount spent must be reduced by 50%.

Fixed Assets and Depreciation

The income tax has made liars out of more Americans than golf.

—Will Rogers

One of my favorite sayings about taxation in the United States is that it's a combination of common sense and arcane rules. Most of this book emphasizes the common sense approach to taxation. Now we must move into an area of arcane rules.

Most businesses purchase items that are subject to *depreciation*. Depreciation is the decrease in the value of an asset over time; it's the allocation of the cost of an asset to the periods in which it is used.

This sounds basic, and many years ago it was. However, now there are many different types of depreciation, including straight-line, ACRS, MACRS, Section 179, "bonus" depreciation, and "economic stimulus" depreciation. Add to this two other issues: *basis* (generally, the purchase price of the item being depreciated) and the Uniform Capitalization Rules. For large entities, depreciation can be a truly bewildering area of tax law.

Luckily, for most small businesses, some general rules apply. This chapter begins by looking at basis and the Uniform Capitalization Rules. Then we look at what assets must be depreciated and the kinds of depreciation. We follow this by looking at leases and amortizable assets and the rules covering amortization. Finally, we look at the typical strategy used by small businesses.

Basis

Basis is the value of the asset being depreciated. The *cost* is what you pay for the asset. It doesn't matter if you pay cash, use a credit card, take out a loan, or exchange another asset for that asset. Basis is the *fair market value* of the asset when you acquire it.

Basis includes ancillary costs of the asset:

- Sales tax,

- Shipping and handling,

- Installation and testing (if required),

- Recording charges and taxes (on real estate), and

- Other similar expenses.

The acquisition of real estate and what is expensed, what is depreciated, and what is amortized are complex. In the section within this chapter on real estate, I give examples of the costs that go in each category.

Uniform Capitalization Rules

The Uniform Capitalization Rules (Section 263A of the Tax Code) require that certain costs be capitalized. However, most small businesses will not be subject to these rules. The rules require that you capitalize direct costs and part of the indirect costs for production or resale activities. This includes the use of inventories, as discussed in Chapter 5. The rules apply if you are producing real or tangible personal property or acquiring property for resale.

However, under Section 1.263A-1(b) of Treasury Regulations, most small businesses will not have to deal with these rules. The rules do not apply to the following:

- Personal property you acquire for resale if the average annual gross receipts of your business are $10 million or less.

- Property you produce if either your indirect costs of producing the property are $200,000 or less or you use the cash-basis method and do not have inventory.

This section is included in this book because a few businesses that are small in size (as far as number of employees) will be subject to these rules. Luckily, most small businesses can ignore this portion of the Tax Code.

▓ **Caution   Seek advice if you are covered by the Uniform Capitalization Rules.** Though some areas of tax are straightforward, the calculations required under the Uniform Capitalization Rules can be complex. If you are covered under the Uniform Capitalization Rules, I *strongly* advise you seek the advice of a tax professional who specializes in this area.

What Assets Must Be Depreciated?

Your business will have many assets, everything from $10 staplers to $100 chairs to $1,000 computers to $10,000 machines. Which of these assets *must* be depreciated? Which *should* be depreciated? Which assets *should not* be depreciated?

Listed Equipment

Congress requires that certain assets called *listed equipment* be depreciated. Listed property includes:

- Passenger automobiles weighing 6,000 pounds or less;

- All other property used for transportation unless excepted;

- Property used for entertainment, recreation, or amusement (including photographic equipment, audiovisual equipment, and communication equipment);

- Computers and related peripherals except if used in a business and owned or leased by the person operating the business. This means that if a partnership or corporation owns a computer, it's listed equipment. However, if a sole proprietor owns a computer, it is *not* listed equipment.

Listed equipment must be depreciated. If the business use of a listed equipment item is 50% or less, you cannot take Section 179 depreciation or special depreciation for that equipment (see later in this chapter). Additionally, if the business use is 50% or less in a year, you must use the straight-line depreciation method for that year.

You may also have to *recapture* depreciation for listed equipment. Depreciation recapture occurs when you use listed property for more than 50% in the prior year, but use it less than 50% in the current year. Under the Tax Code, the excess depreciation is "recaptured" as income. The excess depreciation is the allowed depreciation for the asset (including special depreciation and Section 179 depreciation) less the depreciation that would have been allowed in prior years if you had *not* used the property predominantly for business in the year it was put into service. If you have depreciation recapture, you also increase the adjusted basis of your property by the same amount.

Let's say you purchase a computer and use it 100% for your business in the year of purchase. In the second year you own the computer, you only use it 10% of the time for your business. In the second year, you would have depreciation recapture of the overall excess depreciation.

Cars are the most likely asset where depreciation recapture will be an issue. Let's say you use the actual expense method to determine your automobile expense (as described in Chapter 7). Your business use is 60% of your mileage. In the following year, your business use of your car is only 40%. You will have depreciation recapture. Here's an example of recapture.

You purchase a pickup truck in 2007 for $18,000. The truck is used only for your business from 2007 through 2010. You claimed Section 179 depreciation of $10,000 in 2007. You claimed depreciation of $6,618 in 2007 through 2010. To determine the depreciation allowable when the truck wasn't used predominantly for business, you generally use straight-line depreciation (rather than accelerated depreciation). The straight-line depreciation is 10% of $18,000 in 2007 ($1,800) and 20% of $18,000 in 2008-2010 ($3,600 each year), for a total recalculated allowable depreciation of $12,600. The total depreciation claimed was $16,618. The excess depreciation that is recaptured is $4,018. That amount would be reported as other income on the business return (Schedule C, Form 1065, Form 1120, or Form 1120S).

▓ **Note** **The curious case of cell phones.** On September 27, 2010, President Barack Obama signed the Small Business Jobs Act into law. Buried in this legislation was one section that made business owners and tax professionals happy: Cellular telephones were removed from the listed equipment rules for all tax years beginning after December 31, 2009.

Through 2009, business owners needed to keep excellent records of cell phone usage. The IRS in audits sometimes required calculations of personal versus business usage of cell phones (required under the listed equipment rules).

Today, a cell phone that's for business use is a business expense. This does not mean a cell phone that's for personal use where there's an occasional business call can be taken as a business expense. However, it means you don't have to break out the occasional cost of a personal call from a business cell phone.

Additionally, the IRS considers an employer-provided cell phone to an employee for business reasons to be a *de minimis* fringe benefit and is *not* included in the employee's wages. A cell phone that's provided to promote goodwill, boost morale, or attract employees *is* includable as a taxable fringe benefit.

Large-Cost Items

The idea of depreciation is to recover the cost of an item over its useful life. Consider a stapler (an asset that costs a minimal amount). A stapler costing $10 might last ten years. It doesn't make sense to allocate the cost of a $10 asset over ten years.

Now consider a $10,000 machine used in a manufacturing process. The machine may also last ten years. Here, allocating all of the cost to the year of purchase doesn't make sense. The machine will provide value over ten years, so its cost should be allocated over its ten-year life. This is done through depreciation.

(As will be noted later in this chapter, Congress allows through Section 179 Depreciation and bonus depreciation for you to recover the cost of the asset in the year of purchase.)

Businesses generally get to decide where to draw the line for large-cost items for depreciation. Items that cost $1,000 or more are generally depreciated; items costing under $500 generally are not depreciated. Drawing the line somewhere between $500 and $1,000 is reasonable.

Other Depreciable Items

Most things that are depreciated are obvious. However, a few items are depreciated that you wouldn't expect. Here are some of them.

Real Estate

Building and improvements are depreciated; however, land *never* depreciates.

■ **Tip** **Allocation for land.** Suppose you purchase a commercial building for $200,000 that you plan on renting to a tenant. Your basis is $200,000 (plus costs of purchase), right?

Wrong. Land never depreciates, and the building sits on land. Unless you separately lease the land, you *must* allocate a portion of the purchase price to land. This is usually done by using the most recent property tax assessment.

Assume that the most recent assessment statement shows a total value (land and buildings) of $180,000 and that the land is worth $18,000. That equates to land being 10% of the value. It is then reasonable to allocate 10% of the purchase price, or $20,000, to land. The remaining $180,000 becomes the depreciable basis of the building.

Patents and Copyrights

Some intellectual property is depreciated. The value of a patent or a copyright you acquire is depreciated. A patent or copyright is depreciated using the straight-line method over the remaining useful life (the remaining term granted to it by the government).

Computer Software

Most computer software is expensed. Say you purchase QuickBooks, a standard accounting package. The cost is generally not high enough to require it to be considered a capital asset.

However, some commercial software is quite expensive. That computer software will either be an intangible asset or a depreciable asset. Computer software is depreciated over a *three-year life* using the straight-line method if all of the following are true:

- It is readily available for purchase by the general public,
- It is subject to a nonexclusive license, and
- It has not been substantially modified.

Computer software that does *not* meet the foregoing conditions and is of a large cost is amortized. (Amortizable assets are discussed later in this chapter.)

Types of Depreciation

Many children's stories begin, "Once upon a time . . ." So might the story of depreciation. Many years ago, there was only one kind of depreciation: *straight-line depreciation*. In straight-line depreciation, you take the basis of the asset, divide that by the useful life of the asset, and you get the depreciation. Today, rental real estate, computer software, and intellectual property are the major types of assets that still use straight-line depreciation.

In 1971, Congress adopted class life asset depreciation ranges. Under this system (which went by the acronym ADR), you could choose between several different depreciation methods: straight-line, declining balance, and sum of years digits.

In 1981, Congress decided to make more changes. The Accelerated Cost Recovery System (ACRS) was adopted. Only the declining balance system and straight-line depreciation were allowed for assets. The present Modified Accelerated Cost Recovery System (MACRS) was adopted by Congress in the Tax Reform Act of 1986.

There are two types of depreciation under MACRS: the General Depreciation System (GDS) and the Alternative Depreciation System (ADS). You will probably want to use the GDS; you *cannot* take any special depreciation (bonus or Section 179) under ADS. The only cases where you must use ADS are:

- Listed property used 50% or less in a qualified business,

- Tangible personal property used outside of the United States during the year,

- Tax-exempt use property,

- Two other situations that are very rare.[1]

The benefit of MACRS over straight-line depreciation is that you get a larger amount of depreciation earlier. With straight-line depreciation, the depreciation is the same amount each year. With MACRS, you will get a larger depreciation expense sooner, lowering your income (and tax) today while increasing it in later years.

▨ **Note   You can elect to use ADS or straight-line depreciation.** You may elect to use ADS instead of GDS for any class of property you wish. This election is made by completing line 20 on Part III of Form 4562.

You can also elect out of MACRS and take straight-line depreciation for any class of property. You do this by attaching a statement to your tax return indicating the election you are making and the class of property for which you are making the election.

---

[1] Specifically, these situations are (1) property used predominantly in a farming business and placed in service in a tax year during which an election *not* to use the Uniform Capitalization Rules to certain farming costs is in effect; and (2) property imported from a foreign country for which an executive order is in effect because the country maintains trade restrictions or engages in other discriminatory acts.

The actual method used in MACRS GDS is a combination of the double-declining balance and straight-line depreciation methods. The double-declining balance method is like straight-line depreciation, except it is doubled. Assume that you have an asset with a ten-year life with a basis of $10,000. The depreciation in the first year would be $1,000 using the straight-line method. That's 10% of the basis, or a factor of 0.1000 for the amount of the asset depreciated in the first year. For the *double-declining balance method* we double this factor to 0.2000, so $2,000 would be the amount of depreciation taken.[2] That's the MACRS GDS result. It can also be represented by this formula:

$$\text{Depreciation} = [\text{Basis}] \times 2 \times (1/[\text{Useful Life of Asset in Years}])$$

Note that the basis here is the basis *still left to be depreciated.* In the example, the second-year depreciation would be:

$$\begin{aligned}\text{Depreciation} &= [(\$10,000\text{-}\$2,000)] \times 2 \times (1/[10]) \\ &= \$8,000 \times 2 \times 0.1000 \\ &= \$1,600\end{aligned}$$

But what happens in future years? Eventually, the amount of depreciation taken using the double-declining balance method is less than the amount under the straight-line method. When that happens using MACRS, you switch to the straight-line method. Table 10-1 below shows how this works.

Table 10-1. Example of Depreciation Taken Under MACRS

Year	Beg. Balance	DDB Depr.	S-L Depr.	Depr. Taken
1	$10,000	$2,000	$500	$2,000
2	$8,000	$1,600	$889	$1,600
3	$6,400	$1,280	$800	$1,280
4	$5,120	$1,024	$731	$1,024
5	$4,096	$819	$683	$819
6	$3,277	$655	$655	$655
7	$2,622	$524	$655	$655
8	$1,967	$393	$655	$655
9	$1,312	$262	$655	$655
10	$657	$131	$657	$657

---

[2] Note that depreciation factors are generally expressed to four significant decimal places.

As you may notice, the double-declining balance method does not allow an asset to ever be fully depreciated; that's why there's a switchover to straight-line depreciation under MACRS.

Special Kinds of Depreciation

There are two special kinds of depreciation: Section 179 depreciation and bonus depreciation (currently also called economic stimulus depreciation). These special kinds of depreciation allow you to effectively expense the cost of a depreciable asset in the year of purchase.

Section 179 Depreciation

Section 179 depreciation is named for the section of the Tax Code that authorizes it. Initially, Section 179 depreciation allowed you to expense $25,000 of assets during a calendar year. Congress, however, has increased the dollar limits over the past few years. The maximum Section 179 depreciation for 2012 is $139,000; the current limit for 2013 is $25,000.[3] Note that your ability to take this deduction begins to phase out on purchases of more than $560,000 of assets in 2012 and $200,000 in 2013.

Almost everything qualifies for Section 179 treatment. You can use Section 179 for tangible personal property (including machines, furniture and fixtures, and livestock[4]), computer software, and certain real property.[5]

It might be better to look at what does *not* qualify for Section 179: land and land improvements,[6] and excepted property. The excepted property includes:

- Some property leased to others if you are *not* a corporation,[7]
- Certain property used for lodging (hotels/motels),
- Heating and air conditioning units.

---

[3] I expect Congress to increase this limit for 2013 in either the 2012 "Lame Duck" session following the Presidential election or in early 2013.

[4] Yes, livestock like cows and cattle are depreciated over their useful lives.

[5] Qualified leasehold improvement property, qualified restaurant property, and qualified retail improvement property.

[6] This includes swimming pools, parking lots, wharves, docks, bridges, and fences.

[7] This does *not* include property you manufacture or produce and lease to others.

▓ **Caution** **State limits on Section 179 may be different.** Some states have different rules and limits on Section 179 depreciation. For example, California does *not* conform to the increased amount of Section 179 depreciation. The limit for California tax returns has been and will likely remain at $25,000.

Figure 10-1 illustrates how you take the Section 179 deduction. Note that the form shown is for 2011; the maximum amount (line 1) and the threshold cost before reduction in limitation (line 3) would be $139,000 instead of $500,000 and $569,000 instead of $2,000,000, respectively.

Form **4562**	**Depreciation and Amortization**		OMB No. 1545-0172
	(Including Information on Listed Property)		**20 11**
Department of the Treasury Internal Revenue Service (99)	▶ See separate instructions. ▶ Attach to your tax return.		Attachment Sequence No. **179**
Name(s) shown on return George & Jane Jetson	Business or activity to which this form relates Sch C Consulting		Identifying number 123-45-6789

Part I Election To Expense Certain Property Under Section 179
Note: *If you have any listed property, complete Part V before you complete Part I.*

		(a) Description of property	(b) Cost (business use only)	(c) Elected cost		
1	Maximum amount (see instructions)				1	500,000
2	Total cost of section 179 property placed in service (see instructions)				2	3,069
3	Threshold cost of section 179 property before reduction in limitation (see instructions)				3	2,000,000
4	Reduction in limitation. Subtract line 3 from line 2. If zero or less, enter -0-				4	0
5	Dollar limitation for tax year. Subtract line 4 from line 1. If zero or less, enter -0-. If married filing separately, see instructions				5	
6		MacBook Pro	2,714	2,714		
		Toshiba Monitor	355	355		
7	Listed property. Enter the amount from line 29		7			
8	Total elected cost of section 179 property. Add amounts in column (c), lines 6 and 7				8	3,069
9	Tentative deduction. Enter the **smaller** of line 5 or line 8				9	3,069
10	Carryover of disallowed deduction from line 13 of your 2010 Form 4562				10	
11	Business income limitation. Enter the smaller of business income (not less than zero) or line 5 (see instructions)				11	500,000
12	Section 179 expense deduction. Add lines 9 and 10, but do not enter more than line 11				12	3,069
13	Carryover of disallowed deduction to 2012. Add lines 9 and 10, less line 12 ▶		13			

Figure 10-1. Illustration of electing Section 179 depreciation

You can make a late election to take Section 179 depreciation. To do so, you attach a statement stating you are, "electing the application of Section 179(f) of the Internal Revenue Code" with your amended return.[8] The amended return *must* be filed within the time frame allowed (generally, three years from the due date of the return).

There is one other major restriction regarding Section 179 depreciation: You *must* have positive income to take the deduction. If you do not have positive income, the deduction carries forward to the following year. If the business is a flow-through entity, both the business *and* the individual (or other business entity) taking the deduction must have positive income.

---

[8] This is the normal statement for electing Section 179 depreciation.

Special (Bonus) Depreciation

Congress has enacted various special, or bonus, depreciation rules from time to time. The most recent round of special depreciation is called the economic stimulus qualified property depreciation. For 2012, this allows 50% bonus depreciation on qualified property placed into service.

Like Section 179 depreciation, almost everything qualifies for bonus depreciation. The property must be new (used property does *not* qualify), with a twenty-year or less useful life. Almost all personal property, computer software, and most leasehold improvements qualify. However, qualified restaurant property and qualified retail improvement property are *not* eligible for special depreciation (though they are eligible for Section 179 depreciation).

The advantage of bonus depreciation is that you take 50% of the cost of the property as bonus depreciation (effectively expensed during the first year). This lowers your income and your tax for the year. There is no restriction on the amount of equipment you can purchase in taking bonus depreciation. You are eligible to take bonus depreciation if you purchase $1,000 or $1,000,000 of capital assets during 2012.

▒ **Caution Not all states recognize bonus depreciation.** Just like with Section 179 depreciation, not all states recognize bonus depreciation. For example, California does not conform to this portion of federal tax law.

You can elect out of taking bonus depreciation. To do so, you attach a statement to your return indicating the election you are making and the class of property for which you are making the election.

Unlike Section 179 depreciation, there is no rule requiring that a business have positive income to take bonus depreciation.

Rules and Recordkeeping

We're ready to look at the nitty-gritty of depreciable assets. You should keep a record of your fixed assets. Not only will you need it for your income tax return, you will probably need it for your personal property tax return. Property you own that is depreciated over time is taxed by most local jurisdictions. As usual, keeping good records is half the battle.

Property Class

The Tax Code divides property into different classes based on their useful lives. Property classes range from 3-year property to residential rental property with a life of 39 years. Table 10-2 gives examples of depreciation periods for various assets. Note that any asset type that does not have a class life and has not been designated by law as being some other class is considered to have a 7-year life.

Conventions and First-Year Depreciation

There are two further rules that determine how assets are depreciated in their first year. These are the *half-year convention* and the *midquarter convention*.

Half-Year Convention

Under the half-year convention, assets are considered to be put into service on July 1 no matter what day of the year they were actually put into service. This is the normal means of depreciation during the first year.

For example, say you purchase two machines, one on March 1 and one on September 22. To calculate depreciation, each would be considered put into service on July 1. You would get half the first-year depreciation for each asset.

Midquarter Convention

Congress wrote an exception into the law regarding the half-year convention. If you put into service 40% or more of your depreciable assets during the last three months of the year, you must use the midquarter convention. Under this rule, each asset is put into place during the middle of the quarter of purchase.

Table 10-2. Depreciation Periods for Various Types of Property

Depreciation Period	Types of Property
3 years	Computer software Tractor units for over-the-road use Race horses placed in service before January 1, 2014
5 years	Cars, taxis, buses, and trucks Computers and peripherals Office machines (e.g., copiers) Research and development property Appliances, carpets, furniture, etc. used in residential rentals Most cattle

Depreciation Period	Types of Property
7 years	Office furniture and fixtures (desks, files, etc.) Agricultural machinery and equipment Any property that does *not* have a class life and has not been designated by law as being in any other class
10 years	Vessels, barges, tugs, and similar water transportation equipment A single-purpose agricultural or horticultural structure Trees or vine-bearing fruits or nuts
15 tears	Land improvements (e.g., shrubs, fences, roads, sidewalks, and bridges) Retail motor fuel outlets (including convenience stores)
20 tears	Farm buildings except single-purpose agricultural or horticultural structures
27.5 years	Residential rental property (e.g., an apartment building)
39 tears	Nonresidential rental property (e.g., office building or a home office)

Let's assume you purchase two machines, one on March 1 and one on October 22. Each machine costs $10,000. Because you purchased 40% or more of your depreciable assets during the last quarter of the year, you must use the midquarter convention. The first machine would be considered placed in service on February 15; the second machine would be considered placed in service on November 15.

▨ **Tip   Using Section 179 depreciation to avoid the midquarter convention.** Assets depreciated using Section 179 depreciation do *not* count as being placed in service during the last three months of the year for purposes of determining whether you need to use the midquarter convention. In almost all cases, you want to use Section 179 depreciation with assets purchased at the end of the year to avoid the midquarter convention.

Mid-Month Convention

The half-year and midquarter conventions are used for tangible personal property. The *mid-month convention* is used for real property. Under this convention, property is considered put into service on the middle of the month of purchase.

Date of Purchase vs. Date in Use

We depreciate assets based on the date they are first put into use. Suppose you buy a computer on December 28. For whatever reason, you do not open the box containing the computer and put it into use until January 3. The computer will be considered put into service on January 3, *not* December 28.

Some assets require additional work put into them before being put into service. For example, one of my clients purchased a new truck on May 1. He then had a contractor install refrigeration equipment onto that truck on May 15. The truck went into use on May 15, not May 1. The date put into service for the truck will be May 15.

Calculating Depreciation

If you take Section 179 depreciation, your depreciation will equal the cost of the asset. If you take bonus depreciation, the bonus (special) depreciation will equal half the cost of the asset. If you don't take either method, what is the depreciation? (Or if you take bonus depreciation, what is the rest of the depreciation deduction?)

You can calculate this by hand. The IRS gives instructions on how to do this in Publication 946; I go through two examples below. However, this is an area in which computers and tax preparation software are especially useful.

If I tell my tax software I have a seven-year asset, with a basis of $100,000, put into service on July 17, with bonus depreciation of $50,000, and no Section 179 depreciation, it will tell me that the depreciation deduction is $7,145 (assuming that the midquarter convention does not apply). Why should I spend several minutes calculating depreciation when my computer will do it in several seconds?

It's not only tax software that can calculate depreciation. Many versions of QuickBooks have a *Fixed Assets Manager*. The Fixed Assets Manager will calculate tax depreciation and even include the appropriate convention. The Fixed Asset Manager can use both Section 179 and bonus depreciation. Of course, if you have used either Section 179 depreciation, there's nothing to calculate: Your depreciation deduction is the cost of the asset, although your state depreciation may vary.

Let's go through a couple of calculations.

Example 1. You purchase a machine used in your manufacturing process on July 17 and it is immediately placed in service. This is the only fixed asset you purchase during the year. The machine costs $100,000. You elect full bonus (special) depreciation of $50,000. What is the first-year depreciation?

First, we must determine the class of asset purchased. It's a machine, and from Table 10-2 we can see it has a *seven-year life property*. Because this is the only fixed asset purchased during the year, the half-year convention applies.

Next, we must determine the depreciable basis. To do this, we take the normal basis and subtract any Section 179 or bonus depreciation elected. We take $100,000 and subtract $50,000, so that the depreciable basis is $50,000.

If the machine is not used 100% for business, an adjustment would need to be made for the depreciable basis. That's not necessary in our example.

We then look in the IRS table for the half-year depreciation of a seven-year asset in its first year of depreciation. (The tables are in Appendix A of IRS Publication 946.) The depreciation factor for such an asset is 0.1429. We multiply that factor by the depreciable basis of $50,000 and come up with depreciation of $7,145.

Example 2. You purchase an office building for $120,000, including the land valued at $20,000. The property is commercial (not residential). The sale closes on March 22 and the property is immediately placed in service. What would the depreciation be in the first and second years?

Here, we do not have tangible personal property—this is real property. This is 39-year property (again, refer to Table 10-2).

We next determine the basis for the building. Because land never depreciates, and 39-year property is ineligible for either Section 179 or bonus depreciation, the depreciable basis is $100,000.

Nonresidential real property is depreciated over 39 years using the straight-line method. It doesn't matter what day of the month the building went into service; under the mid-month convention, it will be considered to have gone into service *for purposes of depreciation* on the middle of the month. The depreciation factor from Publication 946 is 2.033%, or 0.02033. We multiply that by $100,000 to get the first-year depreciation of $2,033.

The factor for the second year (indeed, for all years except the first and last years, when the factor is the same) is 2.564%, or 0.02564. That will yield depreciation of $2,564.

Tip   If you do this by hand, check your work! Math errors are now very rare in tax preparation. Computers do an excellent job with math. Assuming you enter the correct class of fixed asset to be depreciated and the correct basis, as well as the correct date of purchase, the computer will calculate the depreciation accurately. It is very easy to misread a table or use the wrong table when calculating depreciation. Appendix A of IRS Publication 946 includes 25 tables on 28 pages.

Leases

Many times, property is rented, or *leased,* instead of being purchased. Some manufacturers do not sell certain products; they only offer them for leases. For example, shuffling machines used in casinos are currently only offered on lease by the manufacturer to casinos.

There are two kinds of leases: *operating* leases and *capital* leases. In an operating lease, there is no option at the end of the lease term for the lessee (the person or business renting the property) to acquire the property, or else the cost is the then-current fair market value of the property. Most automobile leases are operating leases: You must pay the lessor the fair market value of the car to acquire it at the end of the lease term. Under an operating lease, the lessor is only transferring the right to use the property to the lessee. There is no ownership interest granted to the lessee.

Capital leases are different. Here, the lessor gives the lessee the property at the end of the lease or offers it to him for a bargain purchase price, say $1 or $100. A business must capitalize anything acquired through a capital lease.

There are other formats of capital leases. The lease might specify that the lessor is paying interest, or that each payment made by the lessor gives him an increasing percentage of ownership in the asset.

Under an operating lease, the lessor is only transferring the right to use the property to the lessee and there are no ownership rights established. An operating lease causes an expense. Automobile leases were previously discussed (see Chapter 7). Other items that can be expensed through leases will be discussed in Chapter 11.

In a capital lease, the lessee assumes some of the risks of ownership. A capital lease will cause the asset (or a portion of the value of the asset) to be put on the balance sheet, with the asset being subject to the normal rules for depreciation for that class of asset.

Should You Buy or Lease?

It depends.

This really is a complex question, and what *you* should do for your business will depend on what is being acquired, the cost differential in buying or leasing, and the tax consequences. The right answer for your business might be to purchase item 1 but lease item 2. You must evaluate each item on a case-by-case basis.

There are a few things that are always the same when looking at a purchase or an operating lease. I list these in Table 10-3.

Table 10-3. Leasing vs. Buying

	Operating Lease	**Purchase/Capital Lease**
Initial payment	Usually small	Usually large (a much larger down payment is normally required than with a lease)
Ownership	None	You own it
Monthly payments	Lease payments are fully deductible	If bought with a loan, the interest paid is deductible; principal payments are not
Depreciation	None	Depreciable, with Section 179 or bonus depreciation depending on asset class of item

Amortizable Assets

The last portion of this chapter looks at assets that are amortized over their useful lives. We've already covered two such assets earlier in this book: start-up costs and organizational expenses. There are many other such assets. Amortization is used to recover the cost of amortizable assets in the same manner as depreciation is used to recover the cost of fixed assets. Amortization is calculated by taking the cost of the asset and dividing by the useful life (in months). Amortization is always calculated on a straight-line basis.

Most amortizable assets are *intangible assets*. These are things you generally can't touch or hold. The most common type of amortizable asset is a Section 197 intangible asset.

Section 197 Intangible Assets

The Tax Code defines certain items as Section 197 intangible assets. Some of the more common intangible assets are:[9]

- Goodwill,

- Books and records,

---

[9] You can find a complete list in IRS Publication 535.

- Patents, copyrights, formulas, and other intellectual property,[10]

- Government licenses and permits acquired,[11]

- Covenant not to compete.

Section 197 intangible assets are amortized over 180 months (15 years), with an equal amount of amortization expense taken in each month.

When you purchase a home as your primary residence, you are allowed to take a tax deduction for the points paid to acquire the loan. However, you must amortize those points over the life of the loan for a rental property. This falls under Section 461 of the Tax Code. There is no one length of time for the amortization; an equal amount will be taken each month over the life of the loan.

Finally, here are some of the less common kinds of amortizable expenses: pollution control facilities (Section 169 of the Tax Code), some bond premiums (Section 171), some research and experimental expenditures (Section 174), the cost of acquiring a lease (Section 178), and certain forestation and reforestation expenses (Section 194).

A Typical Strategy Used by a Small Business

Most small businesses do not purchase large quantities of or very large dollar amount fixed assets. The strategy used by many small businesses is to use Section 179 depreciation to effectively expense most fixed asset purchases. If the business is losing money (or the owner is, if it's a flow-through entity), then bonus depreciation is elected. This allows the maximum depreciation deduction to be taken in the year so that income (and tax) is lowered.

I need to point out that this may not be the best long-term strategy. Assume a sole proprietor has minimal profit this year, but will have large profits in future years. In this situation it may make sense to not elect any special depreciation. The marginal tax rate this year is going to be relatively low, whereas it will be larger in future years. By not taking special depreciation, the business will have an additional deduction in future years when the tax rate would be higher.

---

[10] Except where the Tax Code specifically states that these should be depreciated.

[11] For example, a taxi medallion or a liquor license you acquire from a previous owner of the medallion or license.

Employees, Payroll Taxes, and Benefit Plans

When you hire staff, have you hired an employee or an independent contractor? There's a huge difference in how each is treated for taxes. Chapter 12 looks at employees and independent contractors, and how each is reported. This chapter also covers the required compensation for an S-corporation shareholder-employee. Payroll taxes are covered in Chapter 13 (both employer and employee taxes). I examine medical expenses and retirement plans in the final two chapters of Part III.

Other Deductions

An income tax form is like a laundry list—either way you lose your shirt.

—Fred Allen

In the previous chapters we looked at the major costs of a business that are deductible. Here we cover most of the other items (except for wages and related expenses). You can call this the A to U of deductible expenses. (It would be nice to call it the A to Z, but there isn't a typical business expense beginning with the letter Z.)

For each of these expense items we'll look at what can and cannot be deducted for the category. The general rule is any expense that is both ordinary and necessary for your business is a deductible business expense.

Advertising

Clearly, advertising your business is a deductible expense. This includes almost any form of advertising:

- Brochures
- Business cards
- Broadcast advertising (radio and television)
- Internet advertising
- Print advertising to the public (newspapers and magazines)

- Trade publication advertising
- Yellow Page advertising
- Billboards

Marketing expenses are usually included within advertising. Most marketing expenses are related to advertising and promoting your business and are included as advertising expenses.

Promotional Expenses

Promotional expenses include a variety of costs your business is likely to incur. For example, promotional goods such as coffee mugs with your logos are part of advertising expenses.

There are some rules regarding promotional items. They must be *de minimis* in cost ($4 or less), be "widely distributed," and have your business's name clearly and permanently displayed on the item. A coffee mug with your business name on it that you give away probably qualifies as a deductible advertising expense.

What about a polo shirt with your name on it? Because most shirts will cost more than $4 each, it will *not* qualify as a giveaway item. However, it may still qualify as an advertising expense if you use it for employees. Such a shirt can clearly be shown to help promote your business and therefore is an ordinary and necessary business expense.

Trade Shows

The costs of attending trade shows that promote your business are included in advertising expenses. However, the cost to travel to the trade show is included in travel expenses; the costs of meals are included in meals and entertainment expenses. Typical deductible costs include registration fees, booth rentals, labor cost for setting up the booth, shipping costs (for sending your booth or materials to the trade show), promotional materials (brochures, promotional items, and the like), audio-visual fees, and Internet connectivity charges. Almost any cost you have to maintain your presence at a trade show (except travel and meals and entertainment) will be deducted as an advertising expense.

Websites

The cost of your website can be an advertising expense. However, it might be more properly expensed in another category. The answer to where the cost of your website should be expensed depends on the purpose of your website and the kinds of expenses incurred.

What is the purpose of your website? If it is used to promote your business, the expenses for it are advertising expenses. That's the case for most websites. All related costs, including hosting, maintenance, and search engine optimization (SEO) expenses, would be deductible under advertising.

However, some websites are used more for internal usage (an intranet). These costs would be categorized as either *computer services and supplies* or as *office expenses*. These categories are discussed later in this chapter.

Where do costs of developing a website go? I've seen website development costs both expensed and capitalized. The answer should be based on what is being developed and the amount of money spent. Relatively small amounts can be expensed; large expenditures should be capitalized. Remember, even if your website development is a capital expense, you can use Section 179 depreciation to effectively expense it in the current year (see Chapter 10).

Bad Debts

What happens when a customer buys products or services from you but doesn't pay? You should make collection efforts, but sometimes these are to no avail. When you end up with a deadbeat customer, you have a bad debt.

There is a major caveat to bad-debt expense: You *must* be an accrual-based business to have bad debt. Remember, a cash-basis business doesn't recognize a sale *until it is paid*. Thus, there can't be bad debt for cash-basis businesses.

For there to be bad debt, the debt must also be either completely or partially worthless. Let's say your accrual-based manufacturing business sells $500 of widgets to a customer. The customer sends you a check for $100 and three months later goes out of business. You would have a $400 of bad-debt expense that would be deductible.

Bad-debt expenses are deducted when you have *certainty* that the debt should be written off. This could be from the customer going out of business, filing bankruptcy, or fruitless efforts at collection.

■ **Note Waiting on bankruptcy.** Assume you're an accrual-basis manufacturer. You've sold $500 of widgets to the Acme Company in December. In January, Acme files for Chapter 11 bankruptcy. In September of the following year, Acme files a reorganization plan with the bankruptcy court, whereby your business would be paid 10 cents on the dollar for what they owe you. Can you write off $450 in September?

No. You must wait for the court to approve the reorganization. In September, there is no *certainty* that you will receive $50. The court could change the plan, and you might receive more or less than the proposed 10 cents on the dollar.

Another form of business bad debts is loans. Let's say your largest supplier is having financial difficulties, and you lend them $5,000. The supplier then goes out of business and the money is not repaid. You have a bad debt of $5,000. Note that bad-debt loans *are* deductible for cash-basis businesses. Similarly, if you guarantee a debt and it becomes worthless, it can become a bad-debt expense if:

- The guarantee was part of your normal business operations,

- You have a legal requirement to pay the debt,

- You made the guarantee prior to it becoming worthless, and

- You had a business purpose for making the guarantee.

Bank Fees

Bank charges for items such as wire transfers, account fees, overdraft charges, are deductible as ordinary and necessary business expenses. The question becomes: Where are these put on a tax return?

Figure 11-1 shows page 1 of Schedule C (used for a sole proprietorship). Figure 11-2 shows page 1 of Form 1065 (used by a partnership or an LLC filing as a partnership). Figure 11-3 shows page 1 of Form 1120 (used by a C corporation). And Figure 11-4 shows page 1 of Form 1120S (used by an S corporation). On all of these forms there is no specific line for bank charges. Clearly they are a deductible expense. So we return to the question: Where do these go on the tax return?

SCHEDULE C (Form 1040)	**Profit or Loss From Business** (Sole Proprietorship)	OMB No. 1545-0074
Department of the Treasury Internal Revenue Service (99)	▶ For information on Schedule C and its instructions, go to *www.irs.gov/schedulec* ▶ Attach to Form 1040, 1040NR, or 1041; partnerships generally must file Form 1065.	20**11** Attachment Sequence No. 09

Name of proprietor		Social security number (SSN)

| A | Principal business or profession, including product or service (see instructions) | B Enter code from instructions
▶ | | | |

| C | Business name. If no separate business name, leave blank. | D Employer ID number (EIN), (see instr.) |

E Business address (including suite or room no.) ▶ ....
   City, town or post office, state, and ZIP code

F Accounting method: **(1)** ☐ Cash **(2)** ☐ Accrual **(3)** ☐ Other (specify) ▶ ....

G Did you "materially participate" in the operation of this business during 2011? If "No," see instructions for limit on losses ☐ Yes ☐ No

H If you started or acquired this business during 2011, check here . . . . ▶ ☐

I Did you make any payments in 2011 that would require you to file Form(s) 1099? (see instructions) . . . ☐ Yes ☐ No

J If "Yes," did you or will you file all required Forms 1099? . . . . ☐ Yes ☐ No

Part I Income

1a	Merchant card and third party payments. For 2011, enter -0- . . .	1a		
b	Gross receipts or sales not entered on line 1a (see instructions) . .	1b		
c	Income reported to you on Form W-2 if the "Statutory Employee" box on that form was checked. **Caution.** See instr. before completing this line	1c		
d	**Total gross receipts.** Add lines 1a through 1c		1d	
2	Returns and allowances plus any other adjustments (see instructions)		2	
3	Subtract line 2 from line 1d		3	
4	Cost of goods sold (from line 42)		4	
5	**Gross profit.** Subtract line 4 from line 3		5	
6	Other income, including federal and state gasoline or fuel tax credit or refund (see instructions) . . .		6	
7	**Gross income.** Add lines 5 and 6 . . . . ▶		7	

Part II Expenses   Enter expenses for business use of your home only on line 30.

8	Advertising	8		18	Office expense (see instructions)	18
9	Car and truck expenses (see			19	Pension and profit-sharing plans .	19
	instructions).	9		20	Rent or lease (see instructions):	
10	Commissions and fees .	10		a	Vehicles, machinery, and equipment	20a
11	Contract labor (see instructions)	11		b	Other business property . . .	20b
12	Depletion	12		21	Repairs and maintenance . .	21
13	Depreciation and section 179 expense deduction (not included in Part III) (see instructions).	13		22	Supplies (not included in Part III) .	22
				23	Taxes and licenses	23
				24	Travel, meals, and entertainment:	
14	Employee benefit programs (other than on line 19) . .	14		a	Travel	24a
15	Insurance (other than health)	15		b	Deductible meals and entertainment (see instructions) .	24b
16	Interest:			25	Utilities	25
a	Mortgage (paid to banks, etc.)	16a		26	Wages (less employment credits).	26
b	Other	16b		27a	Other expenses (from line 48) . .	27a
17	Legal and professional services	17		b	**Reserved for future use** . . .	27b

28	**Total expenses** before expenses for business use of home. Add lines 8 through 27a . . . . ▶		28	
29	Tentative profit or (loss). Subtract line 28 from line 7		29	
30	Expenses for business use of your home. Attach **Form 8829**. Do not report such expenses elsewhere . .		30	
31	**Net profit or (loss).** Subtract line 30 from line 29.			
	• If a profit, enter on both **Form 1040, line 12** (or **Form 1040NR, line 13**) and on **Schedule SE, line 2.** If you entered an amount on line 1c, see instr. Estates and trusts, enter on **Form 1041, line 3.** • If a loss, you **must** go to line 32.	}	31	
32	If you have a loss, check the box that describes your investment in this activity (see instructions).			
	• If you checked 32a, enter the loss on both **Form 1040, line 12,** (or **Form 1040NR, line 13**) and on **Schedule SE, line 2.** If you entered an amount on line 1c, see the instructions for line 31. Estates and trusts, enter on **Form 1041, line 3.** • If you checked 32b, you **must** attach **Form 6198.** Your loss may be limited	}	32a ☐ All investment is at risk. 32b ☐ Some investment is not at risk.

Figure 11-1. Schedule C

Form **1065**		**U.S. Return of Partnership Income**		OMB No. 1545-0099
Department of the Treasury Internal Revenue Service		For calendar year 2011, or tax year beginning _____ , 2011, ending _____ . 20 ___ ▶ **See separate instructions.**		**2011**

A Principal business activity		Name of partnership	D Employer identification number
B Principal product or service	**Print or type.**	Number, street, and room or suite no. If a P.O. box, see the instructions.	E Date business started
C Business code number		City or town, state, and ZIP code	F Total assets (see the instructions) $

G   Check applicable boxes: **(1)** ☐ Initial return   **(2)** ☐ Final return   **(3)** ☐ Name change   **(4)** ☐ Address change   **(5)** ☐ Amended return
  (6) ☐ Technical termination - also check (1) or (2)
H   Check accounting method: **(1)** ☐ Cash   **(2)** ☐ Accrual   **(3)** ☐ Other (specify) ▶ _____
I   Number of Schedules K-1. Attach one for each person who was a partner at any time during the tax year ▶ _____
J   Check if Schedules C and M-3 are attached   . . . . ☐

Caution. Include **only** trade or business income and expenses on lines 1a through 22 below. See the instructions for more information.

Income	**1a**	Merchant card and third-party payments (including amounts reported on Form(s) 1099-K). For 2011, enter -0-	**1a**	
	b	Gross receipts or sales not reported on line 1a (see instructions)	**1b**	
	c	Total. Add lines 1a and 1b	**1c**	
	d	Returns and allowances plus any other adjustments to line 1a (see instructions)	**1d**	
	e	Subtract line 1d from line 1c	**1e**	
	2	Cost of goods sold (attach Form 1125-A)	**2**	
	3	Gross profit. Subtract line 2 from line 1e	**3**	
	4	Ordinary income (loss) from other partnerships, estates, and trusts (attach statement) . .	**4**	
	5	Net farm profit (loss) (attach Schedule F (Form 1040))	**5**	
	6	Net gain (loss) from Form 4797, Part II, line 17 (attach Form 4797)	**6**	
	7	Other income (loss) (attach statement)	**7**	
	8	**Total income (loss).** Combine lines 3 through 7	**8**	
Deductions (see the instructions for limitations)	**9**	Salaries and wages (other than to partners) (less employment credits)	**9**	
	10	Guaranteed payments to partners	**10**	
	11	Repairs and maintenance	**11**	
	12	Bad debts	**12**	
	13	Rent	**13**	
	14	Taxes and licenses	**14**	
	15	Interest	**15**	
	16a	Depreciation (if required, attach Form 4562)	**16a**	
	b	Less depreciation reported on Form 1125-A and elsewhere on return	**16b**	**16c**
	17	Depletion **(Do not deduct oil and gas depletion.)**	**17**	
	18	Retirement plans, etc.	**18**	
	19	Employee benefit programs	**19**	
	20	Other deductions (attach statement)	**20**	
	21	**Total deductions.** Add the amounts shown in the far right column for lines 9 through 20 .	**21**	
	22	**Ordinary business income (loss).** Subtract line 21 from line 8	**22**	

Sign Here	Under penalties of perjury, I declare that I have examined this return, including accompanying schedules and statements, and to the best of my knowledge and belief, it is true, correct, and complete. Declaration of preparer (other than general partner or limited liability company member manager) is based on all information of which preparer has any knowledge.	
		May the IRS discuss this return with the preparer shown below (see instructions)? ☐ **Yes** ☐ **No**
	▶ Signature of general partner or limited liability company member manager ▶ Date	

Paid Preparer Use Only	Print/Type preparer's name	Preparer's signature	Date	Check ☐ if self-employed	PTIN
	Firm's name ▶			Firm's EIN ▶	
	Firm's address ▶			Phone no.	

Figure 11-2. Form 1065 (page 1)

Form **1120**		**U.S. Corporation Income Tax Return**		OMB No. 1545-0123

Department of the Treasury
Internal Revenue Service

For calendar year 2011 or tax year beginning _____ , 2011, ending _____ , 20 _____

▶ **See separate instructions.**

2011

A Check if:						B Employer identification number
1a Consolidated return (attach Form 851)	☐	**TYPE OR PRINT**	Name			
b Life/nonlife consolidated return	☐		Number, street, and room or suite no. If a P.O. box, see instructions.			C Date incorporated
2 Personal holding co. (attach Sch. PH)	☐		City or town, state, and ZIP code			D Total assets (see instructions)
3 Personal service corp. (see instructions)	☐					$
4 Schedule M-3 attached	☐	E Check if: **(1)** ☐ Initial return **(2)** ☐ Final return **(3)** ☐ Name change **(4)** ☐ Address change				

Income	**1a**	Merchant card and third-party payments. For 2011, enter -0-	**1a**		
	b	Gross receipts or sales not reported on line 1a (see instructions)	**1b**		
	c	Total. Add lines 1a and 1b	**1c**		
	d	Returns and allowances plus any other adjustments (see instructions)	**1d**		
	e	Subtract line 1d from line 1c		**1e**	
	2	Cost of goods sold from Form 1125-A, line 8 (attach Form 1125-A)		**2**	
	3	Gross profit. Subtract line 2 from line 1e		**3**	
	4	Dividends (Schedule C, line 19)		**4**	
	5	Interest		**5**	
	6	Gross rents		**6**	
	7	Gross royalties		**7**	
	8	Capital gain net income (attach Schedule D (Form 1120))		**8**	
	9	Net gain or (loss) from Form 4797, Part II, line 17 (attach Form 4797)		**9**	
	10	Other income (see instructions—attach schedule)		**10**	
	11	**Total income.** Add lines 3 through 10	▶	**11**	
Deductions (See instructions for limitations on deductions.)	**12**	Compensation of officers from Form 1125-E, line 4 (attach Form 1125-E)	▶	**12**	
	13	Salaries and wages (less employment credits)		**13**	
	14	Repairs and maintenance		**14**	
	15	Bad debts		**15**	
	16	Rents		**16**	
	17	Taxes and licenses		**17**	
	18	Interest		**18**	
	19	Charitable contributions		**19**	
	20	Depreciation from Form 4562 not claimed on Form 1125-A or elsewhere on return (attach Form 4562)		**20**	
	21	Depletion		**21**	
	22	Advertising		**22**	
	23	Pension, profit-sharing, etc., plans		**23**	
	24	Employee benefit programs		**24**	
	25	Domestic production activities deduction (attach Form 8903)		**25**	
	26	Other deductions (attach schedule)		**26**	
	27	**Total deductions.** Add lines 12 through 26	▶	**27**	
	28	Taxable income before net operating loss deduction and special deductions. Subtract line 27 from line 11		**28**	
	29a	Net operating loss deduction (see instructions)	**29a**		
	b	Special deductions (Schedule C, line 20)	**29b**		
	c	Add lines 29a and 29b		**29c**	
Tax, Refundable Credits, and Payments	**30**	**Taxable income.** Subtract line 29c from line 28 (see instructions)		**30**	
	31	Total tax (Schedule J, Part I, line 11)		**31**	
	32	Total payments and refundable credits (Schedule J, Part II, line 21)		**32**	
	33	Estimated tax penalty (see instructions). Check if Form 2220 is attached ▶ ☐		**33**	
	34	**Amount owed.** If line 32 is smaller than the total of lines 31 and 33, enter amount owed		**34**	
	35	**Overpayment.** If line 32 is larger than the total of lines 31 and 33, enter amount overpaid		**35**	
	36	Enter amount from line 35 you want: Credited to 2012 estimated tax ▶ _____ Refunded ▶		**36**	

Sign Here	Under penalties of perjury, I declare that I have examined this return, including accompanying schedules and statements, and to the best of my knowledge and belief, it is true, correct, and complete. Declaration of preparer (other than taxpayer) is based on all information of which preparer has any knowledge.		May the IRS discuss this return with the preparer shown below (see instructions)? ☐ Yes ☐ No
	▶ Signature of officer _____ Date _____	▶ Title _____	

Paid Preparer Use Only	Print/Type preparer's name	Preparer's signature	Date	Check ☐ if self-employed	PTIN
	Firm's name ▶			Firm's EIN ▶	
	Firm's address ▶			Phone no.	

Figure 11-3. Form 1120 (page 1)

Form **1120S**	**U.S. Income Tax Return for an S Corporation**	OMB No. 1545-0130
Department of the Treasury Internal Revenue Service	▶ Do not file this form unless the corporation has filed or is attaching Form 2553 to elect to be an S corporation. ▶ See separate instructions.	2011

For calendar year 2011 or tax year beginning _____ , 2011, ending _____ , 20___

A S election effective date		Name	D Employer identification number
B Business activity code number *(see instructions)*	TYPE OR PRINT	Number, street, and room or suite no. If a P.O. box, see instructions.	E Date incorporated
C Check if Sch. M-3 attached ☐		City or town, state, and ZIP code	F Total assets *(see instructions)* $

G Is the corporation electing to be an S corporation beginning with this tax year? ☐ Yes ☐ No   If "Yes," attach Form 2553 if not already filed

H Check if: **(1)** ☐ Final return **(2)** ☐ Name change **(3)** ☐ Address change **(4)** ☐ Amended return **(5)** ☐ S election termination or revocation

I Enter the number of shareholders who were shareholders during any part of the tax year . . . . ▶

Caution. *Include only trade or business income and expenses on lines 1a through 21. See the instructions for more information.*

Income

1a	Merchant card and third-party payments. For 2011, enter -0- . . .	1a		
b	Gross receipts or sales not reported on line 1a (see instructions) . .	1b		
c	Total. Add lines 1a and 1b	1c		
d	Returns and allowances plus any other adjustments (see instructions)	1d		
e	Subtract line 1d from line 1c		1e	
2	Cost of goods sold (attach Form 1125-A)		2	
3	Gross profit. Subtract line 2 from line 1e		3	
4	Net gain (loss) from Form 4797, Part II, line 17 *(attach Form 4797)* . . .		4	
5	Other income (loss) *(see instructions—attach statement)*		5	
6	**Total income (loss).** Add lines 3 through 5 . . . . ▶		6	

Deductions (see instructions for limitations)

7	Compensation of officers	7	
8	Salaries and wages (less employment credits)	8	
9	Repairs and maintenance	9	
10	Bad debts	10	
11	Rents	11	
12	Taxes and licenses	12	
13	Interest	13	
14	Depreciation not claimed on Form 1125-A or elsewhere on return (attach Form 4562)	14	
15	Depletion **(Do not deduct oil and gas depletion.)**	15	
16	Advertising	16	
17	Pension, profit-sharing, etc., plans	17	
18	Employee benefit programs	18	
19	Other deductions *(attach statement)*	19	
20	**Total deductions.** Add lines 7 through 19 . . . . ▶	20	
21	**Ordinary business income (loss).** Subtract line 20 from line 6 . . .	21	

Tax and Payments

22a	Excess net passive income or LIFO recapture tax (see instructions) . .	22a		
b	Tax from Schedule D (Form 1120S)	22b		
c	Add lines 22a and 22b (see *instructions for additional taxes*)		22c	
23a	2011 estimated tax payments and 2010 overpayment credited to 2011	23a		
b	Tax deposited with Form 7004	23b		
c	Credit for federal tax paid on fuels (attach Form 4136)	23c		
d	Add lines 23a through 23c		23d	
24	Estimated tax penalty (see *instructions*). Check if Form 2220 is attached . . . . . . ▶ ☐		24	
25	**Amount owed.** If line 23d is smaller than the total of lines 22c and 24, enter amount owed . .		25	
26	**Overpayment.** If line 23d is larger than the total of lines 22c and 24, enter amount overpaid . .		26	
27	Enter amount from line 26 **Credited to 2012 estimated tax ▶** Refunded ▶		27	

Sign Here

Under penalties of perjury, I declare that I have examined this return, including accompanying schedules and statements, and to the best of my knowledge and belief, it is true, correct, and complete. Declaration of preparer (other than taxpayer) is based on all information of which preparer has any knowledge.

_____   _____   _____
Signature of officer   Date   Title

May the IRS discuss this return with the preparer shown below (see instructions)? ☐ Yes ☐ No

Paid Preparer Use Only

Print/Type preparer's name	Preparer's signature	Date	Check ☐ if self-employed	PTIN
Firm's name ▶			Firm's EIN ▶	
Firm's address ▶			Phone no.	

Figure 11-4. Form 1120S (page 1)

On each of these forms is a line labeled "Other Expenses" (Schedule C, line 27a) or "Other Deductions" (Form 1065, line 20; Form 1120, line 26; and Form 1120S, line 19). This is where bank charges and any "other expense" or deduction without a dedicated line on an IRS form is placed.

▒ **Caution   Using "other expenses" on a Schedule C can lead to an audit.** One of the factors used by the IRS to select individual tax returns for examination (audit) is high amounts of other expenses on Schedule C. If at all possible, you should try to avoid large dollar amounts of other expenses. This is not a major issue with business entities filing a Form 1065, Form 1120, or Form 1120S. As noted later in this chapter, you should use Office Expense for many of the charges you would consider as other expenses.

There is one other component of bank charges that should be noted: credit card fees. If you process credit cards, the merchant service charges by your processor are deducted as a bank charge.

Casualty Losses

The Tax Code allows for deductions in the event of a *casualty loss*. That's damage to your business property from fire, theft, vandalism, natural disasters, or some other unexpected or unusual event. A car drove into one of my client's stores: That was a casualty loss.

Just because you suffer a loss, be aware that it may not be a *deductible* casualty loss. Any insurance proceeds you receive or expect to receive lessen the amount of the casualty loss. In the case of my client, his insurance covered him for his loss above his $500 deductible. (The driver who rammed into his store was uninsured.) Thus, his loss was $500.

Like a bad-debt expense, you need *certainty* to take a casualty loss. If you're still negotiating with your insurance company, and you don't know what your loss is, you can't take the loss yet.

Make sure you keep excellent documentation of any casualty losses. If you are a victim of theft, file (and keep) the police report. If your insurance company sends you documentation, keep it. Casualty losses have been abused, so the IRS looks at these deductions carefully.

Business casualty losses are reported on Section B of Form 4684 (Casualties and Thefts). (The IRS has a workbook to help calculate the loss, Publication 584-B.) Once noted on Form 4684, the deductible loss is then transferred to Form 4797 (Sales of Business Property). It will then flow from Form 4797 to your tax return (Form 1040, Form 1065, Form 1120, or Form 1120S).

Unlike with personal casualty losses, there is no reduction of the loss by either $100 or 10% of your adjusted gross income.

Charitable Contributions

You decide to make a charitable contribution from your business. Do you get a deduction on your business tax return? The answer is a definite *it depends*.

For a sole proprietorship, you are the business. Thus, a charitable contribution made by your business is identical to you making the contribution. Such contributions are reported on Schedule A of Form 1040.

When a partnership (or LLC reporting taxes as a partnership) or an S corporation makes charitable contributions, the contributions are separately reported on the owners' Schedule K-1's. They are not considered a deduction for the business entity. However, they do flow through to the owners' individual tax returns (onto Schedule A of Form 1040). If an owner itemizes deductions, he or she will get the benefit of the charitable contributions. The contributions themselves are noted on line 13a of Schedule K on page 4 of Form 1065 (Figure 11-5a) and on line 12a of Schedule K on page 3 of Form 1120S (see Figure 11-5b).

For a sole proprietorship, partnership, LLC, or S corporation, the value of a charitable contribution is the *fair market value* of the contribution.

A C corporation deducts charitable contributions on line 19 of Form 1120 (Figure 11-3). Most charitable contributions by C corporations are valued at their fair market value. However, an exception exists for donations of inventory to a charity that uses the goods to care for the sick, needy, or infants. For such donations, you can add 50% of the difference between the tax basis[1] and the fair market value of the goods (up to a maximum of twice the basis.) Here's an example.

Example: Suppose you have excess inventory of toys you purchased for $2,000 (they are carried on your accrual-basis business books at $2,000). You donate these toys, which have a fair market value of $3,500, to a local hospital, which is a 501(c)(3) charity. The donation would be valued at $3,500 plus 50% of the difference between the fair market value and the basis ($3,500 − $2,000), or 0.5 × ($1,500) = $750, for a charitable donation of $4,250.[2]

---

[1] The value of the donated goods on the books of the company for tax purposes.

[2] There are four requirements for this special donation:

> 1. The donated property must be used solely for the care of the ill, needy, or infants, and in a manner related to the donee's exempt purpose (§170(e)(3)(A)(i) and Reg. 1-170A-4A(b)(2)). A third party cannot use the party unless the use is incidental to the primary use (Reg. 1.170A-44A(b)(2)(ii)).

> 2. Donated property cannot be transferred by the recipient in exchange for money, other property, or services (§170(e)(3)(A)(ii) and Reg. 1.170-A-44A(b)(3).

Form 1065 (2011)					Page **4**
Schedule K		**Partners' Distributive Share Items**			**Total amount**

Income (Loss)	1	Ordinary business income (loss) (page 1, line 22)		**1**	
	2	Net rental real estate income (loss) (attach Form 8825)		**2**	
	3a	Other gross rental income (loss)	**3a**		
	b	Expenses from other rental activities (attach statement)	**3b**		
	c	Other net rental income (loss). Subtract line 3b from line 3a		**3c**	
	4	Guaranteed payments		**4**	
	5	Interest income		**5**	
	6	Dividends: a Ordinary dividends		**6a**	
		b Qualified dividends	**6b**		
	7	Royalties		**7**	
	8	Net short-term capital gain (loss) (attach Schedule D (Form 1065))		**8**	
	9a	Net long-term capital gain (loss) (attach Schedule D (Form 1065))		**9a**	
	b	Collectibles (28%) gain (loss)	**9b**		
	c	Unrecaptured section 1250 gain (attach statement) . .	**9c**		
	10	Net section 1231 gain (loss) (attach Form 4797)		**10**	
	11	Other income (loss) (see instructions) Type ▶		**11**	
Deductions	12	Section 179 deduction (attach Form 4562)		**12**	
	13a	Contributions		**13a**	
	b	Investment interest expense		**13b**	
	c	Section 59(e)(2) expenditures: **(1)** Type ▶ _____ **(2)** Amount ▶		**13c(2)**	
	d	Other deductions (see instructions) Type ▶		**13d**	

Figure 11-5a. Report charitable contributions for a partnership or an LLC on line 13a of Schedule K of Form 1065 (page 4)

Form 1120S (2011)					Page **3**
		Shareholders' Pro Rata Share Items (continued)			**Total amount**
Deductions	11	Section 179 deduction (*attach Form 4562*)		**11**	
	12a	Contributions		**12a**	
	b	Investment interest expense		**12b**	
	c	Section 59(e)(2) expenditures **(1)** Type ▶ _____ **(2)** Amount ▶		**12c(2)**	
	d	Other deductions *(see instructions)* . . . Type ▶		**12d**	

Figure 11-5b. Report charitable contributions for an S corporation on line 12a of Schedule K of Form 1120S (page 3)

However, a C corporation is only allowed to make charitable contributions up to a maximum of 10% of the business's net income. Any contributions in excess of this amount are carried forward to the following year.

▌**Caution**   **Documentation requirements for charitable contributions.** Backup documentation is required for *all* charitable contributions. If you make a donation, keep your canceled check, bank statement, credit card statement, and written receipt or acknowledgment letter from the charity. A written acknowledgment letter is required for all cash contributions of $250 or more. For noncash contributions of $5,000 or more, you will usually need an appraisal. The IRS details this in Publication 1771.

3. The recipient must furnish a written statement to the donor that the above requirements will be met (§170(e)(3)(A)(iii) and Reg. 1.170A-44A(b)(4)).

4. The property must satisfy certain requirements of the federal Food, Drug, and Cosmetic Act (if applicable). Compliance is required not only for the time the contribution is made, but for 180 days preceding the contribution (§170(e)(3)(A)(iv) and Reg 1.170A-4A(b)(5).

Commissions

Commissions you pay to sales representatives are deductible. For a sole proprietorship, they are reported on line 10 of Schedule C; for business entities, they are reported as "other deductions."

▧ **Tip Issue Form 1099-MISC to your representatives.** The IRS requires that if you pay $600 or more to an individual or business for most purposes, you must send the individual or business a Form 1099-MISC at year end to note the amount received. (You do not have to send a Form 1099-MISC to a corporation or for purchases of goods. There are different threshold amounts and rules for royalties and legal fees.)

Computer Services and Supplies

Computer services and supplies (also called *computer supplies and services*) is used for noncapital computer costs such as Internet, some computer peripherals, computer maintenance, and computer supplies. This is an "other expense" for a sole proprietorship (see the "Office Expense" section of this chapter) or an "other deduction" for an LLC, C corporation, or S corporation.

Continuing Education

If you are a professional and must attend continuing education, the costs for the continuing education are deductible. Note that any travel and meals for attending continuing education are reported as travel and meal expenses. Continuing education is included in "other expenses" (for a sole proprietorship) or "other deductions."

Contract Labor

Amounts spent on contract labor related to your business are deductible. This will be covered in depth in Chapter 12. Contract labor for a sole proprietorship is reported on line 11 of Schedule C; it is reported in "other deductions" for other business entities.

Dues and Subscriptions

Dues you pay for professional, business, and civic organizations are deductible unless the organization's primary purpose is providing entertainment facilities to its members. This includes dues paid to professional organizations, trade associations, and civic/public service organizations (such as the Exchange Club or Rotary). No deductions are allowed for dues to a country club or a gym/athletic club. In addition, if any portion of the dues is used for political purposes, that portion is nondeductible.

Subscriptions to magazines (for your waiting room) or for business purposes are deductible.

Dues and subscriptions are reported in "other expenses" (for a sole proprietorship) or in "other deductions" (see "Office Expense" section below).

Education

You have worked as, say, a nurse. You decide to become a tax professional; you take a course to become an Enrolled Agent (a federally licensed tax professional). Can you take a deduction for the cost of the course?

Most likely, the answer is no. You cannot take a deduction for a *new* business or profession, nor can you deduct the cost to meet the basic standards for a profession.

Let's say you've had a business selling office supplies. You decide you want to start selling to your local government. You take a course on selling to government entities. That course would likely be deductible.

▧ **Tip** **Education may be deductible as a personal deduction or credit.** Under the Internal Revenue Code, you can take a tuition and fees deduction and the Lifetime Learning Credit (but not both in the same year). The Lifetime Learning Credit gives you a credit on your taxes for amount paid to "any college, university, vocational school, or other postsecondary education institution eligible to participate in a student aid program administered by the US Department of Education." You can take the Lifetime Learning Credit for tuition, fees, and related expenses for courses that are part of a postsecondary degree program or taken to acquire or improve your job skills. A tax credit reduces your tax; a tax deduction reduces your income.

The tuition and fees deduction covers only tuition and fees (and related expenses) at an eligible institution (the same definition as for the Lifetime Learning Credit). However, the deduction is available for education expenses and not programs for job skills.

Note that there are income restrictions for both the Lifetime Learning Credit and the tuition and fees deduction.

Gifts

Gifts given for business purposes are deductible. However, the maximum deductible amount is $25 per person per year. Any gift in excess of this amount is not deductible.

What if you give a gift to a business and not a specific individual? Is that gift subject to the $25 limitation? If the company to whom you're giving the gift has just one employee, the company and the individual are the same, and the $25 limitation applies. If you give a gift to a large (in number of employees) business and not to one specific individual, the $25 limitation does not apply.

Insurance

Insurance you purchase for your business is generally deductible. This includes:

- Property and casualty insurance
- Liability insurance
- Malpractice and errors and omissions insurance
- Medical insurance for employees
- Workers' compensation insurance
- Business interruption insurance
- Key man insurance

What about your own medical insurance? If you have a sole proprietorship, your medical insurance premiums are deductible directly on Form 1040 (line 29) subject to certain restrictions.[3]

For partnerships and LLCs filing as partnerships, there are two choices for health insurance premiums for owners. If you have an accountable plan, your premiums can be either paid directly by the business or reimbursed. The premiums will be noted as *guaranteed payments* made on Schedule K-1. They will then be deductible as self-employed health insurance on Form 1040 (line 29) just as for sole proprietors.

Medical insurance premiums are deductible by C corporations for both owners and employees. The deduction is taken as part of insurance expenses (other deductions).

---

[3] The most important restriction is that you have enough net income from the business to pay for the premiums.

The situation is different for S corporation owners.[4] As discussed in Chapter 1, an S corporation must add the premiums to wages on Box 1 of the W-2 (but the premiums are *not* included in FICA or Medicare tax). The S corporation owner then takes the health insurance premiums as a deduction on line 29 of Form 1040. The premiums *must* be paid for by the employee; however, the corporation can reimburse the employee for the cost.

Interest

Interest on business loans is deductible. This is true even for a sole proprietorship. This is an exception to the rule that only mortgage interest is deductible. Let's look at an example.

Suppose you obtain a loan to purchase additional inventory for your business. You borrow $25,000 from your bank at a 5% interest rate. The interest you pay is deductible on Schedule C.

Note that a sole proprietor must split out the interest on Schedule C into mortgage interest and all other interest (see Figure 11-1). Other interest is scrutinized by the IRS—only business-related interest is deductible.

This means you should keep *separate business accounts*. There are rules regarding usage and timing of loans. Generally, anything you purchase within 30 days of obtaining a loan will be considered paid for out of the loan proceeds.

If you do *not* keep separate business and personal accounts, allocations must be made between your business and personal usage of the loan. This can become quite complex. The easiest way of handling this problem is to avoid it in the first place by keeping separate accounts.

For all other business entities, interest related to the business is a deductible expense. Of course, interest that is related to personal expenses is not deductible. Prepaid interest for cash-basis taxpayers is also not deductible (but it can be deducted in the year it would normally be paid).

Legal and Professional Fees

Fees paid to attorneys and other professionals (such as tax professionals) are deductible business expenses (assuming, of course, that the expenses are business-related). For business entities other than a sole proprietorship, legal and professional fees are included in "other deductions." A sole proprietor deducts this expense on line 17 of Schedule C.

---

[4] Defined as someone who owns at least 2% of the stock of an S corporation.

Note that legal expenses related to the organization of a business are categorized as *organizational expenses* (see Chapter 3).

Tax preparation expenses for a sole proprietor should be allocated between his business and his other activities. By doing this, a sole proprietor avoids the 2% adjusted gross income limitation on tax preparation on Schedule A. Note that only in rare cases is it reasonable to assume that 100% of the cost of tax preparation relates to the business.

Office Expense

Office expenses are costs directly related to the general operation of the business. This includes postage, Internet expenses, furniture that is not capitalized, and water and coffee service. Office expenses are taken on line 18 of Schedule C for a sole proprietorship and are included in "other deductions" for other business entities.

One thing that is *not* included within office expenses are office supplies. Items such as paper, printer toner, paper clips, and all the other necessary office supplies are included within *supplies* (discussed later in this chapter).

▓ **Tip   Use office expense for many miscellaneous expenses for a sole proprietorship.** Given that the definition of an office expense includes *costs directly related to the general operation of the business,* this is the category of expense to use for many of the costs that would otherwise go as "other expenses" for a sole proprietorship. Bank fees, dues and subscriptions, computer supplies and services, and many other costs related to the general running of a business can be taken as an office expense.

It is important on a tax return to fully disclose your expenses. When I prepare a Schedule C with such costs within office expense, I include a subsidiary schedule that details the costs. It's likely the IRS will not look at the schedule when the return is filed (see Chapter 17); however, should the IRS review the originally filed return, they will see that you provided the necessary details.

Note that this is *not* necessary for other kinds of business entities. The IRS does not generally use "other deductions" for a partnership return (Form 1065) or a corporation return (Form 1120 or Form 1120S) for audit selection.

Rent and Equipment Rental

As discussed in Chapter 6, office rent is deductible. Rent for a storage unit (if used for business purposes) is also deductible.

If you rent office machines (such as a postage meter or photocopier) or rent equipment used in manufacturing, that's also deductible. If the rented item is used to manufacture product, it will be noted within cost of goods sold. However, if it's used anywhere else (such as the copy machine used in an administrative office), it will be noted as rental of machinery and equipment. For a sole proprietorship, it's noted on line 20a of Schedule C; for other business entities, it's included in "other deductions."

Supplies

Office supplies and other supplies used generally within the office are part of *supplies*, not office expense. If it's used on your desk, it's usually part of supplies.

■ **Note   What if you put office supplies within office expense?** You filed your tax return last year and included office supplies within office expense instead of supplies. What should you do?

Most likely, nothing. Yes, your tax return should be complete and accurate. But consider what were to happen if your return were audited and the (say) $500 you deducted as office expense for your office supplies were moved to supplies. Both supplies and office expense are fully deductible "ordinary and necessary" business expenses. Your tax would not change.

If you have not included your office supplies or if you double-deducted that expense, then you need to amend your return and correct the error. From a purely technical standpoint the return has an error, but from a practical standpoint the error is *not* particularly relevant.

Taxes and Licenses

Taxes that you pay as a required part of your business are almost always an ordinary and necessary business expense and are fully deductible. This includes business taxes, business licenses, payroll taxes, property taxes, and sales and use tax.

Income Taxes

You can't deduct your federal income tax as a business deduction on your tax return. The tax you pay is generally not deductible on the same return. However, state income tax paid *is* deductible on a federal tax return. How this is handled depends on the form of business entity.

Sole Proprietorships

A sole proprietor cannot directly deduct the state (and/or local) income tax he pays on his Schedule C (with one exception, discussed next). Instead, the deduction is taken on Schedule A.

The exception is for state and local income tax paid directly by the business entity and not by the sole proprietor. For example, a sole proprietorship operating in New York City must pay the New York City Unincorporated Business Tax. Because that tax is paid directly by the proprietorship, it is a necessary business expense. Another example is a California single-member LLC filing as a sole proprietor (a disregarded entity); the proprietor can take a deduction for the California LLC tax on her federal Schedule C. Of course, you can't deduct state and local taxes on the state and local tax returns.

Partnerships and Corporations

Businesses filing partnership and corporation tax returns deduct the state and local taxes they pay as a tax expense. Again, these taxes will not be deductible on the state and local tax returns.

Self-Employment Tax

If you have earned income other than wages, you must pay the self-employment tax. This tax is calculated on Schedule SE. Sole proprietors and partners (including members of an LLC filing a partnership tax return) generally must pay self-employment tax. Half the self-employment tax paid is a deduction on Form 1040.

Self-employment tax is a separate tax that happens to be collected on income tax returns. It is not an expense of the business, so none of the tax is deductible by the business.

Payroll Taxes

Payroll taxes are an expense of the business and are fully deductible. However, only the *employer's portion* of payroll taxes is deductible; you cannot deduct the *employee's portion* that you remit to the IRS and state tax agencies. Payroll taxes are covered in depth in Chapter 13.

Business Taxes and Business Licenses

License fees (local, state, or national) are clearly deductible as ordinary and necessary business expenses. These are included within taxes and licenses.

Business taxes (*not* income taxes) are another business expense. Many localities and some states collect business taxes from all businesses in their jurisdiction. These are generally based on gross receipts and/or number of employees. Examples of these taxes include Los Angeles's business tax, Washington State's Business & Occupation Tax, and New York City's Unincorporated Business Tax. A business tax is a deductible tax included as part of taxes and licenses.

Property Tax

Property tax paid by your business is included within taxes and licenses. This includes real property tax and personal property tax.

For the sole proprietor, only taxes paid directly by the business can be deducted as a tax of the business. A sole proprietor operating out of his home who has a deductible home office (see Chapter 6) can take a pro rata portion of his property tax on Form 8821. Otherwise, a sole proprietor cannot deduct real property tax on his home as an expense of the business. (The deduction would be taken on Schedule A of Form 1040.)

Sales and Use Tax

Sales and use taxes that you pay are deductible. However, the deduction is normally taken with the item that's purchased. Assume you purchase a case of paper; the sales tax you pay on the paper is expensed with the paper.

Sales tax that your customers pay to you cannot, of course, be deducted by you. You are collecting that money in trust for the sales tax agency. It's not an expense of your business.

■ **Caution   Remember use tax.** If you live in a state with sales tax, you are generally required to pay *use tax* on purchases where sales tax would be owed but was not charged (such as purchases on the Internet or from companies you normally purchase as a reseller). Most sales tax agencies audit businesses regularly, and use tax has become a point of emphasis.

Assume you purchase machines and resell them. You decide to purchase a machine to use as a demonstration model in your office. Because you won't be reselling the machine, you will owe use tax. The use tax you pay will be treated as an additional cost of the machine.

Use tax may be paid separately from sales tax, or it may be paid with the sales tax. You generally must keep sales and use tax records for several years. Recordkeeping requirements are discussed in Chapter 17.

Uniforms

If you purchase uniforms for your employees, the cost of the uniforms is a deductible business expense. This is included in "other expenses" for sole proprietors and "other deductions" for partnerships and corporations.

Utilities

The cost for utilities that your business purchases directly is deductible. But note the word *directly*. If you are operating the business out of your home, most (if not all) of your utility expenses are not direct costs of your business. Instead, they are home costs that can be apportioned to your business if you are eligible to take the home office deduction.

If you have a separate phone line for your business, that can be deducted. A mobile phone that's used exclusively for your business can be deducted. However, a mobile phone that is used for both business and personal expenses must be apportioned. Courts have held that your first phone line in your home is *not* deductible as a business expense.

If you rent an office, all of your utility expenses for the office can be deducted, including gas, electricity, water, sewer, and telephone.

Anything Else

Some businesses have unusual expenses. Just because the expense isn't found in most businesses doesn't mean it can't be deducted. Though the categories noted above cover most of the "other expenses," anything that is both ordinary and necessary can be deducted. Many of these expenses will be categorized under office expense; other items will be included as "other expenses" ("other deductions" for partnerships and corporations).

Employees and Wages

I should fire you, but I don't believe in mixing business with pleasure.

—James Unger

Hiring employees is always a major decision for a small business owner. Many owners outsource some work to independent contractors and other businesses. Still, it is possible you may unwittingly have an employee when you mean to have a contractor.

This chapter focuses on the basics of having employees. We first look at what an employee is and then look at independent contractors. Then we examine the allowed methods to get money from your business based on the type of business entity you have. We look at the special rules that exist in regard to employing your family. Finally, we consider the rules and regulations that impact payroll, employees, and independent contracts and how payroll is reported.

What Is an Employee?

This seems like a trivial question. Aren't employees the people who work for you? Sometimes that's the case, but not always.

Under common law rules, someone is an *employee* if the employer can control what the individual does and how he or she does it. Let's look at a couple of examples.

Example 1. You hire an analyst for your business. You direct him to work from 9 a.m. to 5 p.m. each day in your office. You give him the work he is supposed to analyze for you. The worker and you agree that you can fire him or he can quit at any time. The analyst is an employee.

Example 2. You hire Acme Consultants LLC to analyze a business project for you. Acme assigns George Jetson to do the work. Jetson comes to your office every day from 9 a.m. to 5 p.m. He obtains much of the information from you that's needed to perform the analysis. However, he uses a computer provided to him by Acme, and you can't fire him (nor can he quit). In fact, Jetson is one of the owners of Acme. Jetson is *not* your employee.

Statutory Employees

There's another type of employee, one created by Congress: *statutory employees.* Congress wrote laws (statutes) stating that individuals in certain professions are considered statutory employees. Statutory employees are independent contractors that Congress has said are treated as employees in some ways. To be considered a statutory employee, one must work in one of four professions:

1. A driver who distributes beverages (but not milk) or meat, vegetable, fruit, or bakery products. It could also be a driver who picks up and delivers laundry or dry cleaning, if he or she is your agent or paid on commission.

2. A full-time life insurance sales agent whose principal business activity is selling life insurance or annuity contracts (or both), primarily for one life insurance company.

3. An individual who works at home on materials or goods that you supply that must be returned to you or to a person you name. This is also the case if you also furnish specifications for the work to be done.

4. A full-time traveling or city salesperson who works on your behalf and turns in orders to you from wholesalers, retailers, contractors, hotel operators, and so on. The goods sold must be merchandise for resale or supplies for use in the buyer's business operation. The work performed for you must be the salesperson's principal business activity.

Statutory employees must also meet all three of the following conditions:

1. The service contract states or implies that substantially all the services are to be performed personally by them.

2. They do not have a substantial investment in the equipment and property used to perform the services (other than an investment in facilities for transportation, such as a car or truck).

3. The services are performed on a continuing basis for the same payer.

There are special rules used in reporting wages for statutory employees, discussed later in this chapter.

What Is an Independent Contractor?

Independent contractors are individuals who are not employees whom you hire to perform work for you. These are usually people working on specific self-directed projects.

Independent contractors do *not* include business entities you hire for project work. If you hire Acme Consultants, and Acme is a legal business entity (a corporation or an LLC), Acme is not an independent contractor. This is true even if Acme is just one individual who has formed a corporation.

▓ **Caution**   **Get a W-9 form so you know what you're dealing with.** Form W-9 is a request for a taxpayer to provide you with his or her taxpayer identification number. Suppose you hire Acme Consultants. Have you hired a corporation, an LLC, or an individual who has filed a fictitious business name statement?

The solution is to have the business complete and return a Form W-9. The form is signed under penalty of perjury, so you're allowed to consider the form accurate (unless told otherwise).[1]

Single-member LLCs are generally ignored for tax purposes. Assume you hire Acme Consultants, a single-member LLC. George Jetson, the principal of Acme, tells you that Acme is an LLC, so you assume it's a partnership for tax reporting purposes. As my mother tells me, *never assume.* Unless Jetson elected a corporate status for Acme, for tax purposes Acme is equivalent to a sole proprietorship.

This is important because of reporting issues (discussed at the end of this chapter). Some independent contractors must be reported to state agencies. All independent contractors and LLCs are subject to information returns: If

---

[1] You can't ignore your own personal knowledge. If you know the completed form is wrong, you *must* use your knowledge. Also, if you receive a name and taxpayer identification number mismatch notice from the IRS, you may have to make changes.

you pay an individual or an LLC $600 or more during a calendar year, you must issue a Form 1099-MISC to the contractor.

Independent Contractor or Employee?

Sometimes the situation is murky on whether an individual is an employee or an independent contractor. The IRS uses a seven-factor test to determine if a worker is an employee or an independent contractor. The test is subjective, but it looks at the underlying factors of the relationship (from IRS Publication 15-A):

1. Training that the business gives to the worker. Businesses train employees; independent contractors use their own training methods.

2. The extent to which the worker has unreimbursed business expenses. Most businesses reimburse employees for business expenses; independent contractors are responsible for their own expenses.

3. The extent of the worker's investment. Independent contractors tend to (but not always) have significant investment in their tools and/or facilities.

4. The extent to which the worker makes his or her services available to the relevant market. Independent contractors generally look for multiple opportunities and will advertise or have a business location.

5. How the business pays the worker. An employee is usually guaranteed a regular wage amount. This generally shows an individual is an employee (even if he also receives a commission). Independent contractors generally receive a flat fee or are paid for time and materials. (Certain professions are paid hourly even if they are independent contractors.)

6. The extent to which the worker can realize a profit or loss. Employees can't earn a profit, whereas independent contractors can.

7. The type of relationship. Here, the IRS looks at whether there was a written contract, whether the business provides the worker with employee-type benefits (i.e., insurance, pension, vacation, sick pay), the permanency of the relationship, and the extent to which services performed by the worker are a key aspect of the regular business of the company. Permanency

usually indicates an employer–employee relationship. If a worker performs key aspects of a business, that usually indicates the right to direct the worker (which would make the worker an employee).

The Tax Court uses a similar seven-factor test:[2]

1. The degree of control exercised by the principal.

2. Which party invests in work facilities used by the individual.

3. The opportunity of the individual for profit or loss.

4. Whether the principal can discharge the individual.

5. Whether the work is part of the principal's regular business.

6. The permanency of the relationship.

7. The relationship the parties believed they were creating.

Let's assume you hire an independent contractor to assemble products in your plant. Other than the fact that you're paying the individual as a contractor, that's a position that would normally be considered an employee. The person files his tax return and is shocked to discover he owes significant tax (from the self-employment tax). He decides to tell the IRS (or the state labor department) about your employment practices. The government investigates and determines that the individual was an employee. Now you are subject to back taxes, penalties, interest, and possible fines from the labor department.

▨ **Note   A man scorned.** A few years ago, I prepared tax returns for a man who worked at a local media company. He was paid as an employee the prior year. In the current year, he was paid as an employee until the company he worked at was bought out. He was then paid as an independent contractor. The following year, they switched and again paid him as an employee.

My client was confused about this. I asked him if his duties had changed at any time. They had not; he worked in the production department and was clearly an employee during the entire time. I explained what the law was: that he should have been treated as an employee. I advised him that we could note this issue to the IRS on his tax return. He could also complain to the Labor Board in his state.

We marked the return, and he also complained to the Labor Board. He told me he was upset with his company because he had to pay taxes when he shouldn't have had to do so. (If the proper tax

---

[2] See, for example, *Blodgett v. Commissioner*, T.C. Memo 2012-298, http://ustaxcourt.gov/InOpHistoric/BlodgettMemo.TCM.WPD.pdf.

had been withheld, he would not have owed tax.) He may also have been annoyed that someone else received a promotion instead of him.

Both the federal and state governments investigated this firm and found their employment practices in the year in question were in violation of various laws. The company ended up paying a significant fine. As for my client, he ended up getting a new job with another, far more reputable employer.

Federal and State Rules Do Not Always Match

Some states have different rules defining the employer versus independent contractor issue. For example, California has significantly tighter rules on what an independent contractor is. California's Employment Development Department has a publication (DE 38, available at www.edd.ca.gov/pdf_pub_ctr/de38.pdf) that can be used to determine if an individual is an employee or an independent contractor. You can also ask for a written determination in California.

It is possible (though unlikely) that an individual could be considered an independent contractor under federal rules but an employee under state rules. Anyone with a truly unclear situation should consider obtaining legal advice from an attorney specializing in labor issues.

Temporary Employees

It's very common to hire temporary employees ("temps") from an employment agency. These individuals are employees of the agency. You are hiring an agency to provide you with workers. Although you can remove an individual worker from a job, he or she will still be employed by the agency. Such individuals are *not* considered to be either employees or independent contractors of your business.

Leased Employees

Leasing of employees is a relatively new employment practice. The employee-leasing company pays the employees and is responsible for benefits. The idea is that the "employer" doesn't have to deal with the human resources issues, and the employee-leasing company handles all the back-office paperwork.

Unlike temporary employees, leased employees are generally long-term. Whether this is a viable relationship depends on state law. In some states, having a leasing company pay the employees while the "employer" makes the decisions on hiring or firing is allowed. However, in other states, if the leasing company does not have the right to hire or fire, the actual employer is considered to be the true employer rather than the employee-leasing company. Anyone considering using an employee-leasing company should carefully check your state law; you may need to consult with an attorney specializing in this area.

Reporting Independent Contractors

Many states now require businesses to report the independent contractors they hire. Generally, this is required at the same reporting level as for issuance of Form 1099-MISCs to the contractors ($600 or more in a calendar year).

▓ **Note**   **The law firm with no employees.** It's hard for me to imagine a law firm with no employees (except a one-person firm). However, such a firm exists. Well, that should be *existed*.

In Baton Rouge, Louisiana, there is a law firm called Donald G. Cave, a Professional Law Corporation. The Cave firm had no employees. It was an S corporation (as you will see later in this chapter, the owner of an S corporation must be paid a reasonable salary). The three associate attorneys and the law clerk were considered to be independent contractors. The IRS felt these individuals should be classified as employees. The Cave firm lost with the IRS and went to Tax Court.

The Tax Court agreed that all involved were employees.[3] Cave was held to be a statutory employee (as a principal stockholder of an S corporation). The associate attorneys and the law clerk were all held to be employees. "We conclude on the basis of all of the relevant facts and circumstances that the associate attorneys were petitioner's common law employees. Three of the five specific factors—degree of control, investment in facilities, and permanence of the relationship—indicate an employer-employee relationship, and the remaining factors are neutral." Similarly, the court felt that the factors all favored the law clerk being an employee.

The Cave firm appealed the case to the Fifth Circuit Court of Appeals, which held that the Tax Court was correct in its decision.[4]

Statutory Nonemployees

There are some individuals who are *never* considered employees. That's because Congress has written laws (statutes) stating that these individuals are

---

[3] *Donald G. Cave, A Professional Law Corporation v. Commissioner,* T.C. Memo 2011-48, www. ustaxcourt.gov/InOpHistoric/Cave.TCM.WPD.pdf.

[4] *Donald G. Cave, A Professional Law Corporation v. Commissioner,* Fifth Circuit, No. 11-60390, www.ca5.uscourts.gov/opinions%5Cunpub%5C11/11-60390.0.wpd.pdf.

not employees. There are three categories of such individuals: direct sellers, licensed real estate agents, and certain companion sitters.

Direct sellers and real estate agents are considered to be self-employed for all federal tax purposes if:

- Substantially all payments for their services as direct sellers or real estate agents are directly related to their sales or output and *not* based on the number of hours worked; and

- Their services are performed under a written contract providing that they will not be treated as employees for federal tax purposes.

Direct Sellers

There are three categories of direct sellers:

1. Persons engaged in selling (or soliciting sales of) consumer products in the home or business other than in a permanent retail establishment.

2. Persons engaged in selling (or soliciting sales of) consumer products to any buyer on a buy-sell basis, deposit-commission basis, or a similar basis prescribed by regulations, for resale in the home or business other than in a permanent retail establishment.

3. Persons engaged in the trade or business of delivering or distributing newspapers or shopping news (including services related to such delivery or distribution).

Note that direct selling specifically includes individuals who attempt to increase direct sales activities of their direct sellers (recruits) and who earn income based on the productivity of their recruits. This includes providing motivation and encouragement, imparting knowledge, and recruiting.

Licensed Real Estate Agents

Licensed real estate agents are statutory nonemployees. Also in this category are individuals who appraise real estate if their income is based on sales or other output.

Companion Sitters

Companion sitters are individuals who furnish personal attendance, companionship, or household care services to children or individuals who are disabled or elderly. A companion sitting placement service will *not* be considered the employer if the service does not receive or pay the salary or wages of the sitters and is compensated by the sitters or the persons who employ them on a fee basis. Companion sitters who are not employees of a companion sitting placement service are generally treated as self-employed for federal tax purposes.

S Corporation Rules for Owners

S corporations are flow-through entities. One of the benefits of an S corporation is that the distributions from the company are not subject to employment taxes. However, there's a caveat to this: S corporation owners who materially participate in the business *must* pay themselves a reasonable salary.

What's a Reasonable Salary?

The Tax Code does not provide the definition of a reasonable salary. However, we can look at a few examples to help us determine what is and isn't reasonable. (Note that the rule looks at total compensation, so it is possible that some fringe benefits will count toward salary. However, S corporation fringe benefits are limited.)

Example 1. Consider Unprofitable Widgets, Inc., an S corporation. Unfortunately, Unprofitable Widgets lost money in their current tax year. The sole stockholder of the business materially participates in the business. What is a reasonable salary for a business that's losing money?

Common sense applies here. A business that's losing money should try to cut the losses. The Tax Code does not force Unprofitable Widgets to have a larger loss. In this situation, a reasonable salary is no salary at all.

Example 2. Consider John Doe, a certified public accountant (CPA). Doe is the 100% stockholder of his one-man CPA firm, an S corporation. His firm earns about $200,000 a year (net). He decides to pay himself $10,000 a year.

That's not reasonable. Even large accounting firms, notorious for paying low starting salaries for new employees, can't pay just $10,000. It also doesn't pass the smell test. If I asked you whether 5% of the income of the business was reasonable, what would you think?

▓ **Caution   The IRS is looking at compensation.** In a recent case, an Iowa CPA (who owned his own S corporation) paid himself $24,000 a year. The CPA firm made approximately $200,000 during the year in question. The IRS investigated and felt that was not reasonable compensation and increased his compensation to $91,044 (total) for the year. The IRS assessed back taxes, penalties, and interest that the CPA paid. The CPA then sued the IRS in District Court and attempted to recover the taxes paid.

The CPA lost in both District Court[5] and the Court of Appeals.[6] Both courts held that $24,000 was not a reasonable amount of compensation; the IRS's position that the compensation should be increased to $91,044 was upheld.

Today, the IRS has lots of low-hanging fruit from which to choose. There are many S corporations where principals are being paid nothing or a very small annual salary; the IRS has been concentrating its enforcement activities on those businesses. However, that doesn't mean you can pay yourself a very small salary relative to the net income of your business. As the foregoing case illustrates, the IRS can go after businesses where 12% of the net income was paid as salary.

There are no hard-and-fast rules as to what is reasonable. This will always depend on the facts and circumstances. If your business makes $200,000 and you are paying yourself $100,000, that will likely be considered reasonable. But if your business makes $200,000 and you pay yourself $10,000, it will be hard to justify that as reasonable.

Employing Family Members

There is no prohibition in the law against employing family members. Other than general labor laws, you may employ your spouse or children.[7] However, the employment tax rules can be different in this situation.

Child Employed by Parents

Payments for services of a child under age eighteen who works for his or her parent(s) in a trade or business are *not* subject to Social Security or Medicare

---

[5] *David E. Watson P.C. v. United States,* US District Court for the Southern District of Iowa, Central Division, 4:08-cv-442, http://ia700202.us.archive.org/4/items/gov.uscourts.iasd.37557/gov.uscourts.iasd.37557.35.0.pdf.

[6] *David E. Watson P.C. v. United States,* Eighth Circuit Court, No. 11-1589, www.ca8.uscourts.gov/opndir/12/02/111589P.pdf.

[7] Be aware that there are laws regulating the employment of minors.

taxes if the trade or business is a sole proprietorship or a partnership in which each partner is a parent of the child.

Payments for the services of a child under age twenty-one who works for his or her parent in a trade or business are not subject to Federal Unemployment Tax Act (FUTA) tax.

All payments for services are subject to income tax withholding (regardless of age). Additionally, Social Security, Medicare, and FUTA taxes must be withheld or paid if the child works for:

- A corporation (even if it is controlled by the child's parent[s]);

- A partnership, unless the child's parents are the only partners; or

- An estate, even if it is the estate of a deceased parent.

Payroll taxes are covered in depth in the next chapter (Chapter 13).

One Spouse Employed by the Other Spouse

The wages for the services of one spouse who works for the other spouse *are* subject to Social Security and Medicare taxes but are *not* subject to FUTA tax.

However, if the spouse works for a corporation (even if it is controlled by the other spouse) or a partnership (even if the other spouse is a partner), Social Security, Medicare, and FUTA taxes are required. Income tax withholding is always required.

Employing one spouse by the other spouse is a strategy used for certain medical plans. This is discussed in Chapter 14.

Parent Employed by a Child

Wages of a parent employed by a child are exempt from FUTA tax. However, Social Security and Medicare taxes are required.

Reporting Rules for Payroll

There are various required reporting rules for employees on payroll and independent contractors. The rules for payroll taxes are covered in the next chapter. Here, the focus is on reports sent out regarding the actual wages or service income.

Employees

You must provide every employee with a Form W-2 on or before January 31 after the year of employment. Note that you *cannot* download this form from the Internet for your use. Employment tax forms are printed on special paper; you must order these forms from the IRS (www.irs.gov/Businesses/Online-Ordering-for-Information-Returns-and-Employer-Returns) or other providers. Form W-2 is shown in Figure 12-1.

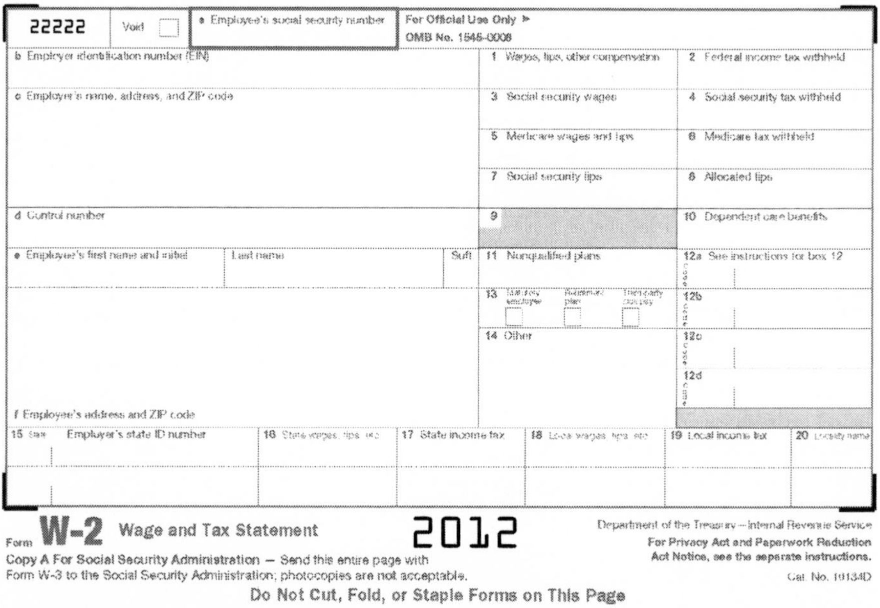
22222
Void
a Employee's social security number
For Official Use Only ▶
OMB No. 1545-0008
b Employer identification number (EIN)
1 Wages, tips, other compensation
2 Federal income tax withheld
c Employer's name, address, and ZIP code
3 Social security wages
4 Social security tax withheld
5 Medicare wages and tips
6 Medicare tax withheld
7 Social security tips
8 Allocated tips
d Control number
9
10 Dependent care benefits
e Employee's first name and initial
Last name
Suff.
11 Nonqualified plans
12a See instructions for box 12
13 Statutory employee / Retirement plan / Third-party sick pay
12b
14 Other
12c
12d
f Employee's address and ZIP code
15 State Employer's state ID number
16 State wages, tips, etc.
17 State income tax
18 Local wages, tips, etc.
19 Local income tax
20 Locality name
Form W-2 Wage and Tax Statement 2012
Department of the Treasury—Internal Revenue Service
For Privacy Act and Paperwork Reduction Act Notice, see the separate instructions.
Cat. No. 10134D
Copy A For Social Security Administration — Send this entire page with Form W-3 to the Social Security Administration; photocopies are not acceptable.
Do Not Cut, Fold, or Staple Forms on This Page

Figure 12-1. Form W-2

The W-2 reports an employee's wages and taxes withheld, along with identification information for both the employer and employee.

Form W-3 summarizes all of the W-2s you have. Your Form W-3 and the Social Security Administration's copies of the W-2 forms are due to the Social Security Administration on the last day of February (if filed by paper) or the last day of March (if filed electronically). Form W-3 is shown in Figure 12-2.

You may also have to file your W-2 forms with your state. Some states obtain this information directly from the Social Security Administration; some states do not. It may depend on whether you file by paper or electronically.

DO NOT STAPLE

Form W-3 Transmittal of Wage and Tax Statements 2012

Send this entire page with the entire Copy A page of Form(s) W-2 to the Social Security Administration (SSA).
Photocopies are not acceptable. Do not send Form W-3 if you filed electronically with the SSA.
Do not send any payment (cash, checks, money orders, etc.) with Forms W-2 and W-3.

Reminder

Separate instructions. See the 2012 General Instructions for Forms W-2 and W-3 for information on completing this form.

Purpose of Form

A Form W-3 Transmittal is completed only when paper Copy A of Form(s) W-2, Wage and Tax Statement, is being filed. Do not file Form W-3 alone. Do not file Form W-3 for Form(s) W-2 that were submitted electronically to the SSA (see below). All paper forms **must** comply with IRS standards and be machine readable. Photocopies are **not** acceptable. Use a Form W-3 even if only one paper Form W-2 is being filed. Make sure both the Form W-3 and Form(s) W-2 show the correct tax year and Employer Identification Number (EIN). Make a copy of this form and keep it with Copy D (For Employer) of Form(s) W-2 for your records. The IRS recommends retaining copies of these forms for four years.

E-Filing

The SSA strongly suggests employers report Form W-3 and Forms W-2 Copy A electronically instead of on paper. The SSA provides two free e-filing options on its Business Services Online (BSO) website:

• **W-2 Online.** Use fill-in forms to create, save, print, and submit up to 50 Forms W-2 at a time to the SSA.

• **File Upload.** Upload wage files to the SSA you have created using payroll or tax software that formats the files according to the SSA's *Specifications for Filing Forms W-2 Electronically (EFW2)*.

W-2 Online fill-in forms or file uploads will be on time if submitted by April 1, 2013. For more information, go to *www.socialsecurity.gov/employer* and select "First Time Filers" or "Returning Filers" under "BEFORE YOU FILE."

When To File

Mail Copy A of Form W-3 with Form(s) W-2 by February 28, 2013.

Where To File Paper Forms

Send this entire page with the entire Copy A page of Form(s) W-2 to:

**Social Security Administration
Data Operations Center
Wilkes-Barre, PA 18769-0001**

Note. If you use "Certified Mail" to file, change the ZIP code to "18769-0002." If you use an IRS-approved private delivery service, add "ATTN: W-2 Process, 1150 E. Mountain Dr." to the address and change the ZIP code to "18702-7997." See Publication 15 (Circular E), Employer's Tax Guide, for a list of IRS-approved private delivery services.

For Privacy Act and Paperwork Reduction Act Notice, see the separate instructions.

Cat. No. 10159Y

Figure 12-2. Form W-3

For example, California requires employers who file W-2 and W-3 forms electronically to also file with the state; however, those who file by paper with the IRS do not have to file with California.

Independent Contractors

You must report payment to both independent contractors and LLCs of $600 or more in a calendar year on Form 1099-MISC. Like employment tax forms, you cannot print this form off the Internet; you must order the form from the IRS. Form 1099-MISC is shown in Figure 12-3.

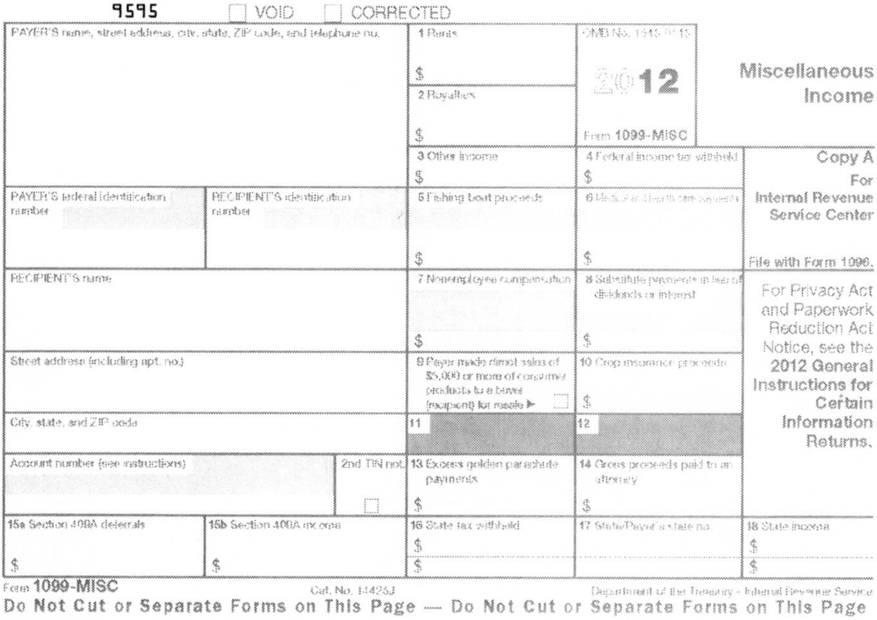
9595 VOID CORRECTED

PAYER'S name, street address, city, state, ZIP code, and telephone no.

1 Rents $

2 Royalties $

2012 Form 1099-MISC

Miscellaneous Income

3 Other income $

4 Federal income tax withheld $

Copy A For Internal Revenue Service Center

File with Form 1096.

PAYER'S federal identification number

RECIPIENT'S identification number

5 Fishing boat proceeds $

6 Medical and health care payments $

RECIPIENT'S name

7 Nonemployee compensation $

8 Substitute payments in lieu of dividends or interest $

For Privacy Act and Paperwork Reduction Act Notice, see the 2012 General Instructions for Certain Information Returns.

Street address (including apt. no.)

9 Payer made direct sales of $5,000 or more of consumer products to a buyer (recipient) for resale ▶

10 Crop insurance proceeds $

City, state, and ZIP code

11

12

Account number (see instructions)

2nd TIN not.

13 Excess golden parachute payments $

14 Gross proceeds paid to an attorney $

15a Section 409A deferrals $

15b Section 409A income $

16 State tax withheld $ $

17 State/Payer's state no.

18 State income $ $

Form 1099-MISC Cat. No. 14425J Department of the Treasury - Internal Revenue Service

Do Not Cut or Separate Forms on This Page — Do Not Cut or Separate Forms on This Page

Figure 12-3. Form 1099-MISC

If you hire an independent contractor, his or her earnings are reported in Box 7, Nonemployee Compensation. You also note your information (name, address, and taxpayer identification number) and the independent contractor's personal information (name, address, and taxpayer identification number). You must send Form 1099-MISC to the recipients on or before the last day of January following the year-end.

As with Form W-2, a cover page is used when sending Forms 1099-MISC to the IRS. (This form is sent to the IRS, not the Social Security Administration.) The cover page form is Form 1096 (Figure 12-4). This form is used to transmit various information returns to the IRS.

Form 1096 and the associated Forms 1099-MISC must be mailed to the IRS on or before February 28. The electronic filing deadline is March 31. Note that Form 1096 is used for a variety of information returns, including Form W-2G, Form 1098, Form 1099-DIV, Form 1099-INT, and many more.

You may or may not have to submit Forms 1099-MISC to your state. Each state handles these forms differently, so check with your state tax department to see if you must file these forms with your state.

■ **Caution   The Deadlines are different for Form W-3 and Form 1096.** You may have noticed that the government copy of Form 1096 is due on February 28 and the government copy of Form W-3 is due on the last day of February. In three of every four years, that's the same date. However, in a leap year (such as 2016), Form 1096 is due on February 28 while Form W-3 is due on February 29.

If you're wondering about the reason is for the difference, it's because that's how Congress wrote the law for these forms. If you're wondering about the logic is behind this, unfortunately you're asking the wrong person.

Other Reporting Requirements

As mentioned earlier, you may also have to report your independent contractors to your state when you hire them. Note that some states require you to report these contractors *every year*.

Penalties

The federal government charges penalties for failing to file information returns. These penalties start at $30 per return and increase to $100 per return, with a maximum penalty of $1,500,000 per year ($500,000 for small businesses).

Do Not Staple   6969

Form **1096**	Annual Summary and Transmittal of	OMB No. 1545-0108
Department of the Treasury Internal Revenue Service	U.S. Information Returns	2012

FILER'S name

Street address (including room or suite number)

City, state, and ZIP code

Name of person to contact	Telephone number	**For Official Use Only**
Email address	Fax number	

1 Employer identification number	2 Social security number	3 Total number of forms	4 Federal income tax withheld $	5 Total amount reported with this Form 1096 $

6 Enter an "X" in only one box below to indicate the type of form being filed.   7 If this is your final return, enter an "X" here ▶ ☐

W-2G 32	1097-BTC 50	1098 81	1098-C 78	1098-E 84	1098-T 83	1099-A 80	1099-B 79	1099-C 85	1099-CAP 73	1099-DIV 91	1099-G 86	1099-H 71	1099-INT 92
☐	☐	☐	☐	☐	☐	☐	☐	☐	☐	☐	☐	☐	☐

1099-K 10	1099-LTC 93	1099-MISC 95	1099-OID 96	1099-PATR 97	1099-Q 31	1099-R 98	1099-S 75	1099-SA 94	3921 25	3922 26	5498 28	5498-ESA 72	5498-SA 27
☐	☐	☐	☐	☐	☐	☐	☐	☐	☐	☐	☐	☐	☐

Return this entire page to the Internal Revenue Service. Photocopies are not acceptable.

Under penalties of perjury, I declare that I have examined this return and accompanying documents, and, to the best of my knowledge and belief, they are true, correct, and complete.

Signature ▶   Title ▶   Date ▶

Instructions

Reminder. The only acceptable method of filing information returns with Internal Revenue Service/Information Returns Branch is electronically through the FIRE system. See Pub. 1220, Specifications for Filing Forms 1097, 1098, 1099, 3921, 3922, 5498, 8935, and W-2G Electronically.

Purpose of form. Use this form to transmit paper Forms 1097, 1098, 1099, 3921, 3922, 5498, and W-2G to the Internal Revenue Service. Do not use Form 1096 to transmit electronically. For electronic submissions, see Pub. 1220.

Caution. If you are required to file 250 or more information returns of any one type, you must file electronically. If you are required to file electronically but fail to do so, and you do not have an approved waiver, you may be subject to a penalty. For more information, see part F in the 2012 General Instructions for Certain Information Returns.

Who must file. The name, address, and TIN of the filer on this form must be the same as those you enter in the upper left area of Forms 1097, 1098, 1099, 3921, 3922, 5498, or W-2G. A filer is any person or entity who files any of the forms shown in line 6 above.

Enter the filer's name, address (including room, suite, or other unit number), and TIN in the spaces provided on the form.

When to file. File Form 1096 as follows.

• With Forms 1097, 1098, 1099, 3921, 3922, or W-2G, file by February 28, 2013.

• With Form 5498, file by May 31, 2013.

Where To File

Send all information returns filed on paper with Form 1096 to the following:

If your principal business, office or agency, or legal residence in the case of an individual, is located in	Use the following three-line address
Alabama, Arizona, Arkansas, Connecticut, Delaware, Florida, Georgia, Kentucky, Louisiana, Maine, Massachusetts, Mississippi, New Hampshire, New Jersey, New Mexico, New York, North Carolina, Ohio, Pennsylvania, Rhode Island, Texas, Vermont, Virginia, West Virginia	Department of the Treasury Internal Revenue Service Center Austin, TX 73301

For more information and the Privacy Act and Paperwork Reduction Act Notice, see the 2012 General Instructions for Certain Information Returns.   Cat. No. 14400O   Form **1096** (2012)

Figure 12-4. Form 1096

Stautory Employees

There are special rules on reporting statutory employees. Statutory employees' wages are reported on Form W-2 (Figure 12-1). The box labeled "statutory employee" should be checked. Note that there are also special rules as to which payroll taxes statutory employees are subject to; this is covered in Chapter 13.

Payroll Taxes

For every benefit you receive a tax is levied.

—Ralph Waldo Emerson

Once you have employees and payroll, you have the obligation to collect, file, and pay payroll taxes. This is true for all businesses with wages, from a small two-person concern to a nonprofit to the largest corporations.

There are three kinds of taxes you will collect: taxes on employees, taxes on both employees and employers, and taxes on employers. Personal income taxes are a tax paid solely by the employee, but an employer collects and remits to the IRS and state tax agencies. FICA (Social Security and Medicare withholdings) is a tax paid by both the employee and employer; the employer collects this tax and remits it to the IRS. Unemployment insurance is a tax paid solely by employers to both the IRS and state tax agencies. This chapter looks at all of these taxes.

Before You Have Employees

Before you hire your first employee, you will have to have an employer identification number (EIN). This is true even if you are a sole proprietor. An EIN is a taxpayer identification number (TIN). EINs were first used solely for businesses with employees. EINs are nine digits, in the format 12-3456789.

Businesses besides sole proprietors must apply for an EIN when their business commences. The EIN will be used for tax filing. You do not need a new EIN for your business when you hire employees if you already have an EIN.

You can obtain an EIN on the phone, by fax, by mail, or online.[1] Information is available on applying for an EIN on the IRS website.

You may also need to apply for a state employment identification number. Some states use the EIN as the state identification number. However, many states assign their own number. Make sure you check with your state on how to apply for your state number.

Taxes on Employees

Each of your employees must pay federal (and state) income taxes. The government wants everyone to pay as they go. Income tax is withheld from their paycheck. You must then remit the withheld tax to the IRS and your state tax agency.

The amount of tax withheld out of each employee's paycheck is based on how often you pay your employees (weekly, biweekly, semi-monthly, or monthly), their marital status (single or married), and the number of withholding allowances they claim. You must provide your employees with Form W-4, Employee's Withholding Allowance Certificate. The employee completes this form and returns it to you. You then use this form to compute the withholding (or provide it to your payroll company for them to do so).

Most states piggyback off the federal form. However, some states (Alabama and California) have an equivalent state form that can be completed.

Federal income tax is reported on Form 941 or Form 944 (see the "Reporting Payroll Taxes" section later in this chapter).

Some states and localities have local taxes paid solely by employees. Examples of these include California's state disability insurance and Pennsylvania's unemployment tax.

Note that statutory employees (see Chapter 12) never have income tax withheld from their pay.

Trust Fund Taxes

Before we go further into payroll taxes, there's a key point to understand. When you collect a tax that's not on you (the business) but you are responsible for paying it, you become the government's agent. Payroll taxes you collect on behalf of the government are called *trust fund taxes*.

---

[1] For applying online, see www.irs.gov/Businesses/Small-Businesses-&-Self-Employed/Apply-for-an-Employer-Identification-Number-(EIN)-Online.

Federal trust fund taxes are personal income tax and the employee's portion of FICA (discussed in the next section). The government considers this to be "their money." When this money is not remitted in a timely fashion, the IRS *always* investigates. If you want to get in trouble with your taxes, simply don't remit your trust fund taxes. That will almost guarantee you will soon have the IRS looking at your business.

Corporate officers and business owners can be held *personally liable* for payment of trust fund taxes. If you are an officer of a corporation that does not remit its trust fund taxes, the IRS and your state tax agency can force you to pay.

For the small business owner, this means there is no way to escape potential personal liability. As will be discussed later in this chapter, the key is to use a reputable payroll company.

▓ **Note   Owner of delivery business is held liable for nearly $700,000 of payroll taxes.** Charles Colosimo, owner of a Des Moines, Iowa, delivery business, had a bookkeeper who likely got him into trouble. Back in 2004, Colosimo learned that the IRS was wondering where missing payroll tax returns were. He asked his accountant (who was not an employee of his company) to follow up on it. The accountant discovered that the outside bookkeeper apparently never filed the payroll tax returns and kept the money that should have been remitted to the IRS. Because his business made payments to other vendors, the district court held that Colosimo was personally liable for the taxes once he knew that money was owed to the IRS. Colosimo appealed; the Eighth Circuit Court of Appeals upheld the ruling of the district court.[2]

Taxes on Employees and Employers

There is one tax paid by both employees and employers: FICA. FICA stands for the Federal Insurance Contributions Act. This tax, introduced during the Great Depression, funds Social Security and Medicare.

Employees and employers pay equal amounts of FICA. Tax is withheld for Social Security until the employee reaches the Social Security wage base for the current year.[3] For 2013, the wage base is $113,700. Both employees and

---

[2] *Colosimo v. United States*, Eighth Circuit Court of Appeals, No. 10-1593, www.ca8.uscourts. gov/opndir/11/01/101593P.pdf.

[3] Although called a "wage base," it really is a *wage maximum*. Once an employee has earned the wage base, there no longer is any withholding for Social Security.

employers must pay 6.2% of the employee's wages as the Social Security component of FICA.[4]

Additionally, 1.45% of an employee's earnings are withheld for the Medicare portion of FICA. Employers must match this, too. There is no maximum on Medicare.

Let's look at a couple of examples of how FICA is calculated.

Example 1. An employee earns $20,000 during the first payroll period of the year. What are the FICA taxes for both employee and employer?

Because this is the first payroll of the year, the wage base has not been reached, and all of the pay is subject to both the Social Security and Medicare components of FICA. The Social Security component is $20,000 × 6.2% = $1,240. The Medicare component is $20,000 × 1.45% = $290. The employer will need to withhold $1,530 from the employee's pay ($1,240 for Social Security and $290 for Medicare). The employer will match those amounts when he remits his or her payroll taxes.

Example 2. An employee earns $20,000 during this payroll period. He has already earned $103,400 of gross wages during the year (the Social Security wage base is $113,400). What are the FICA taxes employee and employer?

The first $10,000 of the employee's pay will be subject to Social Security tax. Once he reaches that, he or she will have earned the Social Security base wage. The Social Security component is $10,000 × 6.2% = $620. Medicare is not impacted by reaching the Social Security wage base; thus, as in example 1, the Medicare component is $290. The employer will need to withhold $910 from the employee's pay ($620 for Social Security and $290 for Medicare). The employer will match those amounts when he remits his or her payroll taxes.

One thing to note is that FICA is not impacted by how frequently you pay employees. FICA is based solely on the amount you are paying your employees.

The employees' portion of FICA taxes is considered a trust fund tax. Responsible individuals can be held personally liable for these taxes when not remitted to the IRS.

There are a few groups that are exempt from FICA: civilian federal government employees hired prior to 1984 (they pay the Medicare portion of FICA but are exempt from the Social Security component), some state and local

---

[4] In 2012, the employee's social security FICA tax rate was 4.2% and the employer's was 6.2%. The 2% reduction for employees is not expected to be continued into 2013.

government employees who are covered by state pension plans, and some college students who work for their universities.

Statutory employees are only subject to FICA if all of the following conditions apply:

1. The service contract states or implies that substantially all of the services are to be performed personally by them.

2. They do not have a substantial investment in the equipment and property used to perform the services (excluding transportation equipment such as a car or truck).

3. The services are performed on a continuing basis for the same payer.

FICA taxes are reported on Form 941 or Form 944 (see the "Reporting Payroll Taxes" section later).

Taxes on Employers

There are some payroll taxes paid solely by employers. On the federal level, there's the Federal Unemployment Tax Act (FUTA). On the state level are state unemployment taxes.

FUTA

FUTA is a tax on employers designed to help fund state unemployment programs. FUTA covers the federal portion of unemployment insurance and half the cost for extended unemployment benefits. States can also borrow from a FUTA fund if their unemployment insurance fund is short of money.

The FUTA tax rate is 6.0% on the first $7,000 of gross earnings of each employee per year. However, a credit is automatically applied; this is called the "FUTA credit reduction" and is based on the employer paying into the state unemployment insurance fund. This credit is normally 5.4%. Thus, the normal effective FUTA tax rate is 6.0% − 5.4% = 0.6%.

■ **Caution   FUTA credit reduction reduced in some states.** Many states have had to borrow from the FUTA fund to fund their own unemployment insurance funds. However, many states have not paid back the FUTA fund. Under the law, if a state has a loan balance for two consecutive years, and the full amount of the loan is not repaid by November 10 of the second year, the FUTA credit is reduced. The reduction is 0.3% of the credit for the first such year; the reduction is increased by 0.3% for each subsequent year. The reduction decreases the credit, increasing the FUTA tax owed.

In 2011, twenty-one states were impacted by the FUTA credit reduction. For 2012, eighteen states and the Virgin Islands will be impacted by the credit reduction. The list of states subject to a credit reduction is available on the Department of Labor's website.[5] The largest credit reductions are for the Virgin Islands (1.5%) and Indiana (0.9%).

FUTA does not apply on all wages. The following are exempt from FUTA:

1. Wages for services performed outside of the United States.

2. Wages paid to a deceased employee or his or her estate in any year after the year of the employee's death.

3. Wages paid by a parent to a child under age twenty-one, paid by a child to a parent, or paid by one spouse to the other spouse.

4. Wages paid by a foreign government or international organization.

5. Wages paid by a state or local government, or by the US federal government.

6. Wages paid by a hospital to interns.

7. Wages paid to newspaper carriers under age eighteen.

8. Wages paid by a school to a student of the school.

9. Wages paid by an organized camp to a student.

10. Wages paid by nonprofit organizations.

11. Certain statutory employees.[6]

FUTA is reported annually on Form 940 (see "Reporting Payroll Taxes" later in this chapter).

State Unemployment Insurance

Once you have employees, you must pay into your state's unemployment insurance fund. Some states base the tax on the first $7,000 of gross wages paid to each employee; however, other states have a much higher wage limitations. For example, Hawaii bases it on the first $38,800 of wages and Washington bases it on the first $38,200 of wages. Generally, you will be

---

[5] See http://workforcesecurity.doleta.gov/unemploy/docs/reduced_credit_states_2012_final.xls

[6] Statutory employees of classes 2 and 3 (see Chapter 12) are *not* subject to FUTA. However, statutory employees of classes 1 and 4 are subject to FUTA.

rated by your state based on how many unemployment claims are made against you. The more claims made, the higher the tax that will be paid.

Other State Taxes

Some states have other employer-only taxes that must be paid. California has an Employment Training Tax (the current rate is 0.1% on the first $7,000 of wages). You will need to check with your state to determine if you are liable for any other payroll taxes.

EFTPS

There are only two methods allowed for making federal payroll tax payments: the Electronic Federal Tax Payment System (EFTPS) (http://www.eftps.gov) and using the payment voucher with Form 940, Form 941, or Form 944. Many businesses will have to make federal payroll tax payments prior to completing a quarterly Form 941 or an annual Form 940 or Form 944 (this is discussed later in this chapter in "Filing Your Taxes"). If your business is required to make such payments, the *only* way to do so is through EFTPS.

EFTPS allows you to make almost all federal tax payments (not just payroll taxes) using the Internet. Once you enroll in EFTPS you can login and schedule your payments in advance. There is no charge to enroll in or use EFTPS.

EFTPS also allows you to verify that your payroll company is actually making your payroll tax deposits. This is another reason to enroll in this system.

▨ **Caution   Paying payroll taxes twice is no fun.** What happens when you use the wrong payroll service provider? Many businesses in North Carolina found out in 2008.

James McLamb of Raleigh was chief financial officer of the Castleton Group, a payroll service company in the Research Triangle Park area. McLamb had a unique (and illegal) method of handling payroll taxes. He would calculate the correct amount of tax for the clients, accept those remittances, and then change the numbers to much lower figures. He used the lower figures when reporting the payroll to the IRS and the North Carolina Department of Revenue. This resulted in $8 million of payroll taxes that the IRS never received (with an additional amount owed to North Carolina).

McLamb received a sentence of two and a half years in prison and was ordered to pay restitution of $8 million.[7] Although justice may have been served for McLamb, it didn't help the clients of

---

[7] See, for example, "Ex-CFO of bankrupt benefits firm sentenced to prison" at www.wral.com/news/local/story/5964918/.

Castleton. If McLamb doesn't pay restitution (which is apparently what happened), the businesses that used Castleton will have to pay their payroll taxes again.

This isn't the only such occurrence. Unfortunately, I've written about several instances of payroll companies absconding with funds in my tax blog over the last few years. Here's another example.

Vincent Mangione operated two payroll services near Buffalo, New York. He did the same scheme as McLamb—he filed fraudulent payroll tax returns without the knowledge of his clients.[8] Mangione pleaded guilty to tax evasion and bank fraud, but the employers are still liable for the payroll taxes ($800,000 in this case).

Should You Use a Payroll Service?

After I've just pointed out examples of payroll services that did anything but provide good service to your clients, you might come to the conclusion I'm against using a payroll service. On the contrary, I *strongly suggest* that if you have payroll you use a *reputable* service.

Note the emphasis on "reputable." This is not an area in which to skimp. You are personally liable for the trust fund taxes. If you use a reputable payroll company and a mistake is made, the company will make good on the mistake. (This assumes you are paying for full payroll service, including having the payroll company make the payroll tax deposits.)

The major issue with payroll is liability. You are liable if mistakes are made. A reputable payroll processing company will stand behind their work. They will correct their mistakes. If you pay for full payroll service (including having the payroll company make the tax deposits), and you can correctly report the hours worked by your employees, you should not have any major problems with your payroll.

Even if you use one of the two largest payroll processing companies in the United States, I recommend you verify that the deposits are made. The phrase "trust, but verify" holds well.

---

[8] See the US Department of Justice press release at www.justice.gov/usao/nyw/press_releases/ Mangione.pdf.

Form **940for 2011:** Employer's Annual Federal Unemployment (FUTA) Tax Return
Department of the Treasury — Internal Revenue Service

850111

OMB No. 1545-0028

(EIN)
Employer identification number [ ][ ] — [ ][ ][ ][ ][ ][ ]

Name *(not your trade name)*

Trade name *(if any)*

Address

Number   Street   Suite or room number

City   State   ZIP code

Type of Return
(Check all that apply.)

☐ a. Amended

☐ b. Successor employer

☐ c. No payments to employees in 2011

☐ d. Final: Business closed or stopped paying wages

Prior-year forms are available at *www.irs.gov/form940.*

Read the separate instructions before you complete this form. Please type or print within the boxes.

Part 1:   Tell us about your return. If any line does NOT apply, leave it blank.

1a   If you had to pay state unemployment tax in one state only, enter the state abbreviation .   1a [ ][ ]
1b   If you had to pay state unemployment tax in more than one state, you are a multi-state
employer . . . .   1b ☐   Check here.
Complete Schedule A (Form 940).

2   If you paid wages in a state that is subject to CREDIT REDUCTION . . . .   2 ☐   Check here. Complete
Schedule A (Form 940).

Part 2:   Determine your FUTA tax before adjustments for 2011. If any line does NOT apply, leave it blank.

3   Total payments to all employees . . . .   3 [   ] •

4   Payments exempt from FUTA tax . . . .   4 [   ] •

Check all that apply: 4a ☐ Fringe benefits   4c ☐ Retirement/Pension   4e ☐ Other
4b ☐ Group-term life insurance   4d ☐ Dependent care

5   Total of payments made to each employee in excess of
$7,000 . . . .   5 [   ] •

6   Subtotal (line 4 + line 5 = line 6) . . . .   6 [   ] •

7a   Total taxable FUTA wages (line 3 – line 6 = line 7a) (see instructions) . . . .   7a [   ] •

7b   Line 7a FUTA wages paid before 7/1/2011   7b [   ] •   x .008 =   7c [   ] •

7d   Line 7a FUTA wages paid after 6/30/2011   7d [   ] •   x .006 =   7e [   ] •

8   FUTA tax before adjustments (line 7c + line 7e = line 8) . . . .   8 [   ] •

Part 3:   Determine your adjustments. If any line does NOT apply, leave it blank.

9   If ALL of the taxable FUTA wages you paid were excluded from state unemployment tax,
multiply line 7a by .054 (line 7a x .054 = line 9). Go to line 12 . . . .   9 [   ] •

10   If SOME of the taxable FUTA wages you paid were excluded from state unemployment tax,
OR you paid ANY state unemployment tax late (after the due date for filing Form 940),
complete the worksheet in the instructions. Enter the amount from line 7 of the worksheet . .   10 [   ] •

11   If credit reduction applies, enter the amount total from Schedule A (Form 940) . . . .   11 [   ] •

Part 4:   Determine your FUTA tax and balance due or overpayment for 2011. If any line does NOT apply, leave it blank.

12   Total FUTA tax after adjustments (lines 8 + 9 + 10 + 11 = line 12) . . . .   12 [   ] •

13   FUTA tax deposited for the year, including any overpayment applied from a prior year .   13 [   ] •

14   Balance due (If line 12 is more than line 13, enter the excess on line 14.)
• If line 14 is more than $500, you must deposit your tax.
• If line 14 is $500 or less, you may pay with this return. (see instructions) . . . . .   14 [   ] •

15   Overpayment (If line 13 is more than line 12, enter the excess on line 15 and check a box
below.) . . . .   15 [   ] •

▶ You MUST complete both pages of this form and SIGN it.   Check one: ☐ Apply to next return.   ☐ Send a refund.

Next ▶

For Privacy Act and Paperwork Reduction Act Notice, see the back of Form 940-V, Payment Voucher.   Cat. No. 112340   Form **940** (2011)

Figure 13-1a. Form 940 (page 1)

850211

Name *(not your trade name)*	Employer identification number (EIN)

Part 5: Report your FUTA tax liability by quarter only if line 12 is more than $500. If not, go to Part 6.

16 Report the amount of your FUTA tax liability for each quarter; do NOT enter the amount you deposited. If you had no liability for a quarter, leave the line blank.

16a 1st quarter (January 1 – March 31) . . . . 16a ☐ .

16b 2nd quarter (April 1 – June 30) . . . . 16b ☐ .

16c 3rd quarter (July 1 – September 30) . . . . 16c ☐ .

16d 4th quarter (October 1 – December 31) . . . . . . 16d ☐ .

17 Total tax liability for the year (lines 16a + 16b + 16c + 16d = line 17) 17 ☐ .   Total must equal line 12.

Part 6: May we speak with your third-party designee?

Do you want to allow an employee, a paid tax preparer, or another person to discuss this return with the IRS? See the instructions for details.

☐ **Yes.** Designee's name and phone number

Select a 5-digit Personal Identification Number (PIN) to use when talking to IRS ☐ ☐ ☐ ☐ ☐

☐ **No.**

Part 7: Sign here. You MUST complete both pages of this form and SIGN it.

Under penalties of perjury, I declare that I have examined this return, including accompanying schedules and statements, and to the best of my knowledge and belief, it is true, correct, and complete, and that no part of any payment made to a state unemployment fund claimed as a credit was, or is to be, deducted from the payments made to employees. Declaration of preparer (other than taxpayer) is based on all information of which preparer has any knowledge.

✗ **Sign your name here**

Print your name here

Print your title here

Date / /

Best daytime phone

Paid preparer use only   Check if you are self-employed . . . ☐

Preparer's name		PTIN	
Preparer's signature		Date	/ /
Firm's name (or yours if self-employed)		EIN	
Address		Phone	
City	State	ZIP code	

Figure 13-1b. Form 940 (page 2)

Reporting Payroll Taxes

There are three forms used to report federal payroll taxes: Form 940, Form 941, and Form 944. Your state tax agency will have its own forms that you must use. If you use a payroll service, your payroll service company will complete the forms on your behalf and may also file the forms and make any required tax payments.

Form 940

Form 940 is used for the annual FUTA tax return. All employers with payroll must complete this form. If your FUTA tax is more than $500 for the year, you are required to make payroll tax deposits (using EFTPS or deposits on your behalf by your payroll service company). If your FUTA tax is $500 or less, you can pay the full amount when filing the form. Form 940 is due on January 31 (following the year you are reporting). You get ten extra days, until February 10, if you deposited all FUTA tax when due. Form 940 is shown in Figure 13-1.

Form 944

Form 944 is one of two forms used to report FICA and federal income tax withheld. Form 944 can *only* be used if the IRS notifies you in writing to use it. The form is designed so that the smallest employers—those with annual liability for Social Security, Medicare, and withheld federal income tax is $1,000 or less—will file and pay these taxes only once a year on a fee basis instead of every quarter. Form 944 is shown in Figure 13-2.

Form **944 for 2012:** **Employer's ANNUAL Federal Tax Return**

Department of the Treasury — Internal Revenue Service

OMB No. 1545-2007

Employer identification number (EIN)

Name *(not your trade name)*

Trade name *(if any)*

Address

Number   Street   Suite or room number

City   State   ZIP code

Who Must File Form 944

You must file annual Form 944 instead of filing quarterly Forms 941 only if the IRS notified you in writing. You must also file Form 944 (or Form 944 (SP)) for 2012 if you filed Form 944-SS or Form 944-PR in 2011 and you did not request to file Forms 941-SS or Forms 941-PR for 2012.

Instructions and prior-year forms are available at *www.irs.gov/form944*.

Read the separate instructions before you complete Form 944. Type or print within the boxes.

Part 1: Answer these questions for this year. Employers in American Samoa, Guam, the Commonwealth of the Northern Mariana Islands, the U.S. Virgin Islands, and Puerto Rico can skip lines 1 and 2.

1   Wages, tips, and other compensation **1**

2   FEDERAL income tax withheld from wages, tips, and other compensation **2**

3   If no wages, tips, and other compensation are subject to social security or Medicare tax **3** ☐ Check and go to line 5.

4   Taxable social security and Medicare wages and tips:

	Column 1		Column 2	
4a Taxable social security wages		× .104 =		For 2012, the employee social security tax rate is 4.2% and the Medicare tax rate is 1.45%. The employer social security tax rate is 6.2% and the Medicare tax rate is 1.45%.
4b Taxable social security tips		× .104 =		
4c Taxable Medicare wages & tips		× .029 =		

4d Add *Column 2* line 4a, *Column 2* line 4b, and *Column 2* line 4c **4d**

5   Total taxes before adjustments (add lines 2 and 4d) **5**

6   Current year's adjustments (see instructions) **6**

7   Total taxes after adjustments. Combine lines 5 and 6 . . . . **7**

8   Total deposits for this year, including overpayment applied from a prior year and overpayment applied from Form 944-X, 944-X (PR), 944-X (SP), 941-X, or 941-X (PR) . . . **8**

9a COBRA premium assistance payments (see instructions) **9a**

9b Number of individuals provided COBRA premium assistance

10 Add lines 8 and 9a **10**

11 Balance due. If line 7 is more than line 10, enter the difference and see instructions **11**

12 Overpayment. If line 10 is more than line 7, enter the difference _____ Check one: ☐ Apply to next return. ☐ Send a refund.

▶ **You MUST complete both pages of Form 944 and SIGN it.**   Next ▶

For Privacy Act and Paperwork Reduction Act Notice, see the back of the Payment Voucher.   Cat. No. 39316N   Form **944** (2012)

Figure 13-2a. Form 944 (page 1)

Name *(not your trade name)*	Employer identification number (EIN)

Part 2: Tell us about your deposit schedule and tax liability for this year.

13 Check one: ☐ Line 7 is less than $2,500. Go to Part 3.

☐ Line 7 is $2,500 or more. Enter your tax liability for each month. If you are a semiweekly depositor or you accumulate $100,000 or more of liability on any day during a deposit period, you must complete Form 945-A instead of the boxes below.

	Jan.		Apr.		Jul.		Oct.
13a	___.__	13d	___.__	13g	___.__	13j	___.__
	Feb.		May		Aug.		Nov.
13b	___.__	13e	___.__	13h	___.__	13k	___.__
	Mar.		Jun.		Sep.		Dec.
13c	___.__	13f	___.__	13i	___.__	13l	___.__

Total liability for year. Add lines 13a through 13l. Total must equal line 7. 13m ___.__

Part 3: Tell us about your business. If question 14 does NOT apply to your business, leave it blank.

14 If your business has closed or you stopped paying wages...

☐ Check here and enter the final date you paid wages. [_____]

Part 4: May we speak with your third-party designee?

Do you want to allow an employee, a paid tax preparer, or another person to discuss this return with the IRS? See the instructions for details.

☐ Yes. Designee's name and phone number [_____] [_____]

Select a 5-digit Personal Identification Number (PIN) to use when talking to IRS. ☐ ☐ ☐ ☐ ☐

☐ No.

Part 5: Sign Here. You MUST complete both pages of Form 944 and SIGN it.

Under penalties of perjury, I declare that I have examined this return, including accompanying schedules and statements, and to the best of my knowledge and belief, it is true, correct, and complete. Declaration of preparer (other than taxpayer) is based on all information of which preparer has any knowledge.

✗ **Sign your name here** [_____]   Print your name here [_____]

Print your title here [_____]

Date [_____]   Best daytime phone [_____]

Paid Preparer Use Only   Check if you are self-employed ☐

Preparer's name		PTIN	
Preparer's signature		Date	
Firm's name (or yours if self-employed)		EIN	
Address		Phone	
City	State	ZIP code	

Page 2   Form **944** (2012)

Figure 13-2b. Form 944 (page 2)

Form 941

Form 941 is used by most employers to report their FICA and federal income tax withheld. This form is filed for each quarter; the form is due on the last day of the month following the end of the quarter (e.g., April 30 for the first quarter).

There are two types of employers: monthly schedule depositors and semi-weekly schedule depositors. If your tax liability is less than $2,500, you are allowed to pay the balance with the filing of your return. All other depositors must make deposits according to the type of depositor they are.

The type of depositor you are depends on the *lookback period*. For 2013, the lookback period is July 1, 2011, through June 30, 2012. If your payroll deposits during the lookback period are $50,000 or less, you are a monthly schedule depositor; you must make deposits for each month by the fifteenth day of the following month (e.g. by February 15 for January). However, if you accumulate $100,000 or more of payroll taxes you *must* deposit those taxes on the next business day and you automatically become a semi-weekly schedule depositor for the remainder of the current year *and* all of the following year.

If your payroll deposits are more than $50,000 during the lookback period, you are a semi-weekly schedule depositor. You have a much more limited amount of time to make payroll deposits. If your payday is on Wednesday, Thursday, or Friday, you must deposit your taxes by the following Wednesday; if your payday is Saturday, Sunday, Monday, or Tuesday, you must deposit your taxes by the following Friday.

There are penalties and interest if you do not make your payroll deposits in a timely way. If the deposit is due on a weekend or a legal holiday[9] you have until the next business day that is not a holiday or a weekend to make your payroll deposit.

Form 941 is shown on Figure 13-3.

---

[9] It must be a legal holiday in the District of Columbia. Congress wrote the Tax Code referencing that a holiday for federal tax purposes is a holiday recognized by the District of Columbia. For example, Emancipation Day is a holiday in the District of Columbia (April 16, or the closest weekday if April 16 falls on a Saturday or Sunday). Emancipation Day is not a recognized federal holiday, but it is for federal tax purposes.

Form **941 for 2012:** Employer's QUARTERLY Federal Tax Return

(Rev. January 2012)   Department of the Treasury — Internal Revenue Service

950112

OMB No. 1545-0029

Employer identification number (EIN)	☐☐ – ☐☐☐☐☐☐☐
Name *(not your trade name)*	
Trade name *(if any)*	
Address	
	Number Street Suite or room number
	City State ZIP code

Report for this Quarter of 2012
(Check one.)

☐ 1: January, February, March

☐ 2: April, May, June

☐ 3: July, August, September

☐ 4: October, November, December

Prior-year forms are available at *www.irs.gov/form941.*

Read the separate instructions before you complete Form 941. Type or print within the boxes.

Part 1:   Answer these questions for this quarter.

1 Number of employees who received wages, tips, or other compensation for the pay period
   including: *Mar. 12* (Quarter 1), *June 12* (Quarter 2), *Sept. 12* (Quarter 3), or *Dec. 12* (Quarter 4) **1** [_____]

2 Wages, tips, and other compensation . . . . **2** [_____]

3 Income tax withheld from wages, tips, and other compensation . . . . **3** [_____]

4 If no wages, tips, and other compensation are subject to social security or Medicare tax ☐ Check and go to line 6.

		Column 1		Column 2	
5a	Taxable social security wages .	[_____]	× .104 =	[_____]	
5b	Taxable social security tips . .	[_____]	× .104 =	[_____]	
5c	Taxable Medicare wages & tips.	[_____]	× .029 =	[_____]	

5d Add *Column 2 line 5a, Column 2 line 5b,* and *Column 2 line 5c* . . . . **5d** [_____]

5e Section 3121(q) Notice and Demand—Tax due on unreported tips (see instructions) . . **5e** [_____]

6 Total taxes before adjustments (add lines 3, 5d, and 5e) . . . . **6** [_____]

7 Current quarter's adjustment for fractions of cents . . . . **7** [_____]

8 Current quarter's adjustment for sick pay . . . . **8** [_____]

9 Current quarter's adjustments for tips and group-term life insurance . . . . **9** [_____]

10 Total taxes after adjustments. Combine lines 6 through 9 . . . . **10** [_____]

11 Total deposits for this quarter, including overpayment applied from a prior quarter and
    overpayment applied from Form 941-X or Form 944-X . . . . **11** [_____]

12a COBRA premium assistance payments (see instructions) . . . . **12a** [_____]

12b Number of individuals provided COBRA premium assistance . . [_____]

13 Add lines 11 and 12a . . . . **13** [_____]

14 Balance due. If line 10 is more than line 13, enter the difference and see instructions . . . **14** [_____]

15 Overpayment. If line 13 is more than line 10, enter the difference [_____] Check one: ☐ Apply to next return ☐ Send a refund.

▶ You MUST complete both pages of Form 941 and SIGN it.   Next ▶

For Privacy Act and Paperwork Reduction Act Notice, see the back of the Payment Voucher.   Cat. No. 17001Z   Form **941** (Rev. 1-2012)

Figure 13-3a. Form 941 (page 1)

950212

Name *(not your trade name)*	Employer identification number (EIN)

Part 2: **Tell us about your deposit schedule and tax liability for this quarter.**

If you are unsure about whether you are a monthly schedule depositor or a semiweekly schedule depositor, see *Pub. 15 (Circular E)*, section 11.

16 Check one: ☐ Line 10 on this return is less than $2,500 or line 10 on the return for the prior quarter was less than $2,500, and you did not incur a $100,000 next-day deposit obligation during the current quarter. If line 10 for the prior quarter was less than $2,500 but line 10 on this return is $100,000 or more, you must provide a record of your federal tax liability. If you are a monthly schedule depositor, complete the deposit schedule below; if you are a semiweekly schedule depositor, attach Schedule B (Form 941). Go to Part 3.

☐ **You were a monthly schedule depositor for the entire quarter.** Enter your tax liability for each month and total liability for the quarter, then go to Part 3.

Tax liability: Month 1 [   ] .

Month 2 [   ] .

Month 3 [   ] .

Total liability for quarter [   ] . Total must equal line 10.

☐ **You were a semiweekly schedule depositor for any part of this quarter.** Complete *Schedule B (Form 941): Report of Tax Liability for Semiweekly Schedule Depositors*, and attach it to Form 941.

Part 3: **Tell us about your business. If a question does NOT apply to your business, leave it blank.**

17 If your business has closed or you stopped paying wages . . . . ☐ Check here, and

enter the final date you paid wages [/ /] .

18 If you are a seasonal employer and you do not have to file a return for every quarter of the year . . ☐ Check here.

Part 4: **May we speak with your third-party designee?**

Do you want to allow an employee, a paid tax preparer, or another person to discuss this return with the IRS? See the instructions for details.

☐ Yes. Designee's name and phone number [   ] [   ]

Select a 5-digit Personal Identification Number (PIN) to use when talking to the IRS. ☐ ☐ ☐ ☐ ☐

☐ No.

Part 5: **Sign here. You MUST complete both pages of Form 941 and SIGN it.**

Under penalties of perjury, I declare that I have examined this return, including accompanying schedules and statements, and to the best of my knowledge and belief, it is true, correct, and complete. Declaration of preparer (other than taxpayer) is based on all information of which preparer has any knowledge.

X **Sign your name here** [   ]

Print your name here [   ]

Print your title here [   ]

Date [/ /]

Best daytime phone [   ]

Paid Preparer Use Only   Check if you are self-employed . . . ☐

Preparer's name	[ ]	PTIN	[ ]
Preparer's signature	[ ]	Date	[/ /]
Firm's name (or yours if self-employed)	[ ]	EIN	[ ]
Address	[ ]	Phone	[ ]
City	[ ] State [ ]	ZIP code	[ ]

Form **941** (Rev. 1-2012)

Figure 13-3b. Form 941 (page 2)

Medical Expenses

He's the best physician that knows the worthlessness of the most medicines.

—Benjamin Franklin

The cost of medical care and health insurance has ballooned over the last several years. The passage of the Affordable Care Act has put these issues into flux.

This chapter explores the tax impact of medical expenses: What can be deducted and how to deduct it. There are tax advantaged plans available for the small business owner; these are examined with the rules and restrictions noted. Finally, the effects of the Affordable Care Act on medical expenses for the small business owner are explored.

The Affordable Care Act

I am certain that every reader is at least somewhat familiar with the Affordable Care Act (ACA, also called Obamacare). The Supreme Court upheld the law in June 2012 based on the taxing authority of Congress. It's definitely a tax; there are twenty items that I've identified in the legislation that are either direct taxes or major changes to tax regulations.

Republicans in Congress and presidential candidate Mitt Romney vowed to repeal the ACA at their first opportunity. Since Obama won reelection, it is highly unlikely that the ACA will be repealed.

However, there are many more legal challenges to the ACA percolating through the courts. The law will return to the Supreme Court in the future, and the Court could strike it down entirely (or a portion of it). This makes planning for medical expenses for the small business owner difficult.

In the remainder of this chapter I reference the changes the ACA made in the law that affect small business owners. (Some of the new taxes affect specific industries and not small business owners.)

Medical Expense Deduction

Individuals are allowed to take an itemized deduction for medical expenses. All qualified medical expenses not deducted elsewhere on the return are eligible to be taken with this deduction. Medical expenses are defined by the IRS as:

> *The costs of diagnosis, cure, mitigation, treatment, or prevention of disease, and the costs for treatments affecting any part or function of the body. These expenses include payments for legal medical services rendered by physicians, surgeons, dentists, and other medical practitioners. They include the costs of equipment, supplies, and diagnostic devices needed for these purposes. . . . Medical expenses include the premiums you pay for insurance that covers the expenses of medical care, and the amounts you pay for transportation to get medical care. Medical expenses also include amounts paid for qualified long-term care services and limited amounts paid for any qualified long-term care insurance contract.* [1]

There are limitations to this deduction. First, you must itemize your deductions. Second, the total deduction must be more than 7.5% of your adjusted gross income (AGI). Let's say your AGI is $100,000 and you have $7,000 of qualified medical expenses. The AGI restriction on your deduction is $100,000 × 0.075 = $7,500. Because the AGI restriction is higher than your qualified medical expenses, you do not get a medical expense deduction.

If the ACA remains the law of the land, your ability to take a medical expense deduction will decrease. Under the ACA, the AGI restriction will increase to 10%. However, for those aged 65 or older, the AGI restriction will remain at 7.5% through 2016.

---

[1] IRS, Medical and Dental Expenses. Publication 502, p. 2, http://www.irs.gov/pub/irs-pdf/p502.pdf.

Health Insurance for the Sole Proprietor or Partnership

Section 162(l) of the Tax Code allows a deduction for health insurance premiums for the sole proprietor and a partner in a partnership (or a member of an LLC taxed as a partnership). This deduction is taken on line 29 of Form 1040.

The sole proprietor (or an LLC treated as a disregarded entity) will simply note his premiums on this line. To take the deduction, the net income from the business must equal or exceed the premiums (you must be profitable to take this deduction). In addition, premiums that cannot be deducted directly on line 29 of Form 1040 can be taken as a medical expense on Schedule A.

The rules are similar for a partnership. A partner can deduct his or her health insurance premiums on line 29. If the partnership pays for the premiums (either directly or by reimbursing the partners), the premiums are deductible by the partnership as guaranteed payments. Guaranteed payments are includable as income for the partner. The partnership can deduct the premiums as a business expense.

The partnership rules make sense: There can be only one deduction taken for any expense. If the partnership gets the deduction, it can't be deductible for the partner and vice versa.

Health Insurance for the S Corporation

The rules for an S corporation are similar to those for a sole proprietor or a partnership, but there is a key difference. A 2% owner of an S corporation can take a deduction for health insurance premiums, just as a sole proprietor or a partner would do. That's where the similarity ends.

For several years it had been unclear exactly how a 2% shareholder in an S corporation handled health insurance premiums. In January 2008, the IRS issued Notice 2008-1 clarifying the rules that apply.[2] The only way for a shareholder-employee to deduct health insurance pretax is that the premiums *must* be included as wages in Box 1 of the shareholder-employee's W-2. These premiums are *not* included in taxable wages for either Medicare or Social Security.

The insurance can be paid directly by the S corporation or the S corporation can reimburse the shareholder-employee. Either way, the deduction is taken

---

[2] See IRS, Notice 2008-1, Special Rules for Health Insurance Costs of 2-Percent Shareholder Employees, http://www.irs.gov/pub/irs-drop/n-08-01.pdf.

only once. (The wages on the shareholder-employee's tax return will be offset by the deduction for health insurance premiums.)

If you have health insurance premiums in an S corporation and handle it in any other manner, the premiums will probably *not* be deductible. The IRS has prescribed only *one* method for handling health insurance premiums for an S corporation.

At least one state treats this situation differently. Pennsylvania considers S corporation health insurance premiums to be deductible by the corporation.

Health Insurance for the C Corporation

A C corporation pays its own tax. Generally, the health insurance premiums paid by a C corporation are deductible. One of the benefits of a C corporation is that it can have a discriminatory plan. The owners can have a "gold-plated" health plan, while employees could have a "bronze" plan. For example, the owners can have a plan with no deductible where they can go to any doctor while employees must use an HMO and pay a deductible.

▓ **Note   The ACA could have an effect on C corporation health insurance deductions.** The ACA is nearly 3,000 pages in length, and there are numerous provisions affecting the tax treatment of health insurance and medical expenses. It appears that the ability to have a discriminatory plan continues with the ACA, but it cannot be guaranteed.

Employing Your Spouse

One issue in obtaining medical insurance for the self-employed is preexisting conditions. The ACA is supposed to eventually ban the usage of preexisting conditions. However, today those conditions can be used to disqualify you from health insurance.

One solution to this dilemma is to have a group plan. In many states, two individuals are enough to be considered to be a group; many states also require all groups to be accepted for health insurance. Hiring your spouse to create such a group is a possible solution for many.

There are some caveats. First, there must be actual wages paid and actual duties performed by your spouse. The wages don't have to be high or the duties taxing, but they both *must* exist. This means you will have payroll and payroll taxes.

Second, employing your spouse will not work for an S corporation owner. The spouse of a more than 2% owner of an S corporation is automatically treated as a more than 2% owner of an S corporation. This forecloses almost all fringe benefits, including health insurance.

There can be an effect on other areas, including retirement plans. It's possible that the owners might not qualify for certain retirement plans.

Medical Benefit Plans

There are a number of medical benefit plans available. Medical benefit plans function are types of plans written into the Tax Code; these include tax credits, Section 105 plans, Section 125 plans, health savings accounts, and other plans. These are generally another form of health insurance (except Section 125 plans).

Tax Credits

One part of the ACA is the small business health care tax credit. This credit is available if you have fewer than 25 full-time equivalent employees with average wages of less than $50,000 a year. The credit can go as high as 35% (it will rise to 50% in 2014).

Unfortunately, there are several issues with this credit. Besides the obvious wage limitations, for many employers, taking the deduction for medical expenses will give a better tax result than taking the credit! If you take this credit, you generally can't take the deduction.

The calculations required for this credit are also complex. The credit is taken on Form 8941. Because the calculations can be complex, and the deduction for medical premiums paid can lead to a better result, few eligible employers are taking advantage of this tax credit.

Section 105 Plans

A Section 105 plan allows small business owners to pay for medical expenses tax-free. This plan is also known as a health reimbursement arrangement (HRA). Section 105 plans offer advantages to both employees and employers.

For the employer, the medical expense reimbursements are tax-deductible. The employer also has flexibility in designing the plan (setting maximum reimbursements, eligibility requirements, and so on). For employees, the biggest advantage is that reimbursements are not considered to be taxable income (as long as the employee doesn't take a medical expense deduction for the reimbursement on his or her tax return).

Section 105 plans have some requirements:

- A written plan document.

- All participants must be employees.

- Expenses that will be reimbursed cannot be reimbursable under any other health insurance policy.

- The plan cannot discriminate in favor of highly compensated employees (including owners) in regard to either eligibility or benefits.

There are various other rules that apply under other laws. Generally, you will need to use an outside administrator if you adopt a Section 105 plan.

Section 125 Plans

Section 125 plans, sometimes called cafeteria plans, are fringe benefit plans. Generally, these are used for medical expenses and health insurance premiums. The Section 125 plans are pretax plans; money contributed into these plans lowers an employee's taxable wages.

Section 125 plans allow for reimbursement of three types of expenses:

- Qualifying insurance premiums.

- Medical expenses.

- Dependent care expenses.

Not every Section 125 plan offers coverage for all three of these expenses to employees. However, this kind of plan must offer at least two of these benefits to employees.

Contributions by employees to this plan are fixed for the calendar year; reimbursements from the plan can be made until March 15 after the close of the year. One drawback is that these are "use it or lose it" plans, so the ability to obtain reimbursements into the next year is helpful.

The medical expenses that qualify under a Section 125 plan include all the expenses that would normally come to mind and numerous others that wouldn't. For example, air-conditioning filters for allergy relief, dyslexia language training, and telephone equipment for the hearing impaired are considered medical expenses under a Section 125 plan.

The major advantage of a Section 125 plan for employees is that expenses are paid with pretax money. An employee participating in such a plan can receive a larger take-home pay based on paying his medical insurance premium with pretax money.

For employers, a Section 125 plan lowers their share of FICA taxes. For a business with twenty employees, each of whom contribute $1,000 into the plan, the savings would be $1,000 × 20 × 7.65% = $1,530.[3]

There is one caveat with a Section 125 plan: The Tax Code prohibits a sole proprietor, partner, most members of an LLC, and a more than 2% owner of an S corporation from participating.

Beginning in 2013, the maximum amount that can be put into a Section 125 plan in a year is $2,500. This is a provision of the ACA.

Health Savings Accounts

Another medical benefit available is the health savings account (HSA). An HSA is a high-deductible medical plan. An HSA functions similar to an individual retirement account. Contributions into the HSA are tax-deductible. Withdrawals for qualified medical expenses are tax-free. Both sole proprietors and businesses can adopt an HSA. Note that contributions made by a business into an employee's HSA are not tax-deductible for the employee.

Both single and family HSAs are available. Note that if married, each spouse can have their own HSA; however, one spouse cannot have a single HSA while the other has a family HSA.

Under the ACA, the cost of HSAs will increase. This is because of how the ACA regulates individual and small group markets. The exact effect is yet to be determined, but you can read a good synopsis on this from Avik Roy in *Forbes*.[4]

Other Plans

Many small business owners get health insurance through their spouse's plan (a spouse might be covered through another employer). That's definitely one strategy that works. Some employers do not offer health insurance. The rules of the ACA will impact this (see later in this chapter).

---

[3] The 7.65% figure is the employer's share of FICA.

[4] Avik Roy, "How Obamacare Will Make Health Savings Accounts More Costly," Forbes.com, April 27, 2012, http://www.forbes.com/sites/aroy/2012/04/27/how-obamacare-will-make-health-savings-accounts-more-costly/.

Other Provisions of the ACA

The remainder of this chapter is devoted to explaining the other provisions of the ACA and how they affect small businesses, although note that there are numerous other provisions in the law. A complete study of the entire law would run thousands of pages. This section is only on provisions of the ACA not previously mentioned herein.

Individual Mandate Tax

The ACA includes a provision that taxes individuals who do not purchase health insurance. The tax begins in 2014 at $95 but increases to the greater of $695 or 2.5% of modified adjusted gross income (MAGI) in 2016. (Families pay three times the individual number for the minimum tax.) This provision affects any individual not covered by health insurance at his or her place of employment (including sole proprietors and partners).

Employer Mandate Tax

This new tax will affect any employer with fifty or more employees that does not offer health insurance. The tax is set at $2,000 per employee beginning in 2014. There is also a $3,000 per employee penalty if the government finds an employer is providing workers with "unaffordable" health insurance.

This edict has several obvious consequences. First, many employers will be reluctant to hire employee number fifty. An employer with forty-nine employees doesn't have to provide health insurance; an employer with fifty must do so. Second, there will be many companies that will switch to part-time employees. Under this procedure, part-time employees working fewer than thirty hours a week do not count toward this mandate.

Health Insurance Reported on W-2s

Employers will have to report health insurance on W-2s in the future. Though not of huge importance (it's just another line item on a tax form), this is another cost for employers.

Medicare Payroll Tax Hike

Beginning in 2013, the Medicare tax is increased by an additional 0.9%. That this increase begins when your MAGI exceeds $200,000 (single) or $250,000 (married filing jointly). This tax increase is for all Americans, whether employed or self-employed.

New Unearned Income Tax

Another provision of the ACA adds a new 3.8% tax on "unearned income." This tax is on singles with MAGI exceeding $200,000 ($250,000 if married filing jointly). Dividends, capital gains, interest, royalties, rents, and passive income from partnerships, S corporations, and trusts are taxed. Some taxpayers may wish to accelerate income into 2012 and postpone deductions into 2013 based on this new tax. (This topic is discussed in Chapter 18.)

Retirement Plans

I need to retire from retirement.

—Sandra Day O'Connor

As far as I know, clocks only move in one direction: forward. With every day, each of us moves toward retirement. One of the benefits of being a small business owner is the ability to tailor a retirement plan to your needs.

Of course, the Tax Code only allows some types of tax-advantaged plans. This chapter looks at those plans and the tax and retirement consequences of each.

The Basics of Retirement Plans

When I first entered the workforce years ago, most employers offered pension plans. Most pension plans are *defined benefit plans*. Given the contributions into the plan by your employer (or by you, or both), a formula is used to determine the amount of your benefits. Pension plans are still offered by a few employers (mostly for government employees).

Today, most employers offer *defined contribution plans*. The most common of these is the 401(k) plan, named after the section of the Tax Code that allows the plan. Many employers offer these plans, which allow employees to take a portion of their salary and invest that toward their retirement. Some employers match some or all of these contributions, which gives an extra incentive for employees to make contributions.

Most retirement plans have the money in the plan growing tax-free until you start making withdrawals. When you make the withdrawals, you pay income tax on the withdrawn money. The theory is that you will either be in a lower tax bracket at retirement (so your tax will be lower) or the time value of the money will offset the tax (because you didn't have to pay tax on the money until retirement).

There are a couple of retirement plans that work differently. These are *after-tax* retirement plans. The Roth IRA and Roth 401(k) plans are such vehicles. For these, you invest after-tax money—money on which you've already paid income tax. The Roth plans still have the investment growing tax-free. At retirement, you do not pay tax on your withdrawals.

There are advantages and disadvantages to both pre-tax and after-tax retirement plans. There is no one right choice for everyone. You will need to weigh the advantages and disadvantages of each plan and choose the one or ones that are right for your situation. It may be that none of these plans is the right choice for you.

The Traditional IRA and the Roth IRA

Most people are aware of the traditional *Individual Retirement Account* (IRA). IRAs were introduced by the Tax Reform Act of 1986. These accounts allow you to take up to $5,000 of what would be taxable income ($6,000 if you are age 50 or older) and invest it. (The contribution limit increases for 2013 to $5,500. The $1,000 extra "catch-up" contribution expires after 2012. Of course, Congress could extend it; see Chapter 18 for discussion on extenders.) You can begin taking penalty-free withdrawals at age fifty-nine and a half; you *must* begin to take withdrawals at age seventy and a half.

You can take withdrawals earlier than the minimum age; however, if they are not for a prescribed reason, you will pay a 10% penalty tax.[1] No matter when you withdraw money from an IRA, the withdrawal is subject to income tax.

Traditional IRAs are a tax-deferral retirement plan: Your tax is deferred until retirement.

Both traditional IRAs and Roth IRAs are personal retirement accounts. These accounts are not related to your business. All Americans can have an IRA, whether they are employed or self-employed.

---

[1] California also charges a 2.5% penalty tax on proscribed withdrawals.

Table 13-1 presents the 2012 traditional IRA modified adjusted gross income (MAGI)[2] deduction limits if you are *not* covered by a retirement plan at your business. If you are covered by a retirement plan, Table 13-2 gives you the IRA MAGI deduction limits. The 2013 deduction limits are presented in Table 13-3 (if you are not covered by a retirement plan) and Table 13-4 (if you are covered by a retirement plan).

Table 13-1. 2012 IRA MAGI Deduction Limits If Not Covered by a Retirement Plan at Work.

Filing Status	Full Deduction	Phase Out	No Deduction
Single, head of household	No limit	Not applicable	Not applicable
Married filing jointly (spouse not covered)	No limit	Not applicable	Not applicable
Married filing jointly (spouse covered)	$173,000 or less	$173,000 to $183,000	$183,000 or more
Married filing separately	Not applicable	$0 to $10,000	$10,000 or more

Table 13-2. 2012 IRA MAGI Deduction Limits If Covered by a Retirement Plan at Work.

Filing Status	Full Deduction	Phase Out	No Deduction
Single, head of Household	$58,000 or less	$58,000 to $68,000	$68,000 or more
Married filing Jointly	$92,000 or less	$92,000 to $112,000	$112,000 or more
Married filing Separately	Not applicable	$0 to $10,000	$10,000 or more

---

[2] MAGI is your adjusted gross income (AGI) with any deductions for the foreign earned income exclusion, student loan deductions, IRA (and SEP IRA) contributions, and deductions for higher education costs added back.

Table 13-3. 2013 IRA MAGI Deduction Limits If Not Covered by a Retirement Plan at Work.

Filing Status	Full Deduction	Phase Out	No Deduction
Single, head of household	No limit	Not applicable	Not applicable
Married filing jointly (spouse not covered)	No limit	Not applicable	Not applicable
Married filing jointly (spouse covered)	$178,000 or less	$178,000 to $188,000	$188,000 or more
Married filing separately	Not applicable	$0 to $10,000	$10,000 or more

Table 13-4. 2013 IRA MAGI Deduction Limits If Covered by a Retirement Plan at Work.

Filing Status	Full Deduction	Phase Out	No Deduction
Single, head of household	$59,000 or less	$59,000 to $69,000	$69,000 or more
Married filing jointly	$95,000 or less	$95,000 to $115,000	$115,000 or more
Married filing separately	Not applicable	$0 to $10,000	$10,000 or more

---

■ **Caution** **You can be covered by a retirement plan at work when you're not contributing to it.** What does "covered by a retirement plan" mean? It does *not* mean that you are contributing into a retirement plan; rather, it means that you *can* contribute into the plan. If your employer offers you a retirement plan to which you are eligible to contribute, you are considered covered by it regardless of whether you contribute.

A Roth IRA is different from a traditional IRA. With a Roth IRA, you are contributing *after-tax* money. As mentioned previously, your contributions grow in a Roth IRA tax-free until retirement. Unlike a traditional IRA, when you withdraw money from a Roth IRA, no tax is due. Table 13-5 lists the AGI[3] contribution limits for 2012 to a Roth IRA; Table 13-6 gives the 2013 limits.

---

[3] These income limits are also based on your MAGI.

Table 13-5. 2012 Roth IRA Income Limits.

Filing Status	Full Contribution	Phase Out	No Contributions
Single, head of household	$110,000 or less	$110,000 to $125,000	$125,000 or more
Married filing jointly	$173,000 or less	$173,000 to $183,000	$183,000 or more
Married filing separately	Not applicable	$0 to $10,000	$10,000 or more

Table 13-6. 2013 Roth IRA Income Limits.

Filing Status	Full Contribution	Phase Out	No Contributions
Single, head of household	$112,000 or less	$112,000 to $127,000	$127,000 or more
Married filing jointly	$178,000 or less	$178,000 to $188,000	$188,000 or more
Married filing separately	Not applicable	$0 to $10,000	$10,000 or more

There is one other very important rule about IRAs and Roth IRAs: You can only contribute to either a Roth IRA or a traditional IRA in the same year; you *cannot* contribute to both.

Self-employed individuals can contribute to IRAs or Roth IRAs if they meet the income restrictions. However, there are other retirement plans that allow larger contributions.

You have until the tax filing deadline of the year in question (without extensions) to make your contributions to a traditional or Roth IRA (generally, April 15 of the following year).

Finally, you cannot take a loan from a traditional or Roth IRA. Loans are allowed from some other kinds of retirement plans.

The SEP IRA

The Simplified Employee Pension Individual Retirement Account (SEP IRA) is similar to a traditional IRA. As with a traditional IRA, a SEP IRA allows you to defer income until retirement. The withdrawal rules are identical to traditional IRAs. SEP IRAs allow you to contribute far more toward your retirement than a traditional IRA: up to $50,000 for 2012 and $51,000 for 2013.

The rules are different for a SEP IRA compared to traditional IRAs. There are also two types of SEP IRAs: for the self-employed (without employees) and for businesses with employees.

Self-Employed (No Employees)

A SEP IRA is a simple retirement plan for a business owner who will never have employees. For 2012, you are allowed to contribute up to the *lesser* of:

- 20% of net self-employment income,[4] or

- $50,000.

For 2013, you are allowed to contribute up to the lesser of:

- 20% of net self-employment income, or

- $51,000.

SEP IRAs can be established for business owners of a sole proprietorship, partnership, or LLC taxed as a sole proprietorship or partnership. (Corporation owners can also establish SEP IRAs. However, the SEP IRA for a corporation owner follows the rules for employees. See the next section.)

A SEP IRA has a different deadline than that for a traditional IRA. You have until the *latter* of your timely filed return, including extensions, or the normal tax deadline to establish and fund your SEP IRA. That gives you until October 15 of the following year to fund your SEP IRA.

In a traditional IRA, you designate the year your contribution is for. In a SEP IRA, you do not designate the tax year for the contribution. However, you must keep your own records showing to which year a contribution relates.

Generally, you can make a larger contribution to a SEP IRA than a traditional IRA. The exception will be if your business does not earn much money in a given year. Because a SEP IRA restricts you to 20% of the net self-employment income, a traditional IRA may allow for a larger contribution.

There is one major negative with SEP IRAs: You must treat employees identically. If you have employees and you contribute 20% of your net income toward your SEP IRA, you must contribute 20% of their net income toward their SEP IRA (if they are eligible). This is covered in depth in the next section.

Like traditional IRAs, loans are not allowed from SEP IRAs.

---

[4] Your net self-employment income is your business income minus the deduction for 50% of the self-employment tax.

Employees

SEP IRAs can be established by corporations (S corporations and C corporations) and any other business with employees. It's important to note that you *must* treat all employees identically when you have a SEP IRA.

The SEP IRA contribution limits are different for employees. For 2012, you can contribute up to the *lesser* of:

- 25% of an employee's salary, or
- $50,000.

For 2013, you can contribute up to the *lesser* of:

- 25% of an employee's salary, or
- $51,000.

SEP IRAs have three additional rules that can apply for employees. Employers can make their plans less restrictive, but the maximum restrictions are:

1. Employees must be twenty-one years of age or older.
2. Employees must have three years of service in the past five years.
3. Employees must have earned at least $550 in compensation.

Remember that all eligible employees are treated identically. If you make (say) 25% contributions to the SEP IRA for yourself, you must make 25% contributions for all of your eligible employees. However, you do not have to make the same contribution to a SEP IRA every year. You could make 20% contributions in one year, none in the next year, 12% in the following year, and so on.

SEP IRA contributions are made *solely by the employer*. The contributions made are a business expense for the employer.

SEP IRAs are relatively easy to administer. Unlike many other retirement plans, there are no special filings required.

Keogh Plans

Keogh plans, named for Congressman Eugene J. Keogh, are another type of retirement plan. These are similar to traditional pensions. Keogh plans have the same limits as SEP IRAs. Unlike SEP IRAs, Keogh plans have a relatively high administrative burden. Keogh plans generally require a third-party administrator to set up the plan and administer it. The major benefit of a

Keogh plan is that a participant can also contribute to either a traditional or Roth IRA.

There are two types of Keogh plans. You can have a *defined-contribution plan*. In a defined-contribution plan, the amount contributed per paycheck (either a percentage or a fixed sum) is identical. A *defined-benefit plan* is similar to a traditional pension plan. With a defined-benefit plan, an IRS formula is used to calculate the contributions. A defined-benefit plan can be set up as a profit-sharing plan, in which employees can contribute.

The contribution limits for a defined-contribution Keogh plan is the same as a SEP IRA for employees: up to the lesser of 25% of compensation or $50,000 for 2012 ($51,000 for 2013).

The contribution limits for a defined-benefit Keogh plan is based on the amount needed to eventually produce an annual pension payment of the lesser of $200,000 (for 2012, $205,000 for 2013) or 100% of your average compensation for your three highest-paid years.

As mentioned previously, Keogh plans have a much higher administrative burden. Keogh plans must file either Form 5500 or Form 5500-EZ every year. (Form 5500 must be electronically filed through the Department of Labor, not the IRS. Form 5500-EZ can be paper filed.) Only one-participant plans can file a Form 5500-EZ.

Solo 401(k) and Solo Roth 401(k) Plans

Another type of retirement plan is the solo 401(k) and its cousin, the solo Roth 401(k) plan. These are also called individual 401(k) and individual Roth 401(k) plans. These can only be used by one-person businesses. However, you can generally contribute to a solo 401(k) or solo Roth 401(k) no matter what type of business entity you are.

The annual maximum contribution to solo 401(k) plans is similar to the SEP IRAs maximum: $50,000 for 2012, $51,000 for 2013. For the self-employed, you must subtract your deduction for half the self-employment tax when calculating the maximum contribution.

There is a major difference, though, in how the maximum contribution is calculated. First, you calculate the *salary deferral*. That contribution is considered the "employee's deferral option" and has a maximum of $17,000 for 2012 ($17,500 for 2013). Like IRAs, a "catch-up" deferral for those aged 50 or older is also allowed. That contribution has a maximum of $5,500 (for both 2012 and 2013). There's also the employer's contribution. This can be up to 25% of compensation (20% of self-employed earnings). Let's look at an example.

George Jetson is the principal of his consulting practice, a sole proprietorship. In 2012, his business earned $100,000. Jetson is eligible to make a catch-up contribution. What is his maximum contribution to a solo 401(k)? What is his maximum contribution to a SEP IRA? Assume that 50% of the self-employment tax is $7,065.

Let's first calculate the maximum contribution to a SEP IRA. We take the net income of his business ($100,000) and subtract the 50% of self-employment tax ($7,065) to obtain the net self-employment income of $92,935. He can make a 20% contribution to a SEP IRA, or $18,587.

For a solo 401(k), we start with the same calculation of the net self-employment income. The employer portion of the contribution is identical to the SEP IRA contribution, $18,587. The difference is that two additional contributions are allowed. First, there's the employee deferral contribution of $17,000. Second, there's the catch-up contribution of $5,500. That gives a final contribution of $41,087, which is $22,500 more than a SEP IRA.

Note that the maximum contribution to both a SEP IRA and a solo 401(k) is the same (excluding the catch-up contribution). At high income levels, there is no difference in contribution amounts.

You can set up your solo 401(k) to be a solo Roth 401(k) plan. A solo Roth 401(k) plan has the same rules as a solo 401(k) plan except the contributions are after-tax contributions—just like a Roth IRA.

You can take loans from your solo 401(k). The maximum loan is the lesser of $50,000 or 50% of the account balance. Loans must be paid back on an amortization schedule of no more than five years. Payments must be made at least quarterly. Interest must be charged at a "reasonable" rate; this is usually the prime rate plus 1%.

There are some rules regarding solo 401(k)s that make them more restrictive than IRAs and SEP IRAs. Solo 401(k)s must be established prior to the end of the fiscal year (December 31 in most cases). For an unincorporated business, contributions must be made prior to the tax filing deadline (including extensions). For incorporated businesses, funding must be made by fifteen days following the end of the fiscal year for salary deferral contributions; the profit contribution can be made up to the tax filing deadline of the business (including extensions).

There is one other major rule regarding solo 401(k) plans. If the value of the assets in the plan exceeds $250,000, Form 5500 must be filed annually. This can add significant costs to the plan.

The withdrawal rules for solo 401(k) plans are the same as with IRAs (the solo Roth 401(k) withdrawal rules are the same as for Roth IRAs.)

401(k) Plans

If you have employees, you can set up a 401(k) plan. Many brokerage houses and other financial institutions specialize in providing these plans to smaller employers.

A 401(k) plan for a small employer follows the exact same rules as a 401(k) plan for a large business. Employees can elect to have a portion of their pay (up to $17,000 in 2012 and $17,500 in 2013) contributed into the plan. Employers can choose to match a portion of the contributions if they wish. (Matching must be done equally for all employees). There are possible restrictions on contributions for "high-earning" employees. Business owners are *always* included as high-earning employees. Employer matching contributions are a deductible business expense of the company. Employee contributions reduce employees' taxes (income tax and FICA).

401(k) plans must be administered by a third-party administrator. There are annual testing requirements, administrative filings (such as Form 5500), and rules that must be followed.

SIMPLE IRAs

A simpler version of a 401(k) plan is the Savings Incentive Match Plan for Employees Individual Retirement Account. Thankfully, that mouthful is normally referred to as a SIMPLE IRA. SIMPLE IRAs share some features with the better known 401(k) plans. Employees can make a pretax salary reduction (just like 401(k) plans). However, the contribution limits are lower for SIMPLE IRAs than for 401(k) plans. Employees can defer $11,500 for 2012 and $12,000 for 2013. A $2,500 catch-up deferral is allowed for employees 50 years of age or older for 2012 and 2013. Unlike 401(k) plans, SIMPLE contributions defer only income tax, not FICA taxes (Social Security and Medicare).

Employers are required to also make contributions on behalf of their employees. An employer can make either *matching contributions* (where the employer matches the employee's contribution dollar for dollar) or *nonelective contributions* (where the employer contributes 2% of each employee's compensation). If you make matching contributions, the employer must match the first 3% of each employee's deferrals.

Salary reduction contributions (the employee's share) must be made into the SIMPLE IRA within thirty days after the month of the deferral. Employer contributions must be made by the due date of the tax return, including extensions.

SIMPLE IRAs do have some rules. Only employers with 100 or fewer employees can set up a SIMPLE IRA. Employees are not required to make contributions, but the employer *is* required to do so. The withdrawal rules are similar to those of traditional IRAs and 401(k) plans. However, the penalty for an early withdrawal made within two years of the first contribution into a SIMPLE IRA can be up to 25%. SIMPLE IRAs must be formed on or before October 1. If your business comes into being after October 1, the SIMPLE IRA must be formed as soon as "administratively feasible."

SIMPLE IRAs lack the administrative paperwork of 401(k) plans; in that sense, they are far easier than many retirement plans.

■ **Caution   SIMPLE 401(k)s should be avoided.** In addition to SIMPLE IRAs, you can form a SIMPLE 401(k). But unlike SIMPLE IRAs, which are easy to administer, SIMPLE 401(k)s combine the administrative features of a 401(k) plan with the rules of a SIMPLE IRA. The major advantage of a SIMPLE IRA is the administrative ease of the plan. By forming a SIMPLE 401(k), you throw away that simplicity.

Other Retirement Plans

There are many other types of retirement plans; the ones listed in this chapter are the most common kinds. This book is not meant to be a primer on retirement plans (I would need to write a separate treatise to do that). Instead, this chapter is designed to expose you to many of the retirement plans that are available.

There is no one right plan for everyone. Like most things in the tax world, the answer to the question, "What's the correct retirement plan for me?" is: "It depends." Most retirement plans offer tax deferral of current income, but some are after-tax plans that give you the benefit of not paying taxes on the withdrawals. The right retirement plan for you will depend on your situation, your goals, your assets, and your other retirement plans. I strongly recommend you discuss retirement plans with a financial advisor who specializes in this field.

Other Items

Chapter 16 examines the *other* taxes a small business owner may have to pay. Some states and localities tax flow through business entities (partnerships and S corporations); some also have minimum taxes that a business losing money must pay. These are all detailed in this chapter.

Notices from tax agencies, audits, and how to communicate to tax agencies are covered in Chapter 17. The entire audit process, from how returns are selected for examination through the audit, into appeals, and audit reconsideration, is covered.

Chapter 18 covers other topics that don't fit neatly into another chapter. These include tax planning based on the Affordable Care Act, what happens when a business loses money, net operating losses, foreign issues, should you file by paper or electronically, obtaining tax help, whether you should use a tax professional, and selling your business.

Other Taxes

There is no such thing as a good tax.

—Winston Churchill

If federal income tax were not enough, most small business owners will pay many additional taxes, licenses, and user fees. Some of these are paid as part of other costs (such as the telephone excise tax). Most are separately filed and paid for.

In this chapter I cover many of the other taxes that business owners must file and pay. For state income taxes (and local income taxes), the focus is on the differences between the federal tax return and the state and local returns. I examine the basics of how these returns are prepared, the backup documentation required, and other significant rules, regulations, and procedures.

Unfortunately, the list of taxes in this chapter cannot be complete. Our legislators continue to find new and inventive ways of taxing us.

State Income Tax

Most states have a state income tax. If you are lucky enough to reside in Nevada or Wyoming, you can skip this section. These are the only two states that have no state income tax on individuals or businesses. Everyone else has a state income tax return that must be filed.

How this functions depends on the kind of business entity (sole proprietorship, partnership, S corporation, or C corporation) and the tax system of the state. Most states use the federal income tax as the starting point of their tax system in calculating the tax due; a few do not.

Sole Proprietors

A sole proprietor in Alaska, Florida, Nevada, South Dakota, Tennessee, Texas, Washington, and Wyoming can relax regarding state income tax.[1] These states do not have an income tax that affects sole proprietors (including LLCs that file as disregarded entities).

Unfortunately, the residents of the other forty-three states and the District of Columbia must file state income tax returns on their businesses. Generally, the preparation of a sole proprietor's state income tax return is similar to the preparation of his or her federal tax return. The key areas where differences can apply are depreciation, state income taxes, and apportionment of taxes.

Depreciation

Many states conform to federal depreciation rules completely. In those states, your federal depreciation and state depreciation will be identical. However, some states do not conform. In those states, your state depreciation will be different. Where differences exist, generally you will not get the full federal depreciation early in an asset's life; however, you will usually get a larger depreciation deduction later in an asset's life. Here are some states that have differences and how they work.

Table 16-1 lists the states that allow and do not allow "bonus" depreciation. Table 16-2 notes which states do and do not conform with federal Section 179 depreciation. Note that most states that do not conform to the extra 2012 Section 179 depreciation allow the original $25,000 of Section 179 depreciation.

---

[1] South Dakota's financial institution tax impacts solely financial institutions. Any business that must pay this tax should consult a tax professional. Tennessee does have a state income tax, but it is solely on interest and dividends. Washington's Business & Occupation Tax is covered in "Gross Receipts Taxes."

Table 16-1. State Conformity with Bonus Depreciation

Allows Bonus Depreciation	Does Not Allow Bonus Depreciation
AL, AK,[a] CO, KS, LA, MN,[b] MO, MT, NE, NM, ND, OH,[c] OK, UT, WV	AZ, AR, CA, CT, DC, FL,[d] GA, HI, ID, IL, IN, IA, KY, ME, MD, MA, MI, MS, NH, NJ, NY,[e] NC, OR, PA, RI, SC, TN,[f] TX,[g] VT, WI

[a]Not allowed for an oil and gas corporation.
[b]Allowed, but taken over five years.
[c]Allowed, but taken over six years.
[d]For business entities; sole proprietors do not have a FL tax filing requirement.
[e]Allowed only if in the Resurgence Zone or New York Liberty Zone.
[f]For business entities; sole proprietors do not have a TN tax filing requirement.
[g]For business entities affected by the TX margin tax. Sole proprietors do not have a TX tax filing requirement.

Table 16-2. State Conformity with Section 179 Depreciation

Allows $139,000 Section 179 Depreciation	Does Not Allow $139,000 Section 179 Depr.
AL, AR,[a] CO, CT, DE, FL,[b] GA,[c] IL, KS, LA, MA, MI, MN,[d] MS, MO, MT, NE, NM, NY, ND, OK, OH,[e] SC, TN,[f] TX,[g] UT, VT, VA, WV	AZ, CA, DC, HI, ID, IN, IA, KY, ME, MD, NH,[h] NJ, NC, OR, PA, RI, WI

[a]AR allows $133,300 Section 179 depreciation.
[b]For business entities; sole proprietors do not have a FL tax filing requirement.
[c]Except for certain real property that is depreciated.
[d]Allowed, but taken over five years.
[e]Allowed, but taken over six years.
[f]For business entities; sole proprietors do not have a TN tax filing requirement.
[g]For business entities affected by the TX margin tax. Sole proprietors do not have a TX tax filing requirement.
[h]Section 179 limit is $20,000.

These tables are accurate as of the time of this writing, but state tax laws can and do change. You should verify these figures with your state tax department.

Additionally, as of this writing it is unclear if either "bonus" depreciation or the extra Section 179 depreciation will be extended into 2013 by Congress. An extender legislation package is expected to be introduced during the lame duck session following the November election. What tax deductions will be included in that package and the ultimate fate of the legislation are unknown.

State Income Taxes

State income taxes that are deductible on the federal income tax return cannot be deducted on the state income tax return. The most common of these will be California's mandatory LLC tax on an LLC that is a disregarded entity (filing as a sole proprietor).

Apportionment

Most businesses are conducted in one state. However, some businesses will have business conducted in multiple states. If you have *nexus* (a connection) to more than one state, you will need to file a tax return for the other states.

For sole proprietors, this generally means filing a nonresident state income tax return for the other state. Let's look at an example.

Assume your consulting business is in Chicago. You take a four-month assignment in Oklahoma City. Your client in Oklahoma pays you $25,000. The client reimburses you for all of your business expenses in Oklahoma, so the $25,000 is your net business income from Oklahoma. Overall, your business earns $100,000 of net income during the year.

You will need to file an Oklahoma Nonresident/Part-Year Income Tax Return (form 511NR).[2] The income and deductions attributable to Oklahoma will be included on the return. In addition to the $25,000 of business income, 25% of the deduction for self-employment tax[3] and any other Oklahoma-source income will need to be included on the return. (Any other deductions based on business income, such as health insurance premiums, must also be included on a pro rata basis on the Oklahoma return.)

On the Illinois tax return, you can take a credit for the tax paid to the other state. This credit is taken on Schedule CR.[4] Overall, you end up paying the higher of the two states' marginal tax rates.

There can be many complexities when a sole proprietor has to file multiple tax returns. Because state tax laws are not identical across states, treatment of certain kinds of income and deductions can differ. Any business owner facing such a situation should consult with a tax professional.

---

[2] Available from the Oklahoma Tax Commission, http://www.tax.ok.gov/.

[3] Because 25% of the business's income is Oklahoma-source, 25% of the deduction for self-employment tax is Oklahoma-source.

[4] See Schedule CR at http://www.revenue.state.il.us/TaxForms/IncmCurrentYear/Individual/Schedule-CR.pdf.

■ **Caution   Not all tax credits are taken on your state's tax return.** In most cases, the credit for paying taxes to another state is taken on the taxpayer's "home" state tax return. However, in some cases the credit is taken on the other state's return. For example, a taxpayer who is a resident of Oregon and pays California income tax (and vice versa) will take the tax credit on the other state's income tax return. Generally, the instructions to your state's other state tax credit form should list any states where you take the credit on the other state's return.

Partnerships and LLCs Filing as Partnerships

Most partnerships and LLCs filing as partnerships will not owe any tax. However, a few states tax partnerships and LLCs directly. Most states do require a partnership tax return (in some cases, a flow-through entity return) to be filed. Generally, no tax will be due with the filing of the return.

However, a few states directly tax partnerships and LLCs. Table 16-3 lists these states and the tax they impose. The table is based on what is believed to be accurate information as of the date of writing. However, state taxes can change, so you should check with your state tax agency to verify this information.

Table 16-3. State Taxes Imposed Directly on Partnerships and LLCs

State	Tax
California	$800 minimum tax on LLCs. Also must pay a gross receipts tax if receipts are $250,000 or more. Partnerships are not subject to this tax.
Connecticut	Must pay $250 business entity tax.
Illinois	Must pay 1.5% personal property tax replacement income tax.
Kentucky	Limited liability entities subject to minimum $175 tax (increases with gross receipts of more than $3 million). Partnerships are not subject to this tax.
New Hampshire	Subject to 8.5% tax on business profits.
New Jersey	Filing fee tax of $150 per owner if more than two owners.
New York	Subject to filing fee tax from $25 to $4,500 based on gross receipts ($25 if gross receipts are $100,000 or less).
Oregon	Filing fee tax of $150.

State	Tax
Texas	Business margin tax applies to LLCs (including single-member LLCs) and LLPs but *not* partnerships owned by "natural persons." Filing requirement exists for all impacted entities but tax begins at $600,000 of gross income.
Vermont	Must pay business entity tax of $250.
Wisconsin	Has $25 minimum economic surcharge tax on partnerships and LLCs. Tax is greater of $25 or 0.2% of net Wisconsin business income.

Most states require withholding of nonresident partners' portion of state income tax. Let's look at an example of how this is calculated.

Assume you have a New York LLC taxed as a partnership with a member from North Carolina. The LLC has net income of $20,000 each quarter. The North Carolina member has 25% ownership of the LLC. What should the LLC withhold and remit to New York?

Like most states, New York requires withholding at their top individual tax rate. That's currently 8.82%. The North Carolina partner's share of the LLC's income is $5,000 each quarter (25% of $20,000). Thus, the withholding is $5,000 × 0.0882 = $441. This withholding is due to New York on April 15, June 15, September 15, and January 15 (of the following year). New York requires that the appropriate information be entered on Form IT-2658.

Other than these exceptions (the few states that directly tax partnerships and nonresident withholding of partnerships), state tax returns of partnerships tend to be straightforward.

S Corporations

As with partnerships, S corporations are flow-through entities. Generally, there is no direct taxation of S corporations by states. However, there are exceptions to this as noted in Table 16-4.

Table 16-4. State Taxes Imposed Directly on S Corporations

State	Tax
California	$800 or 1.5% tax (whichever is greater) on S corporations. The minimum tax is waived in the S corporation's first year.
Connecticut	Must pay $250 business entity tax.

State	Tax
District of Columbia	The District of Columbia does *not* recognize S corporations. Thus, for DC tax purposes, an S corporation is a C corporation and pays its own tax. Additionally, there is a $250 minimum tax for all businesses in DC.
Georgia	Georgia has a net worth tax on corporations. This is based on the equity (stock, additional paid in capital, and retained earnings) of the business within Georgia. The minimum tax is $10.
Illinois	Must pay 1.5% small business corporation replacement tax (a tax on personal property).
Kentucky	S corporations must pay the limited liability entities tax (minimum $175; increases with gross receipts of more than $3 million).
Massachusetts	Minimum tax of $456. S corporations with $6 million of gross receipts subject to excise tax of 3% (4.5% with $9 million of gross receipts).
Missouri	S corporations must pay franchise tax if more than $10 million of assets.
New Hampshire	Subject to 8.5% tax on business profits.
New Jersey	Minimum gross receipts tax of $375 (increases at gross receipts over $100,000; maximum tax is $1,500).
New York	Subject to minimum tax from $25 to $4,500 based on gross receipts ($25 if gross receipts are $100,000 or less).
North Carolina	Minimum franchise tax of $35 or 0.15% of largest of equity (capital stock, surplus, undivided profits), investment in NC tangible property, and appraise value of NC tangible property.
Oregon	Minimum tax of $150.
Texas	Business margin tax applies to S corporations. Filing requirement exists for all S corporations but tax begins at $600,000 of gross income.
Vermont	Must pay business entity tax of $250.
Wisconsin	Has $25 minimum economic surcharge tax on corporations. Tax is greater of $25 or 0.2% of net Wisconsin business income.

Just like partnerships, S corporations must make withholding payments for nonresident shareholders. The calculation is basically identical to that of partnerships and LLCs with nonresident partners.

There are few other differences with state taxation of S corporations from federal taxation.

C Corporations

Because C corporations pay their own tax, generally a business that owes federal corporate tax will also owe state corporate tax. Additionally, many states have minimum corporate taxes. These are noted in Table 16-5.

Table 16-5. States with Minimum Taxes on C Corporations

State	Tax
California	$800 minimum tax on C corporations. The minimum tax is waived in the C corporation's first year.
Connecticut	Must pay $250 business entity tax.
District of Columbia	There is a $250 minimum tax for all businesses in DC.
Georgia	Georgia has a net worth tax on corporations. This is based on the equity (stock, additional paid in capital, and retained earnings) of the business within Georgia. The minimum tax is $10.
Kentucky	C corporations must pay the limited liability entities tax (minimum $175; increases with gross receipts of more than $3 million).
Massachusetts	Minimum tax of $456.
Mississippi	Minimum tax of $25.
Montana	Minimum tax of $50.
New Jersey	Minimum tax of $500.
New Mexico	Minimum tax of $50.
New York	Subject to minimum tax from $25 to $5,000 based on gross receipts ($25 if gross receipts are $100,000 or less).
North Carolina	Minimum franchise tax of $35 or 0.15% of largest of equity (capital stock, surplus, undivided profits), investment in NC tangible property, and appraise value of NC tangible property.
Ohio	Minimum tax of $50.
Oregon	Minimum tax of $150.
Rhode Island	Minimum tax of $500.
South Carolina	Minimum license fee tax of $25.
Tennessee	Minimum franchise tax of $100.
Utah	Minimum tax of $100.

State	Tax
Vermont	Minimum tax of $250 (small farm corporations, $75).
West Virginia	Minimum tax of $50.
Wisconsin	Has $25 minimum economic surcharge tax on corporations. Tax is greater of $25 or 0.2% of net Wisconsin business income.

Most states begin with federal taxable income to calculate a C corporation's state taxable income. However, there are exceptions (such as Iowa). Business owners operating as C corporations in those states may wish to consider using a tax professional.

Local Income Taxes

Some areas of the country are subject to local income taxes. These can be on the city, county, or regional level. Here are states where you might be subject to local income taxes:

- Indiana (county tax paid as part of state income tax filing)

- Kentucky (Lexington and Louisville regions have separate income tax filings)

- Michigan (several cities, including Detroit, Grand Rapids, and Saginaw have city income taxes)

- Missouri (Kansas City and St. Louis have city income taxes)

- New York (New York City and Yonkers have individual income taxes collected on the state income tax return; New York City has separate business tax returns required for all businesses; the Metropolitan Commuter Transportation Mobility Tax (MCTMT) is also due from business owners and the self-employed in the New York City metropolitan area)

- Ohio (almost every city in Ohio has a city income tax; some school districts have school district income taxes)

- Pennsylvania (many cities and counties have income taxes)

Most city and local income taxes are based on federal income tax. Generally, preparation of the returns themselves is straightforward.

I spotlight two cities for their income taxes: New York City and Philadelphia.

Business owners in New York City must pay New York City income tax on their state tax returns. They must also file an MCTMT return. An individual conducting a successful business in New York City can easily have a marginal tax rate in excess of 50%.

In Philadelphia, a business owner must pay three additional taxes. There's the school district income tax (on interest and dividends), the business privilege tax, and the net profits tax. A business owner in a nearby suburb might have to pay a county tax, but would avoid the other three taxes.

▨ **Tip   Make sure you look at local taxes when you locate your business.** Make sure you check out all the business taxes, licenses, registration fees, and gross receipts taxes you may be subject to before you decide on a location.

Excise Taxes

From time to time, Congress has imposed excise taxes on various industries. The most famous of these is the telephone excise tax. It was originally designed to pay for the Spanish-American War of 1898. Like most taxes, once it started it wasn't stopped even after the war ended.

Many excise taxes are on the retail cost of an item. For example, cigarette and other tobacco taxes are a form of excise tax. Both the federal and state excise taxes are based on a package of cigarettes being sold. Some excise taxes are taxes on gross receipts.

Generally, the information you need to prepare the return will be a portion of the information needed to prepare your federal tax returns. Depending on the tax, you may also need exact sales figures (e.g., number of packages sold). Depending on the tax, returns are due monthly, quarterly, or annually.

Gross Receipts Taxes

Several states and many local governments have gross receipts taxes. These are taxes on the receipts of your business. Gross receipts taxes exist in Delaware, Hawaii, Texas, and Washington. You will find them in many cities (usually called a "business tax"), such as Los Angeles.

Delaware Gross Receipts Tax

Delaware imposes a gross receipt tax on sellers of goods and service providers. The tax rate depends on business activity and range from 0.1037% to 2.0736%.

However, there is an exclusion in most categories of $80,000 per month; thus, most small businesses will not owe any tax. Note that there is an annual fee for most businesses of $75.

Hawaii General Excise Tax

Hawaii's general excise tax is commonly thought of as the state's sales and use tax. It's also a tax on income from most types of business activities within the state. The tax is a gross receipts tax, and depending on the business activity the tax rate is 0.15%, 0.5%, or 4%. The 0.15% rate is on commissions from insurance sales. The 0.5% rate is on wholesaling, producing, and manufacturing. Most other business activities, such as retailing, services, and contracting, are taxed at 4%.

The tax is commonly passed on by retail outlets to consumers as a sales tax. However, the tax is on the seller, not the consumer. More information on the Hawaii general excise tax is available from the Hawaii Department of Taxation.[5]

Texas Franchise Tax

Texas does not have personal income tax. However, it does have a business tax (the Texas franchise tax). That tax is based on the least of three calculations:

- Total revenue minus cost of goods sold;

- Total revenue minus compensation;[6] or

- Total revenue times 70%.

Unless your business has significant gross revenue ($600,000 or more) you will not owe this tax. However, you still need to file a tax return. The tax rate varies from 0.5% (most wholesalers and retailers) to 1.0% (most other entities). There is a 0.575% rate for entities with less than $10 million in revenue.

Washington Business & Occupations Tax

Washington state does not have a state income tax. Instead, there is the Business & Occupations (B&O) tax. This on the gross receipts of a business. Almost all businesses must pay this tax. Each business activity has its own tax rate. The most common rates are 0.471% for retailing, 0.484% for wholesaling and manufacturing, and 1.8% for service industries.

---

[5] See the FAQ at http://www6.hawaii.gov/tax/a7_faq.htm#get.

[6] "Compensation" is defined as wages and benefits but does not include contract labor.

Businesses in Washington must register with the Washington Department of Revenue (DOR). Based on the information in the application, the DOR will assign the business to a category, and determine the required frequency of filing returns (monthly, quarterly, or annually).

Other Gross Receipts Taxes

Many cities have gross receipts taxes. Often, these are called "business license fees." However, when you look at the paperwork you discover that the cost is based on your gross receipts. Locations with gross receipts taxes include Los Angeles; Bellevue, Washington; and many cities in West Virginia.

Sales and Use Taxes

If you are a wholesaler or in retail, it's likely you will need to collect your state's sales tax. If you are in Alaska,[7] Delaware, Montana, New Hampshire, or Oregon, you can skip this section; your state does not have a sales tax.

States with sales tax also have *use taxes*. A use tax is identical to a sales tax; it's on goods you purchase for your own use that were not charged sales tax. Suppose you purchase a machine from out of state. As discussed in Chapter 2, the seller will probably not charge you sales tax. However, you owe the equivalent of sales tax—use tax—on the purchase. If you have a sales tax license, you usually report the use tax on the sales tax return.

Some states also tax services. New Mexico's gross receipts tax functions as the state's sales tax; most services in New Mexico are subject to the tax. Other states that charge sales tax on services include Florida, Hawaii (as part of the general excise tax), and South Dakota.

The starting point in preparing a sales tax return is your total sales. You then generally subtract sales for resale and out-of-state sales. (There are some other adjustments, too.) Note that you must have the correct documentation to justify not charging sales tax on any transaction. Most state tax agencies require a form of resale certificate. For example, California requires a resale certificate signed by the purchaser. Florida, though, requires a copy of the sales tax license of the purchaser. Since the Florida license is annual, a reseller must obtain a copy of the license each year. Make sure you obtain the correct documentation for your state.

How often you file and pay sales tax depends on your state and the size of your business. It could be monthly, quarterly, or annually. Also, in some states you may file every twelve months, but the filing is not based on a calendar year.

---

[7] Some local governments in Alaska do levy sales taxes.

▨ **Caution** **Sales tax audit rates are high.** Most sales tax agencies have high audit rates. In a sales tax audit, you will need to justify all nontaxable transactions. You will need to show you either paid sales tax on all purchases of goods and machines for your own use or paid use tax on those items. In Florida, this includes paying use tax on rent if your landlord doesn't charge you sales tax.

Real Property Taxes

If your business owns real property, you will probably pay property tax on that property. Your local assessor (usually a county-level function) will assess your land and buildings. You will then receive a property tax bill. Depending on the location, the bill can be paid in one to four installments.

Some jurisdictions assess properties annually. If you believe an error has been made in assessing your property, you need to file an appeal of the assessment. Depending on the locality, you may have as few as thirty days to challenge an assessment. Most of the time when you receive the tax bill, it will be too late to challenge the assessment.

For the most part, there is little work involved for the business owner with regard to real property taxes.

Personal Property Taxes

In most jurisdictions you also have to pay personal property taxes. These are due on machinery, equipment, supplies, and in some locations, inventory. These are generally administered on the local level. However, in Maryland the state Department of Assessments and Taxation is responsible for personal property tax.

Generally, you self-report the personal property on hand. If you have multiple locations, you need to submit a separate report for each location. Most jurisdictions list the personal property you have from prior years. You note items added and disposed.

Some states (such as Maryland) charge a filing fee for the report. Most locations do not charge anything for the filing. However, you will receive a personal property tax assessment that must be paid.

Local Business Licenses

Most local jurisdictions charge for business licenses. Generally, there is a nominal charge for the license. However, some locations charge more than

$1,000 for a business license—in some cases, much more. The 2011 Kosmont-Rose Institute Cost of Doing Business Survey[8] noted that a retail business license in Akron, Ohio, costs $112,500. Chicago and Naperville, Illinois, are also expensive; they cost $125,000 and $100,000, respectively.

Most jurisdictions charge a standard fee; some also charge based on the number of employees. You should check with your local government agencies to determine the costs and other requirements.

Some locations mandate an occupancy permit. Others may require a visit by a zoning employee. If you are opening a restaurant, the local health district will probably inspect your premises. If your business involves hazardous waste, the fire department or hazardous waste agency may require you to purchase a permit. The local licenses can add up. Make sure you budget accordingly.

User Fees

You probably pay user fees every day without realizing it. Tacked on to utility bills you will see a potpourri of fees; these are examples of user fees. My telephone bill contains a "local telecommunications tax." That's a user fee I'm paying to use my phone.

Generally, these fees are small. However, if you need a government permit, you may find yourself paying a much higher user fee. Where a building permit used to be, say, $100, it might now be $500. You don't have a choice but to pay these fees. The key is to include such fees in your budget for your business.

Other Taxes

Although the list in this chapter contains the major taxes and government fees you will pay, it is by no means complete. Legislators are always looking to expand revenue, so no activity is safe from taxation.

Many taxes are hidden; this is especially true if you travel. Your hotel room might be $100 per night, but that's before taxes. Besides the ubiquitous sales tax, you might see a hotel destination tax, a resort zone tax, a building zone tax, a stadium tax, an airport user fee tax, and many others. It's rare when you see a tax cut or eliminated. Unfortunately, like the excise tax that paid for the Spanish-American War and continued for more than 100 years after the end of the war, most taxes live forever.

---

[8] See "2011 Kosmont-Rose Institute Cost of Doing Business Survey Report," at http://www.reuters.com/article/2011/11/28/idUS186751+28-Nov-2011+BW20111128.

Dear Valued Taxpayer: When You Hear from the IRS

The nine most terrifying words in the English language are, "I'm from the government and I'm here to help."

—Ronald Reagan

One of the most terrifying events for a business owner (or for any taxpayer) is receiving mail from the IRS. Perhaps the scariest possible Halloween costume is that of an IRS auditor. If you really want to put fear into someone, just say, "I'm from the IRS and I'm here to help."

As will be discussed in this chapter, the more successful you are, the more likely you are to be audited. The IRS is a collection agency. If you make $100,000 and your neighbor makes $1 million, and you both cheat on your taxes by underreporting your income by 10%, the IRS should get a better result by auditing your neighbor—there's more tax to potentially recover. The IRS knows that's the case; generally, if you earn more money, you are more likely to be audited.

No one can give you a strategy to completely prevent your returns from being audited, and that's because some examinations are truly random. This chapter looks at what you should do if you are audited, and the best way to survive an audit with the least possible amount of pain.

What to Do When You Get an IRS Notice

The most important thing to do when you get a notice from a tax agency is to open it. Perhaps you would be surprised to find out that many taxpayers don't open notices from tax agencies because they are scared. Not opening the mail won't make the notice go away! The IRS will send you a second notice. If the notice involves assessment of tax, after two notices the IRS will assess the tax. If you don't file a Tax Court petition within ninety days of the IRS assessing the tax, your options become paying the tax and filing a lawsuit after waiting six months or going through audit reconsideration. (All of these will be discussed later in this chapter.) It's *always* easier (and cheaper) to timely respond to an IRS notice.

▓ **Note**   **The IRS never initiates emails to taxpayers.** If you receive an email supposedly from the IRS, it is almost certainly spam or a phishing email. Unfortunately, emails in the name of the IRS (or other tax agencies) in an attempt to obtain personal information are now common. You can forward the email, including headers, to phishing@irs.gov. Whatever you do, do **not** click on any links or attachments in the email. After forwarding the email, you should permanently delete it.

You should read the notice and see what the IRS wants. (In the later sections of this chapter I'll go over the more common types of IRS notices.) If you use a tax professional, immediately send him or her a copy of the notice. Your professional should be able to give you advice on what you need to do.

Some IRS notices are benign. If you amend your return, you will receive a notice letting you know that your amended return has been processed. Some notices may ask for additional information. Others will state that you've made a math error on your return. Another set of notices allege that you've left one or more items off your return. Most of the other notices relate to examinations and collection activity.

You have a limited amount of time to respond to an IRS notice. Depending on the kind of notice, it can be as few as ten days. It is very important that you respond on a timely basis; if you don't, you may lose rights that you have.

▓ **Tip** **Make sure you keep your address current with the IRS.** When you move, notifying tax agencies of your new address likely won't make your list of things to do. However, it should. The IRS mails all notices. As long as the IRS sends the notice to the address of record for you (generally, the address you used on your last tax return), the notice will be considered received **whether or not you actually receive it!** You can use Form 8822 to change your address with the IRS. As discussed later in this chapter, you should mail the form by certified mail, with a return receipt requested so that you have proof the IRS received it.

Once you send a response to the notice, you may wait weeks for a response. Although a taxpayer has a specific amount of time to respond to an IRS notice, the IRS can almost always take as long as they wish. Unfortunately, it can be "hurry up and wait" when you correspond with a tax agency.

If you've ever served on jury duty in a criminal matter, you know that defendants are innocent until proven guilty. In the tax realm, things are different. *You are generally presumed guilty until proven innocent.*

The US tax system is based on self-reporting. You prepare a return, and what you submit to the IRS (and other tax agencies) is presumed correct, subject to the right of the agency to examine (audit) your return. Congress and the courts decided that because the system is based on self-reporting, the judgment of the IRS is presumed correct. Thus, IRS notices are presumed correct; you must prove they are incorrect. Generally in an audit, you must prove all of the numbers shown on your return are accurate.

There are times when the burden of proof shifts to the IRS. However, these cases are rare. (I'll note the most common occurrence later in this chapter.) As has been emphasized throughout this book, it is vital that you keep excellent records. If you have proof of the numbers on your tax return, an audit may be an annoyance, but it's unlikely to result in you paying additional tax.

Types of Audits

When the IRS sends you a notice, it can be for many different reasons. We now look at the common types of notices and audits that you might encounter.

Math errors are exactly what they are called: The IRS believes you made a mistake involving math on your return. These notices are different from all of the other types of notices. If the error results in a change to your return, the IRS immediately assesses the additional tax (or sends you a refund). As with all notices, the IRS assumes it is correct. With a math error, the IRS is allowed to immediately make the change. Unlike other notices, generally you do not have to respond to this kind of notice.

The next kind of notice is an Automated Underreporting Program (AUR) notice. The IRS computer system has flagged your return; it believes that you left something out or there is some other error. You are given thirty days to respond to the notice. If you don't respond, the IRS will send you a second notice giving you thirty more days to respond. If you continue to ignore the notice, the IRS sends you a *notice of deficiency*. The IRS has now assessed the additional tax; you generally have ninety days to file a case in Tax Court or the tax is permanently assessed. (There are ways of fighting the IRS even after tax has been assessed; those are covered later in this chapter.)

The remaining kinds of notices are notices of audit. There are three types of audits: correspondence, office, and field.

Correspondence audits are generally limited. The IRS asks you to mail documentation on a few items. You mail the information to the IRS; the IRS then sends you a response in the mail.

Office exams are also limited, usually dealing with one to five items. The IRS will have helpfully set up a day and time for you to come into their local office (hence, "office audit"), though you can change the day and time. You will bring the backup documentation for the items the IRS is examining.

Field exams are the most searching kinds of audits; these are the audits that most individuals think of when they hear the words "IRS audit." A field exam is an audit usually conducted at a taxpayer's place of business—in the "field" rather than in the office (hence, field audit). Most audits are now done by correspondence rather than being performed in the field. Field audits are the most expensive for the IRS; they are usually reserved for difficult returns, complex issues, and project work. (Project work is discussed later in this chapter.)

In a field audit, the examiner can expand the audit to other issues on the return or other years that are open. These audits are the riskiest for taxpayers.

The goal of the IRS in an examination (audit) is for you to have paid the correct amount of tax for the year in question. It is possible to obtain a refund in an audit. It is also possible for you to owe substantial amounts of tax, penalties, and interest.

Math Errors

Many years ago, math errors on tax returns were common. When I graduated from college, computers occupied whole rooms; today, my cell phone is more powerful than those computers.

If you prepare your return by hand, it's relatively easy to make a math error. Tax forms are complex, and if the instructions tell you to add lines six and ten and you add lines seven and ten, you have made a mistake.

Math error notices are different than all of the other notices in this chapter. Unless you owe additional tax because of the error, the IRS does *not* expect you to respond. In almost all cases, the IRS's correction will be accurate.

However, occasionally the IRS computers will make a mistake with a math error notice. I've seen this happen with negative numbers: The IRS changed the negative number to a positive and a "math error" was created.

If you believe there was no math error, you will need to provide proof that the original calculations were correct. Usually, you need to print a copy of the form in question. Write out an explanation of why the originally submitted return was correct. Mail the explanation, along with a copy of the notice and supporting data using certified mail, return receipt requested, to the IRS office that sent you the notice.

▨ **Tip**   **Always mail your response using certified mail, return receipt requested.** The IRS gives you the option of faxing a response. Unfortunately, you have no proof that the IRS received the fax. Although you can print a report showing that you ***sent*** something via fax to the IRS, there's no proof that the agency ***received*** it. I've sent responses via fax only to have the IRS state that they were never received. Unless I'm actually speaking with an individual from the IRS (or it is a field examination matter; see later in this chapter), I ***always*** send my responses using certified mail. With certified mail, you have proof that courts will accept that whatever you sent to the IRS was received. Unless you use the tracking information off the US Postal Service's website, you should use return receipt requested. The USPS purges the online information after one year.

▨ **Note**   **Why is the IRS sending me a notice from a different service center than the one that processed my return?** The IRS balances its workload among nine service centers. Only four service centers currently process individual returns (Atlanta, Austin, Fresno, and Kansas City); two others (Cincinnati and Ogden) process business returns. Although it is possible that an IRS notice will come from the same service center that processed your return, it is also possible it will come from any of the service centers. The IRS service centers that no longer process returns are in Andover, Massachusetts; Holtsville, New York; and Philadelphia.

AUR Notices

You can identify IRS notices by the notice number. These are usually shown in the top right corner of the notice. Notice labels begin with "CP." This stands for "computer paragraph"; each IRS CP notice is tied to a specific issue.[1]

The most common kind of notice is an AUR notice: a CP2000.

Before we get into how to respond to an AUR notice, here's why the IRS has this program and why it's been expanded: It's a huge profit center. Many individuals receive a notice from the IRS and simply pay it without determining whether the IRS is correct. Don't do that! Many notices are wrong; if you sign the notice and pay the tax, you've agreed to the change(s) made by the IRS and most likely will have no further recourse.

When you read an AUR notice, you will be the first human to read it. These notices are sent out through a completely automated process. Generally, these notices involve "matching" issues. For example, you are a sole proprietor and have received a 1099-MISC regarding work you've done. However, you didn't include that 1099-MISC on your return. Or the IRS thinks you didn't include it on your return. The IRS sends you a CP2000 noting the error that the computer has identified.

The first thing you should do is identify the issue(s) in the notice. The notice will state them, usually listing forms they think weren't included (such as 1099s, K-1s, etc.). This is listed in the Explanation Section. The IRS names the documents, noting "Information Reported to IRS that differs from the amounts shown on your return." The IRS then notes the reasons for the changes. This section references the tax law. The reasons may note that the IRS just needs more information. The IRS will then note the changes to your return. This section shows the recomputation of your return based on the changes made. Sometime the IRS includes additional information.

You should review all of this information and determine if it's accurate. If it is not, print backup paperwork that would show the IRS why the computer is wrong. The IRS includes one or two response forms with the notice. (Sometimes they include two response forms, one if you are sending a payment and one if you are not sending a payment. In some cases the IRS includes only one response form.) Complete the response form. If you believe the IRS is incorrect, write out a letter of explanation. In the letter, make sure you include your name, taxpayer identification number, the tax year, and the AUR number (this will be on page one of the notice in the top-right corner). Mail the response using certified mail, return receipt requested.

---

[1] You can find a list of some of the more common IRS CP notices at http://www.irs.gov/Individuals/Understanding-Your-IRS-Notice-or-Letter.

The IRS will respond in one of several ways. First, the agency may reply stating, "Thank you for your response. We were able to close the matter with the information you provided." That means the matter is closed, and the IRS agrees with you. This will usually be labeled a CP2005 notice.

The IRS may reply they need additional information (this usually is sent as a new CP2000 notice). If so, provide the IRS with whatever has been requested.

The IRS can respond that they disagree with what you've written and they still believe the computer is correct. If so, you will either have to respond again showing why you are correct and the IRS is wrong. This can come as a new CP2000 notice; it may also come as an IRS letter.[2] If you now believe the IRS is correct, you can respond by paying the tax.

If you still disagree with the IRS, you can take the case to their Appeals Department (discussed later in this chapter). You also have the right to file a case in Tax Court (also discussed later in this chapter).

Note that it is possible when you receive an AUR notice that you will agree in part and disagree in part. In that case, you can send a response noting that fact and paying just the amount of additional tax (and interest and penalties, if applicable) with which you agree.

■ **Tip   Ask the IRS if you need additional time to respond.** If you receive a notice from the IRS and need additional time to respond, ask for it. In most cases, the agency will give you thirty additional days to respond. The IRS is aware that it can take time to gather needed information.

How Returns Are Selected for Audit

There are many ways returns are selected for audit. The most common relates to the *differential score* (DIF score) of the return.

All tax returns are given a DIF score. This generally relates to how different a return is from normal. Suppose you are a consultant filing as a sole proprietor. You have $50,000 of gross income. You note travel expenses of $2,345 and meal and entertainment expenses of $44,000 (after the 50% reduction for meals and entertainment). It's hard to believe that a consultant with $50,000 of gross income has $88,000 of meals and only $2,345 of travel. Such a return is likely to receive a high DIF score and be selected for audit.

There are other reasons returns are selected for examination. Every year, the IRS conducts research projects. Some are annual: the agency takes a random

---

[2] The most likely form is Letter 2257C, a balance due notice to a taxpayer.

sample of all returns to see what forms and schedules are leading to the largest nonpayment of taxes.

The IRS also conducts specific research projects. For example, a few years ago they examined random samples of S corporation returns. The IRS was looking to see how big the issue of S corporation owners not taking reasonable salaries was.

Some audits are based on the kind of work in which you are involved. Recently, the IRS began a project in Las Vegas, looking at various service industry personnel to see if all the gratuities they received were being reported on their returns.

Another set of audits relates to a tax professional. Assume that the IRS examines a taxpayer, and discovers that the return had errors that could be the result of malfeasance by a tax professional. The IRS will then select fifteen to thirty additional returns prepared by that tax professional to see if it was an isolated incident or a pattern of fraud.

Generally, the more money you make, the more likely your return is to be examined. The "sweet spot" for audits are sole proprietors who make more than $300,000 a year from their businesses. The highest audit rate, excluding large corporations, is for sole proprietors who make more than $1.2 million.[3]

Any tax professional who tells you he can prevent your return from being audited is lying. Some audits are truly random, and unless that professional has access to the IRS's random number generator, we all have an equal chance of winning that lottery.

Correspondence Audits

The first kind of audit is the correspondence examination. In a correspondence examination, the IRS sends you one of two types of notices. In the first, the agency asks you for additional information regarding something on your tax return. For example, the IRS may ask for proof of your meal and entertainment expenses. You will then have to print backup documentation of the expenses and send that to the IRS.

In the second kind of notice, the IRS sends you the results of the examination. The IRS will have looked at your return and changed various items on it. You are given (generally) thirty days to respond. If you don't respond, the tax is assessed and you receive a notice of deficiency. Tax professionals do not like this form of IRS correspondence audit because of the accusatory nature of it.

---

[3] The very largest corporations are audited for every tax year.

The keys when responding to a correspondence audit are listed below.

1. Respond in a timely way. There will be a deadline. Make sure your response is mailed by the deadline. If you need additional time, ask for it.

2. Send only the information the IRS has requested. If the IRS asks for information on meals and entertainment but not travel expenses, send them the information on meals but not travel. This seems basic, but according to the IRS, taxpayers routinely send the wrong information.

3. Make your response easy to follow. Most of the personnel involved in correspondence audits are former clerk-typists. In days gone by, the IRS needed thousands of typists to transcribe returns. Today, electronic filing has negated the need for legions of typists. The IRS has retrained these former workers; many now handle correspondence audits. Your response should be simple to follow. If needed, label your documentation so that the IRS can easily follow along with your letter.

4. Write your name, taxpayer identification number, and tax year on *every* document you send in. The IRS separates packages even though all the material is supposed to stay together.

Once you send your response in, the IRS will respond as with an AUR notice. The agency may agree with your response, disagree with your response, or ask for additional information. Once you and the IRS agree, you should pay the additional tax (if applicable). If you and the IRS cannot come to an agreement, you have the right to appeal.

■ **Note   Should you use a tax professional for an examination?** When you receive a notice of examination, the IRS will include with the notice two publications, *Your Rights as a Taxpayer*[4] and a publication on the examination process.[5] One of the rights you have is to be represented by a tax professional: an attorney, a certified public accountant (CPA), or an Enrolled Agent.[6]

---

[4] IRS Publication 1, "Your Rights as a Taxpayer," http://www.irs.gov/pub/irs-pdf/p1.pdf.

[5] Either IRS Publication 3498, "The Examination Process," http://www.irs.gov/pub/irs-pdf/p3498.pdf, or IRS Publication 3498-A, "The Examination Process (Examinations by Mail), http://www.irs.gov/pub/irs-pdf/p3498a.pdf.

[6] Only attorneys, CPAs, and Enrolled Agents have the right to represent any taxpayer in an examination with the IRS or other tax agency.

There is a cliché among attorneys, "A lawyer who represents himself has a fool for a client." If the matter is simple—say, you need to provide copies of all of your meal and entertainment expenses— you probably do not need representation.

However, if the matter is complex or you are facing an office or field audit, you should consider representation. It is far too easy to say the wrong thing to the IRS and find what you thought to be a simple matter has expanded into an unholy mess. If I faced an examination, I would get representation for myself, even though I am an Enrolled Agent.

If you do use a tax professional, it's likely you will not be at the examination. As noted above, you might say the wrong thing; if you're not at the audit, you can't say the wrong thing. You also are hiring a professional so that you do not have to be at the examination. While the IRS may insist that you must be there, the law says that you do not need to attend.

Office Examinations

The second type of examination is the office exam. These are conducted at an IRS office: You've received an invitation you can't refuse.

Generally, office exams are limited to a few issues. Common office exams look at a sole proprietor's automobile expenses, travel expenses, and meals and entertainment expenses. However, an office exam can target anything on a return.

Office examiners have experience within their areas. Many have worked for the IRS for years. Today, all office examiners have heavy workloads.

Here are the keys to surviving an office examination.

1. Call the examiner and set up an appointment as soon as practical. If you are going to need forty-five days to obtain some of your backup information, let the examiner know. Most are reasonable as long as you are upfront with them.

2. Prepare full and complete documentation covering just the areas noted on the exam notice. Most office exams cover just a few areas for one tax year. Make copies of all documentation so that you can provide them for the examiner. Make life easy on the examiner, and cross-reference items where needed.

3. Get to the appointment early. If you live in an area like Los Angeles where traffic can be an issue, plan appropriately. You do not want to be late.

4. Treat the examiner as a person, not as a bureaucrat. Employees at the IRS all have jobs to do. Follow the golden rule: Treat them how you would want to be treated.

5. If you have strong documentation in some areas and weak in others, try to start with the areas in which you are strong. As previously noted, office examiners are overworked. If it looks as if you have excellent documentation throughout, the examiner may stop the exam before it reaches your weak areas.

Once the exam is concluded, the examiner will either print the result for you or mail it to you shortly thereafter. If you and the examiner do not agree, you can request a meeting with the examiner's manager. You also have the right to appeal.

Field Examinations

A field examination is the most far-reaching kind of audit. The field examiner is allowed to expand the audit to anything on the tax return.[7] The examination can be expanded to any year that is open, both forward and backward.[8]

The IRS puts its most experienced examiners in field audits. Most have upward of ten years of experience. With the exception of project work, most field exams are the result of a return having a high DIF score (see the discussion earlier in this chapter). Given that these audits have an almost unlimited scope, *I strongly advise anyone facing a field audit to obtain professional representation.* To have representation, you need to sign an IRS Power of Attorney (Form 2848). Note that if the audit is of a married couple filing jointly, both spouses must sign *separate* powers of attorney.

You can tell you are facing a field exam when the initial letter asks you to call to make an appointment, or there's a reference to seeing your premises, or there's a reference that the scope of the exam may be expanded.

As always, prepare full and complete documentation of the information requested. If the information requested is of a complex nature and you need additional time, let the examiner know.

When you hire a representative, he or she should meet with you. The representative will review the documentation and determine if it is everything

---

[7] The examiner's manager does have to approve the audit expansion. However, I've never seen an audit where the manager objected to an audit expansion.

[8] There is generally a three-year statute of limitations on tax returns (three years from the due date of the return or date of filing, whichever is later). Years where the statute of limitations has not expired are considered open years.

that's needed. If not, he or she will let you know what else is needed. A bank account analysis may be conducted (see later in this section). Most likely, the representative will *not* want you to appear at the examination. With the power of attorney, the representative becomes "you."

■ **Tip   There's nothing wrong with saying, "I don't know."** You're at an IRS audit, and the auditor asks for a piece of information about which you're unsure. There's nothing wrong with saying "I don't know." In fact, in such situations that's the best and only response you should provide! *Lying to an IRS employee is a felony.*

If you don't know the answer, let the examiner know that you'll investigate and get back to him or her with the answer. The IRS appreciates candor, and as long as it's a matter where it's reasonable that you might not know the answer, the examiner should be fine with, "I don't know, but I'll get you the answer soon."

I am generally upfront when I am representing a client in a field audit. First, I'm dealing with auditors who usually know the rules. They have seen almost everything that's possible. You generally can't pull the wool over their eyes. If they don't know the tax rules about something, they know whom to ask to get the information.

I also prefer cooperation to confrontation. Audits can involve give and take. If you are completely confrontational in a field exam, the auditor will not be willing to compromise.

■ **Note   When you find yourself sitting across from Attila the Hun.** In my fourteen years as a tax professional, only once have I sat across from a completely confrontational individual from a tax agency. The auditor violated various rules (among them, he contacted my client directly instead of calling me). When I spoke with him, he denied this.

I spoke with his manager and explained the situation to her. The manager said she would talk with him, and the situation would change or she would reassign the examination. The situation improved, and the audit progressed normally.

As mentioned earlier, most IRS employees are hardworking and conduct themselves in a highly professional manner. Unfortunately, the IRS is a large agency and it's inevitable that there will be some unprofessional employees.

In a field examination, unreported income is almost always looked at. Generally, the IRS reviews all of your bank accounts. The agency will conduct a bank account analysis; they will see if all of the deposits into your accounts are reflected on the tax return.

For the sole proprietor, this can become difficult. You may be moving money from one account to another; the IRS will assume that a transfer is income when it really isn't. You will need to show that it's not income. Suppose you receive a gift from your parents and deposit it into your personal bank account. You tell the IRS examiner it's a gift; you will have to prove it by obtaining a photocopy of the deposit. A separate bank account for your business is helpful in examinations as long as you make sure that all of your income and expenses are run through the account.

If you don't cooperate, the IRS has the power to use a summons to get information from banks and financial institutions. (A *summons* is an administrative demand for documentation. It's similar to a subpoena except that it is for a civil matter instead of a criminal matter.) I had an examination where we requested three-year-old information from a bank; they sent my client the wrong information. The IRS was upset with us over our perceived lack of cooperation, so they created a summons for the information. The bank sent the same information to the IRS that they sent us—the wrong information. It did cause some laughs between the auditor and me. Eventually the correct information was sent to us.

A field examination can take a long time to conclude. Field exams can be expanded, and a large volume of information may be needed. Large corporate audits are usually measured in years of time. You can expect an audit of a small business to take a minimum of a few weeks and could take months to conclude.

■ **Note**   **Privilege in audits.** There is no privilege between a tax professional and a client in tax preparation. You are probably familiar with the attorney-client privilege. If you hire an attorney, generally anything you tell that attorney is confidential; the attorney can never reveal any of that information to anyone. There is a *limited* accountant–client privilege in representation (including examinations). However, there's a problem when you assert privilege.

When privilege is asserted, a tax professional will, of course, comply with a client's request. The problem is that when privilege is asserted, the IRS can refer the matter to their criminal investigations unit.

The IRS criminal investigations unit has highly trained accountants who are also federal agents (accountants with guns). Criminal investigators have subpoena power (just like all police agencies). CPAs and Enrolled Agents *must* answer questions when faced with a lawful subpoena.

If an individual is facing a potential criminal tax matter, he or she should hire a tax attorney. These are attorneys who specialize in tax matters. As with all attorneys, there is attorney–client privilege when speaking with a tax attorney. Tax attorneys then can hire a CPA or Enrolled Agent to assist them under a *Kovel letter*.[9] However, the applicability of a Kovel letter has recently been limited, and it may not always be applicable. Your attorney may elect to just provide information to the CPA or Enrolled Agent.

When an Audit Concludes

When the examination concludes, the examiner will give you a closing letter for the audit. It can take one of a several forms.

If you agree with the results, you sign the letter, and tax is assessed (if applicable). If you disagree, the first step would be to discuss the differences with the examiner's manager.

Audits can involve compromising. I've had conversations with managers where we note our disagreements, and we elect to my position on travel expenses but take the IRS's position on meals and entertainment.

If after meeting with the manager you still don't agree with the results, the IRS will send closing documents. If you believe the tax law has been misinterpreted, you can then take the case to IRS Appeals.

IRS Appeals

The mission of IRS Appeals is "to resolve tax controversies, without litigation, on a basis which is fair and impartial to both the Government and the taxpayer in a manner that will enhance voluntary compliance and public confidence in the integrity and efficiency of the Service." Almost any IRS matter where there's a dispute can be taken to Appeals.

Appeals is *not* the place for rehearing an audit. This is where you go if there's a dispute over the tax law, rules, and regulations.

The IRS has set up service center appeals groups. Generally, tax professionals prefer to have appeals hearings heard on the local level. The IRS's most experienced personnel are at local appeals. In most cases, you have the right to have the appeal heard at the local level. At your first opportunity, you need to ask for the case to be moved to the local level.

Here's an example of why tax professionals prefer local appeals. One of my clients was examined (a correspondence audit) for reporting gambling winnings by session (which is allowed). The issue related to him receiving a

---

[9] Named for *United States v. Kovel*, 296 F.2d 918 (2nd Cir., 1961).

W-2G for a larger amount than his total gambling winnings from the session. Was he liable for the amount of the win on the W-2G or for his actual win? The IRS had held that my client was liable for the full amount of the W-2G.

The first year he was examined, the appeal was heard at the service center. The service center appeals officer agreed with the IRS. My client was examined for the same issue the next year. The case was moved to local IRS appeals. The appeals officer called me, and I explained the issue. The appeal was never heard; the appeals officer agreed with our view, and we never had to argue the case.

After Appeals hears the case, a decision will be sent. (Sometimes you will be told the decision at the appeal, but paperwork is always issued.) If you agree with the appeals decision, you sign the documentation (if necessary) and pay the tax (if applicable). If you still disagree, you can, at that time, take your case to Tax Court.

Court

You've gone to appeals and lost, or you received a notice of deficiency and disagree with it. There are three methods available to take a tax case to court. You can pay the tax, wait six months, and file a claim for refund. If the claim is denied, you can then file a lawsuit to recover the tax in either federal district court of the Court of Federal Claims.

The alternative that most pursue is to file a case in Tax Court. The major benefits of Tax Court are you do not have to pay the tax until the case is resolved, there's a "small case" option with relatively looser rules (somewhat similar to small claims court), and it is possible to represent yourself (called *pro se*).

Most cases filed in Tax Court are never heard: Most are settled. There are several reasons for this. First, all cases that are filed in Tax Court are referred to IRS appeals (if they have not already been heard by IRS appeals). Second, the court encourages both the IRS and the petitioner to settle. Finally, IRS attorneys judge a case based on the hazards of litigation. There is almost always a risk with litigation. In the end, less than 10% of cases filed in Tax Court proceed to a trial.

There is no appeal from a small case Tax Court case (no matter which side wins). All other cases can be appealed to the circuit courts of appeal. If your case is appealed, you will need an attorney (even if you represented yourself at Tax Court). Cases can be appealed from a circuit court of appeals to the Supreme Court.

The main reason the Supreme Court hears a tax case is when two of the circuit courts of appeal reach opposite conclusions on the same issue. When that happens, the Supreme Court grants a writ of certiorari and hears the matter. Once the Supreme Court rules on an issue, it is resolved; the Supreme Court is the highest court in the United States.

The two other methods of fighting the IRS in court (district court and the Court of Federal Claims) involve paying the IRS first and then filing a lawsuit against the IRS. Although this can be done, you will almost always need to hire an attorney.

Audit Reconsideration

What happens if your return is examined by the IRS, and you can't find your documentation proving some of your deductions? You lose that portion of the audit and pay the IRS the additional tax. Sometime later, you discover all of the receipts. Do you have any recourse?

You do; the IRS allows for *audit reconsideration*. In audit reconsideration, you must prove that the original conclusion(s) of the examination were incorrect. When you file audit reconsideration, you note the result of the audit, why the result was wrong, and the evidence showing that the conclusion was wrong.

Audit reconsideration can be done if you don't respond to an IRS notice. Assume you receive a CP2000 and ignore it. The IRS assesses the tax. Three months after the tax was assessed, you realize what happened. The CP2000 notes that you supposedly didn't include a 1099-MISC from a vendor on your Schedule C. You look at your return, and you see that you did include it and that you can prove it. This is an excellent example of when audit reconsideration can be used.

Be aware that it can take from three to twelve months (and longer) for your audit reconsideration to be resolved by the IRS. You will receive a letter after your request has been received giving you an estimated timeframe for response. Unfortunately, that estimate is likely to be exceeded.

Finally, audit reconsideration is not the place to refight an audit when you don't have new evidence. You may not like an examiner's conclusions, but unless you have *proof* the examiner was wrong, you should not file audit reconsideration. Such a filing might be deemed frivolous; the IRS can assess a frivolous filing penalty in such a situation.

State Audits

State and local tax agencies can and do conduct examinations. Though these audits are rare (in comparison to IRS examinations), they can be more difficult for the taxpayer. Many states have budgetary difficulties; states have become far more aggressive with examinations to drum up some funds.

One area where states examine returns where the IRS does not is residency. If you move, you may find yourself facing such an exam. The state will look at whether you have cut your ties to your old state. Be aware that rules on residency vary among the states.

Other Topics

His ignorance is encyclopedic.

—Abba Eban

There are several topics that need to be discussed but don't fit neatly into the other chapters. This chapter focuses on these miscellaneous subjects. Just because they're not in a chapter of their own doesn't make them any less essential.

The final matter discussed here is whether you should use a tax professional for preparation, and if you do, what should you tell him or her.

Tax Planning for 2012 Based on the ACA and Expiring Tax Legislation

In most years, tax professionals tell their clients to accelerate deductions into the current year and postpone income. Generally, tax rates are stable; by doing this most individuals decrease their tax in the current year. (The advice is general; there are definitely situations in which it is normally correct to accelerate income and postpone deductions.)

The end of 2012 is different. Tax rates are going up in 2013, perhaps by even more than the Affordable Care Act (ACA) increases (see Chapter 14). In this situation, *for the average individual* income should be accelerated into the current year and deductions postponed (where possible). This will hold for sole proprietors, partnerships, and S corporations.

It is also unclear whether "extender" tax legislation will pass in the lame duck session of Congress. The Bush Tax Cuts expire at the end of 2012. Republicans want to extend all of the cuts; Democrats and President Obama want the cuts to expire to those earning $250,000 or more. There are a number of other tax measures that likely will be considered; among these are a patch for the alternative minimum tax (AMT), an extension of the Estate Tax limitation, and the ability to deduct sales tax as an itemized deduction.

C corporation tax rates are not changing. Thus, there is no special tax planning for the end of 2012 based on the ACA.

When a Business Loses Money

Not every business makes money each year. In fact, most new businesses lose money in their first year. This makes sense: A new business is looking for customers (marketing) more than servicing existing customers. It's not just new businesses that lose money. A business might move into a new product line, and until that line succeeds the business as a whole could lose money.

What is the tax impact of a loss? As usual, the response is "it depends." The factors that will determine the results are your basis and the type of business (sole proprietor, partnership, S corporation, or C corporation). There is one certainty: A business that loses money will not owe tax. Tax is always a percentage of income; anything times zero is zero.[1]

Basis

Basis is a measure of your investment in your business. For a sole proprietor, you always have basis in your business; that's because the business and a sole proprietor are one and the same. As long as a sole proprietor is materially participating in his business, the loss will be taken on the tax return.

There are two types of basis for all other entities: stock (or partner's capital contribution) and loan. Stock basis is the contributions of owners into the business. This includes contributions to purchase the original stock and additional paid-in capital. For partnerships (and LLCs treated as partnerships), it includes all contributions of capital.

The second source of basis is loans to the entity. A loan provides capital to the business. Of course, as the principal of the loan is paid back, the loan basis drops. All loans require interest to be paid, so it is important that interest is charged (and that the business is either paying interest or accruing interest). Note also that a loan must be a loan *to the business*. Let's say your uncle loans you money, and you invest a portion of that money into the business. You

---

[1] As noted in Chapter 16, you may owe state income tax. Some states charge minimum taxes for business entities regardless of income.

have increased your capital contribution (and your stock basis will increase). However, that's not a loan to the business, and you do not have an increase in your loan basis.

You can only take losses up to the amount of your basis. Losses lower your loan basis first, and then lower the stock basis. Let's say you are one of two members of an LLC taxed as a partnership; each of you has an equal percentage ownership of the LLC. Your capital (stock) basis is $50,000. The partnership has no debt, so there is no loan basis. During the current year, the partnership loses $120,000. Your share of the loss is $60,000. However, you are limited by your basis to reporting a $50,000 loss.

■ **Caution Tax software and basis restrictions.** Suppose the scenario just described applies to you, and you have a $60,000 loss, of which you are limited to $50,000 because of your basis. You receive a Schedule K-1 noting your $60,000 loss; this is the only paperwork you receive from the LLC for the tax year. Can you take the additional $10,000 of loss?

You can't. Basis is controlling; because you have no basis, the deductible loss is limited.

There are two issues related to this. First, it's very important that you receive basis statements each year for partnerships and S corporations. This is especially true if different tax professionals prepare the business and personal returns. There's probably no way for the person preparing your individual return to know of the basis issue without the basis schedule.

Second, there is no form to note the basis restriction on the individual's return. What most tax professionals do to note this limitation is attach a subschedule for the K-1 entry, noting the amount shown on the K-1 and the amount of loss unable to be taken due to the basis restriction.

C corporations pay their own taxes. Thus, although the basis does apply to the C corporation, it applies to the *overall* corporate entity and not each stockholder. For a C corporation to take a loss, the entity must have positive basis between owners' equity and loans.

Material Participation

A second issue that affects the ability to take a loss for a sole proprietorship, partnership, or S corporation is *material participation*. To take a loss, the owner must be materially participating in the activities of the business.

Section 469(h)(1) of the Tax Code defines *material participation* to be when one "works on a regular, continuous and substantial basis in operations" of the activity. Temporary Reg. §1.469-5T(a) states that a taxpayer materially participates in an activity if *any* of the following seven tests are met:

(1)The individual participates in the activity for more than 500 hours during such year;

(2) The individual's participation in the activity for the taxable year constitutes substantially all of the participation in such activity of all individuals (including individuals who are not owners of interests in the activity) for such year;

(3) The individual participates in the activity for more than 100 hours during the taxable year, and such individual's participation in the activity for the taxable year is not less than the participation in the activity of any other individual (including individuals who are not owners of interests in the activity) for such year;

(4) The activity is a significant participation activity (within the meaning of paragraph (c) of this section) for the taxable year, and the individual's aggregate participation in all significant participation activities during such year exceeds 500 hours;

(5) The individual materially participated in the activity (determined without regard to this paragraph (a)(5)) for any five taxable years (whether or not consecutive) during the ten taxable years that immediately precede the taxable year;

(6) The activity is a personal service activity (within the meaning of paragraph (d) of this section), and the individual materially participated in the activity for any three taxable years (whether or not consecutive) preceding the taxable year; or

(7) Based on all of the facts and circumstances (taking into account the rules in paragraph (b) of this section), the individual participates in the activity on a regular, continuous, and substantial basis during such year.

If none of these tests are met, the activity is a *passive activity*. Losses from passive activities can only offset income from other passive activities. Let's look at an example of how this works.

You contribute $25,000 to the funding of Acme LLC (taxed as a partnership); you have a 25% share of the income, losses, and capital. You are otherwise uninvolved in Acme's business activities. In its first tax year, the LLC loses $10,000. What portion of the $2,500 loss shown on your K-1 can you take on your personal tax return?

You have basis in the LLC; however, you are not materially participating in it. You cannot take any of the loss.

Passive activity loss limitations are noted on Form 8582. This form is quite complex and contains several worksheets. I strongly advise a business owner with passive losses to consult a tax professional.

If you have passive losses, these losses carry forward to your next tax year. If you have income in the following year from passive activities, the passive losses you have in prior years offset the income.

Type of Business Entity

The type of business entity will determine how a deductible loss is taken on your tax return. The impacts are different for flow-through entities and entities that are directly taxed.

Sole Proprietors

The loss from a Schedule C will flow to the taxpayer's Form 1040. There, it will offset other income items on the tax return. If the taxpayer has no other sources of income, or if the loss is large enough to offset all of the other sources of income, the taxpayer will have a *net operating loss* (NOL). As discussed in the next section, an NOL can generally be carried back exactly two years (say, from 2012 to 2010) or carried forward for up to twenty years.

Partnerships and S Corporations

Flow-through entities do not take the loss themselves. Instead, the loss is shown on Schedule K-1 and taken on the beneficial owners' returns. Assuming the owners meet the basis and material participation tests, the loss will flow to the owners' Form 1040. This loss, like a loss from a sole proprietorship, will offset other sources of income and can lead to an NOL.

C Corporations

C corporations pay their own taxes. A loss by a C corporation leads to an NOL for the corporation. As discussed in the next section, a C corporation NOL is treated differently than an individual's NOL in the Tax Code.

Net Operating Losses

When an individual or C corporation loses money, an NOL is generated. The Tax Code gives an individual two choices when he or she has an NOL. The loss can be carried back exactly two years, or it can be carried forward for up to twenty years.[2] To carry the loss forward, an irrevocable election must be

---

[2] There are some exceptions to the two-year carryback rule. A farming loss NOL can be carried back five years. An NOL due to a theft or casualty can be carried back three years.

attached to the taxpayer's timely filed return (including extensions) electing this treatment. A sample election statement is shown in Figure 18-1.

IRC SECTION 172(b)(3)

Name(s) shown on Return	Identification Number
John Smith	111-22-3333

Tax Year: 2012

Election to Forego the Carryback Period for Net Operating Loss

Pursuant to the Internal Revenue Code, Section 172(b)(3), the taxpayer, John Smith, Irrevocably elects to relinquish the entire carryback period with respect to the net operating loss incurred for the taxable year ended................12/31/2012.

Figure 18-1. Election to forgo the carryback period for an NOL

If the loss is carried back, a taxpayer has two available methods for claiming the loss. An amended tax return can be filed for the year in question (Form 1040X). The taxpayer needs to attach to the Form 1040X all forms and schedules that show the generation of the loss (including any Schedule K-1s) and any tax forms recalculated for the carryback year.

Alternatively, a taxpayer can file an Application for Tentative Refund (Form 1045). Generally, the same documentation must be attached to the Form 1045 as would be attached to the Form 1040X, including Schedule A of Form 1045.

The benefit of using Form 1045 over Form 1040X is that the IRS is required to process a Form 1045 within ninety days of its receipt; there is no guaranteed processing time for Form 1040X. If the IRS does not process a Form 1045 in a timely way, it must pay interest.

An individual should evaluate his or her marginal tax rate in the possible carryback year and the carryforward year. This is to determine whether to carry the loss backward or forward. Generally, you choose to take the loss

---

An NOL attributable to a federally declared disaster for a qualified small business can be carried back three years (a sole proprietorship or partnership with average annual gross receipts of $5 million or less during the three years of the carryback). Note that only the NOL attributable to the disaster itself can be carried back three years.

where the marginal tax rate is higher, so you will get a larger benefit. If the decision is believed to be close, then the loss is normally carried back.

C corporations carry the losses forward, not backward. The carried-forward losses offset income in future tax years. Like losses for individuals, a C corporation can carry an NOL forward for up to twenty years.

■ **Note   States have different rules regarding NOLs.** Each state treats a net operating loss differently. Some states conform to federal law and allow carrybacks; some only allow carryforwards. California, at times, has prohibited using NOLs (though they carryforward for an additional year for each year that taking the NOL was prohibited).

Foreign Issues

There's nothing illegal about having a foreign bank account. However, there are numerous reporting requirements if you have foreign bank accounts. These apply to both individuals and businesses.

Noting You Have a Foreign Financial Account

If you have a foreign financial account, you will need to check a box on your tax return noting that fact. For individuals, this box is located on the bottom of Schedule B (see Figure 18-2). Business entities do not have to answer this question (though partnerships must disclose on Form 1065 no matter whether they must file a Report of Foreign Bank and Financial Accounts).

				Yes	No
	Note. If line 6 is over $1,500, you must complete Part III.				
	You must complete this part if you **(a)** had over $1,500 of taxable interest or ordinary dividends; **(b)** had a foreign account; or **(c)** received a distribution from, or were a grantor of, or a transferor to, a foreign trust.				
Part III **Foreign** **Accounts** **and Trusts** (See instructions on back.)	**7a** At any time during 2012, did you have a financial interest in or signature authority over a financial account (such as a bank account, securities account, or brokerage account) located in a foreign country? See instructions				
	If "Yes," are you required to file Form TD F 90-22.1 to report that financial interest or signature authority? See Form TD F 90-22.1 and its instructions for filing requirements and exceptions to those requirements				
	b If you are required to file Form TD F 90-22.1, enter the name of the foreign country where the financial account is located ▶				
	8 During 2012, did you receive a distribution from, or were you the grantor of, or transferor to, a foreign trust? If "Yes," you may have to file Form 3520. See instructions on back				
For Paperwork Reduction Act Notice, see your tax return instructions.		Cat. No. 17146N	Schedule B (Form 1040A or 1040) 2012		

Figure 18-2. Foreign account questions of Schedule B (Part III)

Report of Foreign Bank and Financial Accounts (FBAR)

Foreign bank and financial accounts must be reported if certain criteria are met. This dates back to the Bank Secrecy Act of 1970. The scope and breadth of the law have been changed and expanded several times since then, most notably by the USA PATRIOT Act.

You need to report all of your foreign financial accounts if you have US$10,000 or more in one or more such accounts. This is determined by taking the maximum balance of each account at any time during the year, summing the maximums, and comparing the sum to $10,000. If it's $10,000 or more, all such foreign accounts must be reported. Note that all amounts in foreign currencies must be converted to US dollars.

The reporting is done on a Report of Foreign Bank and Financial Accounts (Form TD F 90-22.1). This form, called an FBAR, asks for basic information on every foreign account you have. You must report the financial institution name and address, account number, and the maximum balance at any time during the year. Once you must report one account, you must report *all* accounts, even an account with a zero balance.

The requirement to file an FBAR exists for both individuals and business entities. Be aware that if a business entity (a partnership or corporation), has to file an FBAR the signatories of the business account can also have an FBAR filing requirement.

If you have an FBAR filing requirement, you will also need to check a box on your tax return (if you file as an individual or a partnership). This box is located just below the box you check to note that you have a foreign financial account for individuals (see Figure 18-2).

There are severe penalties for not filing an FBAR when required to do so. Penalties for willfully not filing an FBAR *start* at a $100,000 fine and six months in prison. Nonwillful violators can face up to a $10,000 fine and up to six months in prison.

Note that the FBAR is *not* filed with your tax return; it is filed separately. It can be either mailed to the Department of the Treasury or filed electronically through the BSA E-File System.[3] Currently, tax professionals are *not* allowed to file FBARs on behalf of clients. The FBAR filing deadline is June 30 following the year-end. Unlike tax forms, this is a *receipt deadline*. Additionally, there are no extensions for filing an FBAR.

---

[3] The BSA E-Filing System (BSA stands for Bank Secrecy Act) is operated through the Financial Crimes Enforcement Network of the Department of the Treasury.

A sample FBAR is shown in Figure 18-3. Note that all amounts are reported in US dollars. The form must be signed and dated. If the form is for an individual, the title of the signer is left blank.

Form 8938

Beginning with the 2011 tax year, a new law went into effect for those with foreign financial accounts. The Foreign Account Tax Compliance Act (FACTA) was passed by Congress in 2010. The net result of this law is that individuals who maintain large balances in foreign financial accounts will have a new tax form that must be completed, Form 8938. Generally, an individual residing in the United States will need to file Form 8938 if he or she has $50,000 in one or more foreign financial accounts on December 31 or $75,000 on any other day of the year. (If filing a joint return, the amounts are $100,000 on December 31 or $150,000 on any other day of the year.) Like the FBAR, you need to convert all amounts in foreign currencies into US dollars. You generally are required to use the official Department of the Treasury Reporting Rates of Exchange.[4]

Investing in a Foreign Business

There are strict reporting requirements for individuals who invest in a foreign business, be it a partnership, LLC (or the foreign equivalent), or a corporation (or the foreign equivalent). The rules and reporting requirements are beyond the scope of this text. If you invest in such a business, I strongly advise you consult with a tax professional.

---

[4] Available at http://www.fms.treas.gov/intn.html.

TD F 90-22.1

(Rev. January 2012)
Department of the Treasury

Do not use previous editions of this form

REPORT OF FOREIGN BANK AND FINANCIAL ACCOUNTS

Do NOT file with your Federal Tax Return

OMB No. 1545-2038

1 This Report is for Calendar Year Ended 12/31

2 0 1 2

Amended ☐

Part I   Filer Information

2   Type of Filer

a ☑ Individual   b ☐ Partnership   c ☐ Corporation   d ☐ Consolidated   e ☐ Fiduciary or Other – Enter type _____

3 U.S. Taxpayer Identification Number	4 Foreign identification (Complete only if item 3 is not applicable.)	5 Individual's Date of Birth MM/DD/YYYY
111-22-3333	a Type: ☐ Passport ☐ Other _____	
If filer has no U.S. Identification Number complete Item 4.	b Number _____ c Country of Issue _____	01/01/1981

6 Last Name or Organization Name	7 First Name	8 Middle Initial
Smith	John	

9   Address (Number, Street, and Apt. or Suite No.)

3456 Las Vegas Blvd S

10 City	11 State	12 Zip/Postal Code	13 Country
Las Vegas	NV	89199	

14   Does the filer have a financial interest in 25 or more financial accounts?

☐ Yes   If "Yes" enter total number of accounts _____

(If "Yes" is checked, do not complete Part II or Part III, but retain records of this information)

☑ No

Part II   Information on Financial Account(s) Owned Separately

15 Maximum value of account during calendar year reported	16 Type of account a ☑ Bank b ☐ Securities c ☐ Other – Enter type below
11222	

17   Name of Financial Institution in which account is held

Second National Bank of Canada

18 Account number or other designation	19 Mailing Address (Number, Street, Suite Number) of financial institution in which account is held
1234567890	123 W Main St

20 City	21 State, if known	22 Zip/Postal Code, if known	23 Country
Tornoto	ON	A1A 2B2	Canada

Signature

44 Filer Signature	45 Filer Title, if not reporting a personal account	46 Date (MM/DD/YYYY)
John Smith		5/11/13

File this form with: U.S. Department of the Treasury, P.O. Box 32621, Detroit, MI 48232-0621

This form should be used to report a financial interest in, signature authority, or other authority over one or more financial accounts in foreign countries, as required by the Department of the Treasury Regulations 31 CFR 1010.350 (formerly 31 CFR 103.24). No report is required if the aggregate value of the accounts did not exceed $10,000. **See Instructions For Definitions.**

PRIVACY ACT AND PAPERWORK REDUCTION ACT NOTICE

Pursuant to the requirements of Public Law 93-579 (Privacy Act of 1974), notice is hereby given that the authority to collect information on TD F 90-22.1 in accordance with 5 USC 552a (e) is Public Law 91-508; 31 USC 5314; 5 USC 301; 31 CFR 1010.350 (formerly 31 CFR 103.24).

The principal purpose for collecting the information is to assure maintenance of reports where such reports or records have a high degree of usefulness in criminal, tax, or regulatory investigations or proceedings. The information collected may be provided to those officers and employees of any constituent unit of the Department of the Treasury who have a need for the records in the performance of their duties. The records may be referred to any other department or agency of the United States upon the request of the head of such department or agency for use in a criminal, tax, or regulatory investigation or proceeding. The information collected may also be provided to appropriate state, local, and foreign law enforcement and regulatory personnel in the performance of their official duties. Disclosure of this information is mandatory. Civil and criminal penalties, including in certain circumstances a fine of not more than $500,000 and imprisonment of not more than five years, are provided for failure to file a report, supply information, and for filing a false or fraudulent report. Disclosure of the Social Security number is mandatory. The authority to collect is 31 CFR 1010.350 (formerly 31 CFR 103.24) . The Social Security number will be used as a means to identify the individual who files the report.

The estimated average burden associated with this collection of information is 75 minutes per respondent or record keeper, depending on individual circumstances. Comments regarding the accuracy of this burden estimate, and suggestions for reducing the burden should be directed to the Internal Revenue Service, Bank Secrecy Act Policy, 5000 Ellin Road C-3-242, Lanham MD 20706.

Cat. No. 12996D   Form **TD F 90-22.1** (Rev. 1-2012)

Figure 18-3. Sample completed FBAR

Paper or Electronic?

Should you file your returns electronically or use paper? The IRS has an electronic filing mandate; most tax professionals are required to electronically file your returns unless you tell them not to (or the return cannot be electronically filed for some reason). Many states also have an electronic filing requirement. New York is the most aggressive; most tax professionals are required to file all returns electronically unless it cannot be electronically filed for some reason. Even if a client asks me not to file electronically, I have no choice but to do so.

Years ago, electronic returns were more likely to be audited than paper returns. That would be a good reason not to file electronically if that's still the case.

However, it's *not* the case. Let's look at the path a paper return takes when it's sent to the IRS. After payment is separated and deposited, the return goes to a clerk-typist who transcribes the return into the IRS computer system—the same computer system that electronic returns are downloaded into. After returns reach this system, the DIF score (see Chapter 17) for the return is created.

What this means is that rather than a paper return having less chance of an audit, it actually has a greater chance of audit. That's because it's always possible for there to be a transcription error made by the clerk-typist.

I'm a fan of electronic filing. It's easy, you don't have to deal with lines at the post office, and it works. You can also pay electronically (either through your return filer or with Electronic Federal Tax Payment System, EFTPS).

If you don't file electronically, I strongly advise that you mail your returns using certified mail, return receipt requested. You get proof of filing when you do this. Some post offices have automated postal centers where you can purchase certified mail. My supermarket has that machine, too. You can find locations with automated postal centers on the US Postal Service's website (www.usps. com).

Obtaining Tax Help

There's an old saying: You get what you pay for. This can be the case when you're searching for tax information. Although Google and other search engines may be helpful, not everything you read on the Internet is accurate.

When I'm looking for information, my first stop is the IRS's website (www.irs. gov). It has a wealth of information, every federal tax form that exists, and generally sound advice on tax issues. My only quibble with the website is that on issues that are not settled (as far as tax law), the IRS will state that their position is fact, when it is, for now, just a position.

Similarly, if I'm researching a state tax issue, I'll check the state's tax website. Most states have excellent websites, and these have the forms for each state.

If you use a tax professional (see the next section), he or she should be the first person to whom you turn. If you're paying for advice, you should be listening to the individual giving it to you.

Many court decisions are available on the Internet. All of the recent decisions of the Tax Court can be found on its website (www.ustaxcourt.gov). You can also find decisions of the courts of appeal and the Supreme Court on the Web.

You can also do a search on the Internet. Be careful about what you see on the Internet. Court decisions, law, and regulations promulgated under the law are binding; however, even a court decision you read online may no longer be valid. The law (the Tax Code) could have changed or a higher court may have issued a decision that invalidates a lower court ruling.

You should be especially careful reading "advice" on the Internet. It's free, and it's worth exactly what you pay for it. I have a tax blog (http://www.taxabletalk.com). There is a disclaimer on my blog that states: "All of the items below are for information only and are not meant as tax advice. Please consult your own tax advisor to see how each item impacts your own situation."

That's the problem with general advice: It's general. Your situation is based on *your* facts and circumstances, not average or general facts and circumstances. Unless I know all of the facts and circumstances of your situation, I can't give correct advice.

There's another, more important issue with what you may read on the Internet: A lot of what is purported to be true is false. Anyone can say he is an expert. Some people are, and some are not.

Be especially careful of anyone who says "there is no income tax" or any variation thereof. If you use any of these kinds of arguments, you will find yourself in very deep trouble.

■ **Note   How to turn $1 million into nothing.** I don't watch much television, but one show that has had a long and successful run is *Survivor.* The very first winner on *Survivor* was Richard Hatch. He won $1 million back in 2000.

When you win $1 million, it's time to seek tax advice. Hatch did so. The first accountant he went to told him he would owe about $300,000. He didn't like that, so he went to a second accountant, who told him he would owe slightly under $300,000. Hatch asked the accountant what he would owe if he hadn't won *Survivor;* the accountant told him he would receive a $4,700 refund. Hatch asked the accountant for a copy of that return. The accountant provided Hatch with that, though it was stamped "Do Not File." The accountant also told Hatch not to file the return.

Hatch filed that return. After the IRS caught him, he unwisely decided not to accept a plea bargain. He served more than three years in prison and ended up paying the $300,000 of tax, plus penalties and interest. After legal bills and fines, Hatch's winnings from *Survivor* are exhausted. He unwisely ignored the advice of two accountants.

Whatever you do, don't fall for one of the tax-avoidance schemes that are rampant on the Internet. The IRS has a webpage that debunks most of these schemes.[5] Another site that shows the fallacies of these frivolous arguments is the Tax Protester FAQ.[6] If you try one of these snake oil schemes, only bad things will result.

Should You Use a Tax Professional?

There are many thousands of tax professionals in the United States. Some are *enrolled preparers;* they are in one of the three professions with full rights of representation in front the IRS. Those are attorneys, CPAs, and Enrolled Agents. Many tax professionals are unenrolled. The IRS is in the process of requiring all unenrolled tax professionals to obtain a license as a Registered Tax Return Preparer (RTRP). Initially, these preparers will take a test authorizing them to prepare basic tax returns.

Tax professionals provide two major benefits to the public. First, we offer our expertise. Many are skilled in specific areas of tax law. For example, I specialize in two areas: small businesses and gambling. A tax professional operating in his or her area of expertise should know most of the tax information in that area. The result should be that the client will pay the least amount of tax legally possible.

The second benefit is saving time. You do not have to prepare the return. However, you (or a bookkeeper) will have to organize your paperwork for the return to be prepared.

Unfortunately, the US Tax Code is far too complex. Though I and most tax professionals wish for a simpler Tax Code, the reality is the day we will be able to prepare returns on a postcard is years (likely decades) away. Until that day, any taxpayer with a complex return likely has to use a professional.[7]

---

[5] See "The Truth About Frivolous Tax Arguments" at http://www.irs.gov/Tax-Professionals/The-Truth-About-Frivolous-Tax-Arguments-1.

[6] See "The Tax Protester FAQ" at http://evans-legal.com/dan/tpfaq.html.

[7] I really would prefer a simple and straightforward Tax Code. Though it would cut down on some of my business, today's Tax Code is so complex that the majority of taxpayers are forced to use a professional.

Not everyone needs to use a professional. If your return is simple and straightforward, and you have few or no deductions, a tax professional is not going to find any additional deductions. A good example is an individual who does one or two consulting engagements a year. The only deductions that would be available are the expenses of the engagements, the home office deduction (if the individual qualifies for it), and itemized deductions on Schedule A. For such a person, widely available tax software is likely sufficient.

A fellow tax blogger calls all tax software "flawed." I disagree. The software does what you tell it to do. The issue is that if you tell it the wrong thing, the software doesn't know that you've made a mistake. A mistake you make can cascade through a return, causing multiple errors. While the "TurboTax defense" worked for Treasury Secretary Timothy Geithner, it won't work for you or me in an audit with the IRS.

▧ **Note: The TurboTax defense.** Timothy Geithner used the popular tax software TurboTax to prepare his own 2001 and 2002 tax returns. He did not pay $34,000 of self-employment tax he was supposed to have for those two years. This would have been just another story except for one thing: Geithner was nominated for Secretary of the Treasury in 2009. During his confirmation hearings, the issue of his mistake came out, but he took full responsibility. His "TurboTax" defense became the butt of jokes on late night television.

For the rest of us, the TurboTax defense rarely works in court. You are responsible for your return. For example, in *Bartlett v. Commissioner,*[8] the petitioner blamed TurboTax for the errors. The court came up with a different conclusion: "It is apparent that a portion of the information petitioner entered into the TurboTax program was incorrect; hence the mistakes made (which resulted in the underpayment) were made by petitioner, not TurboTax. TurboTax is only as good as the information entered into its software program. See Bunney v. Commissioner, 114 T.C. 259, 267 (2000). Simply put: garbage in, garbage out."

If You Use a Tax Professional

There are many things that tax professionals wish all clients did. Here's a partial list of the things that you should know.

1.   Submit all of your government paperwork. We usually need to see all of your tax paperwork. That means *every* Form 1099, 1098, K-1, W-2, and W-2G.

---

[8] See *Bartlett v. Commissioner,* T.C. Memo 2012-254 at http://www.ustaxcourt.gov/InOpHistoric/BartlettMemo.TCM.WPD.pdf.

2. Make sure you let your professional know about any significant tax events in your life. Most tax professionals will provide clients with an organizer. One of the questions in my organizer is "Did your marital status change during the year?" Another question is, "Are there any new dependents or children this year?" I've had clients forget to tell me about marriages, divorces, and children. When they review the draft of their return and ask, "Where's my spouse?" I have a puzzled look on my face and say, "You got married?" If you don't tell your tax professional about these items, he or she won't know.

3. Complete the organizer. Tax law changes and the questionnaire helps your professional correctly complete your return.

4. If you have an appointment, keep it and be prepared for it; if you're not ready, change your appointment. Tax professionals are incredibly busy in the weeks prior to the April 15 filing deadline. Be considerate of your professional's time.

5. Keep good records! During the preparation of your return, your professional may need to look at some of your records. This will likely include records for fixed assets purchased during the year, issues related to possible misclassifications, and any timing issues (whether an item should be in the current tax year or a future year). If your professional is asking for an item, there's usually a good reason behind it.

6. Tell your professional about significant business issues. Tax professionals aren't clairvoyant. If you don't tell your professional about the issue, it will remain unknown to the professional.

7. It's better to extend than amend. If you are not going to be ready by the tax deadline (March 15 for calendar year corpora-tions, April 15 for individuals and partnerships), let your profes-sional know as early as possible. Provide your best guess of your income so that an extension can be prepared for you. Your professional can probably electronically file the extension for you, too.

■ **Caution   An extension is just an extension of time to file, not pay.** An extension allows you more time to prepare your return. You need to prepare an estimate of your income to determine whether you owe any tax. With the estimate, your professional will prepare an estimate of tax you owed, so that you can pay the tax by the original tax deadline and avoid penalties.

---

8. Let your preparer know if you're now operating in multiple states or if there are any nexus issues. If your preparer doesn't know that you've begun operating in another state, he or she won't prepare the additional state tax return.

■ **Caution** **State extension rules vary.** Some states give an automatic extension, and no paperwork need be filed. Some states require an extension to be filed. Some states require not only a filed extension but also that 80% or 90% of the tax due be paid for the extension to be considered valid.

---

9. Don't email sensitive information to your professional. Most tax professionals have web portals for the secure uploading and downloading of information. Email is fast, but not secure.

10. Get your paperwork in as early as possible. If you have a complex return, plan on getting your paperwork in earlier rather than later. Your tax professional may need additional time to correctly prepare your returns.

11. If you turn in your paperwork after your professional's deadline, expect to go on extension. Almost every tax professional has a deadline for receiving your paperwork.

When I first began preparing tax returns, "tax season" was not nearly as compressed as it is today. Unfortunately, individuals now must wait for 1099s and K-1s, and these tend to come later and later. Additionally, Congress has had the tendency to pass legislation in December that affects tax returns due shortly after the new year.

Above all, tax professionals simply don't have any time to waste in the days prior to the tax deadlines. If you are prepared for your appointment or you submit everything that's needed to your tax professional, he or she will be appreciative.

Selling Your Business

Back in the height of the real estate boom, a man knocked on my front door and asked me, "Would you sell your home for $675,000?" I had no plans to move, so I declined. However, it did get me thinking about the exit strategy for my business.

There are many ways of ending a business. There are different tax consequences of each. This section looks at the tax issues involved with each.

▓ **Tip Get professional help if you are selling your business.** The advice in this section is general. Selling a business isn't general; it's very specific based on your situation. This is an area where you almost always should consult an attorney and a tax professional.

There are two methods (generally) for selling a business: sale of stock and sale of assets. The facts and circumstances will determine which is right for you. It's probably also something that will be negotiated. (Most sales end up being sales of the assets of the business. This is because the purchasers rarely want the liability for the past actions of the business.) An attorney should give you advice so that your liability for the business ends with the sale. There will be legal documents (from the sale itself, a nondisclosure agreement, an agreement to stay on as a consultant, and potentially more). Your tax professional can tell you the ramifications of the deal depending on how it is structured.

You may also need a business broker to market the sale of your business. Business brokers can market a business. Not all business sales need a broker, but it is something to be considered.

Estate Planning Considerations

"Bad things happen to good people," goes the cliché. Most individuals have a written will. If you don't have one yourself, your state has one already for you; every state has a law governing inheritances of individual who die *intestate* (without a will). If you have children or will have a complex business, you should see an estate planning attorney *immediately* if you don't have a will (or other estate plan). Estate law varies from state to state, so this is an area where you need to find a local professional. Do it properly today, and should an unforeseen event happen, things will go far smoother.

Capital Gains, Installment Sales, and Assets

When a business is sold, it can be a sale of the business or a sale of the assets. Either way, the business owner will have a capital gain. The gain is dependent on the value on the books of what is being sold.

Assume I am selling the assets of my business for $100,000. Those assets have a value of $50,000 (after depreciation). In this simple example, I would have a capital gain of $50,000. Assuming I've owned the business (and the assets) for more than one year, the gain would be taxed as a long-term capital gain.

Many sales of businesses are structured as installment sales. There are other rules for installment sales, too; generally, each year's payments will be attributed partially to interest and partially to the sale. Interest income is taxed as ordinary income. If you have an installment sale, you will need to complete Form 6252. More information on installment sale rules is available in Publication 537.[9]

When a business is sold, in most cases the IRS requires an Asset Acquisition Statement (Form 8594) be completed. Both the buyer and seller complete the form; the information on the assets should be identical on both forms. There are seven classes of assets that are noted, including cash (Class I), personal property (Class II), mark-to-market assets[10] and accounts receivable (Class III), inventory (Class IV), Section 197 intangibles (Class VI), and goodwill (Class VII).[11] All other assets are Class V assets. Allocations are very important, because the sale of a business increases the risk of audit.

Sole Proprietors

When a sole proprietor ends a business, sometimes he or she will sell the business; other times, the business just closes. If you close the business, there are generally no tax consequences because you are the business. If you sell the business, capital gains and/or installment sales will apply.

Partnerships

If the partnership (or an LLC taxed as a partnership) is sold, there will be capital gains and possibly installment sales considerations. If the partnership dissolves, the assets of the partnership must be distributed. There can be potential tax consequences from the distribution.

If a sale is designed as a sale of the assets, the partnership might live on for some time. This is especially true in an installment sale. The assets are transferred to the purchaser in exchange for cash and a note. The partnership likely won't dissolve until the note is paid off. Once the final payment is made, the partnership can be dissolved.

A partnership (or an LLC taxed as a partnership) should consider having a buy/sell agreement among the partners (or members). What happens if in a two-person partnership the partners no longer get along? Having a buy/sell agreement ahead of time allows for the orderly dissolution of the partnership. It also can cover the buyout of the heirs of a partner.

---

[9] IRS, *Installment Sales*, Publication 537, http://www.irs.gov/pub/irs-pdf/p537.pdf.

[10] *Mark-to-market* assets are assets that have been adjusted to the their current value at the end of each year: marked (adjusted) to the market (current value). This will be found in banks and other financial institutions. Few other entities use mark-to-market accounting.

[11] This list is not complete; see the instructions for Form 8594 at http://www.irs.gov/pub/irs-pdf/i8594.pdf for the complete list.

Corporations

When the stock of a C or S corporation is sold, it's like selling any other stock. There will be a capital gain reported (and possibly an installment sale). If the assets are sold, the corporation may continue until the final payment is made on the sale.

If a corporation dissolves, the assets of the corporation will be distributed. If the assets are not fully depreciated, this can result in a taxable event for those receiving the assets (a deemed asset sale).

Conclusion

About every twenty-five years, tax law goes through a major change. The last such occurrence was the Tax Reform Act of 1986. We're due for that major change, and I expect it to occur by the end of this decade. I'm hopeful we will see a major simplification of the Tax Code, but until that happens we have to live with the code as it is.

I've emphasized one thing repeatedly in this book: Keep good records! It is *by far* the most important thing you can do. If you have good records, it will be relatively easy to recover from a tax mistake. Also, an audit will likely be an annoyance rather than a *costly* annoyance.

As I said at the beginning of this book, tax law is a combination of common sense and arcane rules. If you use common sense regarding your taxes and keep good records, your tax returns won't be taxing events.

A democratic government is the only one in which those who vote for a tax can escape the obligation to pay it.

—Alexis de Tocqueville

$$\boxed{I}$$

Index

CPSIA information can be obtained at www.ICGtesting.com
Printed in the USA
LVOW061931220113

316781LV00001B/2/P